John Elwyn

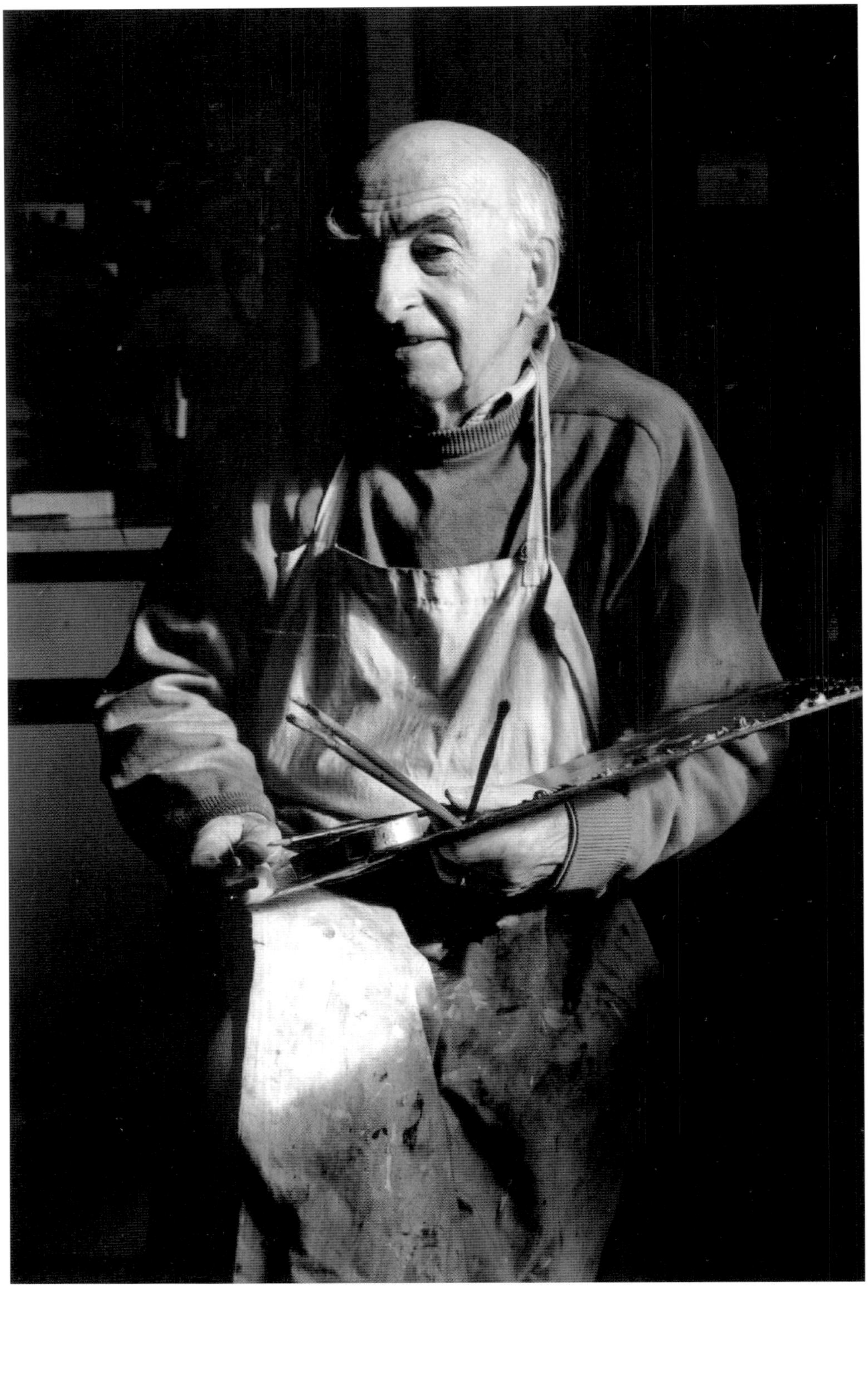

John Elwyn
February 1996

John Elwyn

Robert Meyrick

Scolar Press

Published by
Scolar Press
Gower House
Croft Road
Aldershot
Hants GU11 3HR
England

Ashgate Publishing Company
Old Post Road
Brookfield
Vermont
05036-9704
USA

First published 2000

British Library Cataloguing in Publication Data
A CIP record of this book is available from the British Library
ISBN 0 7546 0062 9

Produced for the publisher by
John Taylor Book Ventures, Faringdon, Oxfordshire
Designed by Peter Guy
Printed in Singapore

Contents

	Foreword by Sir Kyffin Williams RA	6
	Introduction and Acknowledgements	7
	List of Colour Plates	9
	Chronology	10
Chapter 1:	young and easy under the apple boughs: *a childhood in Wales*	13
Chapter 2:	and fire green as grass: *the war years*	23
Chapter 3:	and the sabbath rang slowly: *chapel days remembered*	36
	Colour Plates I–XIX	49
Chapter 4:	famous among the barns: *establishing a reputation*	65
Chapter 5:	once below a time I lordly had the trees and leaves: *nature remodelled*	78
	Colour Plates XX–XXXV	81
Chapter 6:	golden in the heydays of his eyes: *the Cardiganshire landscape revisited*	103
	Colour Plates XXXVI–XLV	113
	Notes	122
	APPENDICES AND BIBLIOGRAPHY	
1:	Exhibitions	125
2:	Public Collections	128
3:	Holidays	128
4:	Books, Catalogues and Principal Reviews	129
5:	Obituaries	130
6:	Television and Radio Programmes	130
7:	Illustrations: illustrated books, dust wrappers and Radio Times	130
8:	Further Reading: British Landscape	130
9:	Further Reading: Art in Wales in the 20th Century	130
	Photographic credits	131
	Index	132

Foreword

JOHN ELWYN was a real artist who knew what he wanted to do and quietly settled down to do it. What he achieved was work of such merit that it will take its place permanently in the artistic history of Wales. John was a clear-headed man who looked at his own world of Wales and loved what he saw. He loved the people, the farms, the chapels, the winding roads and the small and tidy fields and guided by this obsession he gave to Wales something of great worth.

Yet he did more than that, for his natural creative curiosity led him into the world of the abstract in which his personal sense of colour was allowed to burst onto his canvases; but John's heart was in his native Ceredigion and his painting of it was to become one of the foundation stones in the development of Welsh art after the Second World War.

Much has happened in Welsh art since those days, but looking back at all the many paintings in many different styles that have poured from the brushes of Welsh artists, the work of John Elwyn will always stand out and be admired, for John loved the land he painted and the people who lived in it and had the talent to communicate that love to others.

Sir Kyffin Williams RA
President, Royal Cambrian Academy

Introduction and Acknowledgements

SINCE THE EIGHTEENTH CENTURY artists have found inspiration in the sublime mountains of Snowdonia, and the romantic coastal scenery and industrialised landscape of Wales, but unlike John Elwyn few have been drawn to the isolated farming communities in the west. His paintings are evocative interpretations of the landscape and people of his native south Cardiganshire; the landscape around Newcastle Emlyn sustained his painting for over sixty years. The paintings celebrate his Welsh heritage, sense of Welsh identity and love of narrative; these have been the raw material of poets in the Welsh bardic tradition from the medieval poetry of Dafydd ap Gwilym to that of Dylan Thomas and other twentieth-century Anglo-Welsh writers. Like these poets, John Elwyn consistently drew from his own observations, experiences and memories, inspired by his feelings towards the landscape, its people, their language and long-established social traditions. The Welsh have a word to convey this affection for a community, the love of a locality and regional character: *Brogarwch*.

Until the nineteenth century, British art was often characterised by regional variation; artists first became known in their locality and more widespread recognition may have followed. In these days of world markets and global economies, words such as local, provincial and indigenous have become tarnished. As horizons widen, contemporary artists compete within the international arena and it has become difficult to distinguish between works produced in New York, London or Sydney. John Elwyn's paintings, however, are the product of his immense knowledge of the countryside and experience of living in Wales. His paintings of its landscape and people developed clearly within the British landscape tradition, but are observed from a peculiarly Welsh perspective. In that respect he proudly described himself as an 'indigenous' artist. When he left Cardiganshire in 1938 in search of training, employment and recognition there was neither the cultural nor economic climate in Wales to support practising artists. Although John Elwyn lived in Hampshire for almost fifty years, Wales remained his spiritual home. This passion for the homeland is not uncommon amongst Welsh ex-patriots, and the nation has long since paid tribute to this phenomenon in the popular expression *gorau Cymro, Cymro oddi cartre* (the best Welshman is the Welshman away from home).

I was introduced to John Elwyn in 1993 by Michael Francis, Assistant Keeper in the Department of Pictures and Maps at the National Library of Wales, when he invited me to curate and write the catalogue for a retrospective exhibition of the artist's work in his eightieth year. I was privileged to come to know John Elwyn as a friend, and to have played a small part in the renewal of interest in his work. We shared many pleasurable days together at his studio in Winchester, in Aberystwyth, and revisiting childhood haunts in rural south Cardiganshire as he recalled his formative years. The catalogue essay that accompanied the retrospective exhibition provided a structure on which to build this monograph, to examine the artist's career in the context of art in post-war Wales, and assemble here the facts and circumstances of his life that undoubtedly had a bearing on the paintings. It seemed apposite to head each chapter with a line from John Elwyn's favourite poem, *Fernhill* by Dylan

Thomas; a poem about his memory and perception of the landscape experienced during his childhood in Wales.

John Elwyn led a fairly uneventful life devoted to his art; always patient and unhurried, always absorbing life around him with a refreshing optimism and quiet humour, his positive attitude towards life is evident in so much of the work he produced. Like many Welshmen the artist used two forenames when, in the 1940s, he chose to be known professionally as 'John Elwyn'. It has never seemed appropriate, therefore, to refer to him as 'Mr Elwyn', or to his paintings as 'Elwyns'. With this in mind he is referred to consistently throughout the text as 'John Elwyn'. Where possible John Elwyn's own words have been used to convey his intentions; his unpublished autobiographical notes helped me build a fuller picture of his early experiences in Wales which were to shape his art and his attitude towards the landscape and its inhabitants.

I would sincerely like to thank Gillian Davies, the artist's widow, for her hospitality and willing contribution of information. Since John Elwyn's death in November 1997, Gillian has been unstinting in her support of this publication and generous in allowing me continued access to her husband's private correspondence, photographs, record books and press cuttings. All the letters have now been deposited in the National Library of Wales where they are in the process of being catalogued. I am indebted to the art galleries and private collectors who have agreed to works being reproduced; every effort has been made to locate and acknowledge the owners. I am also grateful to all John Elwyn's friends and acquaintances who have provided recollections about the artist and responded to my requests for information, among them Joyce Eaborn, Anthony Eyton RA, the late Doreen Jones, Garrick Palmer, Vivian Pare, Leonard Renton, John Ward RA, Andrew Watchorn and particularly Alexander and Jennifer Coombe-Tennant for granting access to the Winifred Coombe-Tennant papers. Geoff Hassell has been of invaluable assistance, patiently answering my inquiries to help locate John Elwyn's peers at the Royal College of Art, and Ainsleigh Davies, an enthusiastic collector of John Elwyn pictures, kindly allowed me to use his extensive archive of press cuttings, exhibition catalogues and other ephemera. I would like to express my appreciation to Sir Kyffin Williams RA for his affectionate and insightful foreword, and to Neil Holland for reading the manuscript and offering perceptive and constructive criticism. And finally, but of course not least, I have a deep sense of gratitude to John Elwyn, who regrettably did not live to see this handsome volume which I hope is a fitting testament to one of Wales' most distinguished artists, whose paintings, in their subject and distinct character, have contributed significantly to the British landscape tradition. His paintings, fortunately, remain as a permanent reminder of their creator, his gentle nature, generosity of spirit and warmth of character.

Colour Plates

All measurements are in inches, height precedes width.

I: *Picnic in Cilgwyn Woods*
1940, oil on canvas 16 x 20
[Professor and Mrs Derec Llwyd Morgan]

II: *The Stillness of the Roots*
1944, ink and watercolour on paper 14½ x 22½
[Peter Wakelin]

III: *Everyman*
1944, ink and watercolour on paper 11 x 15
[Robert Meyrick]

IV: *A Social Tea Party*
1949, oil on board 10½ x 14
[The Artist's Estate]

V: *The Faithful Few*
1949, oil on board 11½ x 18½
[National Library of Wales, Aberystwyth]

VI: *The Hymn Critics*
1949, oil on board 13 x 19
[The Artist's Estate]

VII: *Suliau Mebyd*
(Sundays of my Youth)
a.k.a. *Before the Meeting*
1950, oil on board 23 x 35
[National Library of Wales, Aberystwyth]

VIII: *Southsea Front*
1951, oil on board 18½ x 24½
[Frances and Nicolas McDowall]

IX: *Family Outing, Southsea*
1951, oil on canvas 20 x 30
[Homer Sykes]

X: *After the Rain (Gosport)*
1952, oil on board 20 x 24
[Robert Meyrick]

XI: *Wool Dyers*
1950, oil on canvas 20 x 30
[Gillian Arthur]

XII: *The Sweeper*
1952, oil on board 20 x 11
[Frances and Nicolas McDowall]

XIII: *Miners Returning Home over Waste Ground*
1951, oil on board 14 x 20
[The Arts Council of Wales]

XIV: *The Egg*
1952, oil on board 20 x 24
[Frances and Nicolas McDowall]

XV: *The Sailor's Return*
1952, oil on canvas 20 x 24
[Martin Tinney Gallery]

XVI: *Funeral in the Snow*
1953, oil on canvas 20 x 24
[Present whereabouts unknown]

XVII: *The Farmer's Wife*
1953, oil on canvas 16 x 20
[Robert Meyrick]

XVIII: *The Milky Way*
1953, oil on canvas 20 x 24
[National Museum and Art Gallery of Wales, Cardiff]

XIX: *The Pet Cockerel*
1953, oil on canvas 30 x 50
[Powys Education Authority]

XX: *The Mothers I*
1954, oil on canvas 20 x 16
[Newport Museum and Art Gallery]

XXI: *Ydlan yn Sir Aberteifi*
(The Rickyard) 1954,
oil on canvas 20 x 24
[Glynn Vivian Art Gallery, Swansea]

XXII: *The Adventurer*
1954, oil on canvas 20 x 24
[Robert Meyrick]

XXIII: *The Derelict Barn*
1955, oil on canvas 24 x 30
[Martin Tinney Gallery]

XXIV: *Windfalls*
1956, oil on canvas 30 x 40
[Contemporary Art Society for Wales / National Library of Wales, Aberystwyth]

XXV: *Glyn Jones*
1956, oil on canvas 20 x 30
[the late Doreen Jones]

XXVI: *Carmarthenshire Green*
1957, oil on canvas 40 x 30
[Newport Museum and Art Gallery]

XXVII: *Barn Walls*
1956, oil on canvas 20 x 24
[Dr and Mrs Huw Bevan Jones]

XXVIII: *Shoni Winwns*
1958, oil on canvas 36 x 28
[Robert Meyrick]

XXIX: *Glamorgan*
1960, gouache on paper 13 x 17
[The Shell Art Collection at the National Motor Museum, Beaulieu]

XXX: *Green Approaches*
1959, oil on board 24 x 36
[Wil Aaron]

XXXI: *Cardiganshire Meadows*
1959, oil on canvas 29 x 38½
[National Library of Wales, Aberystwyth]

XXXII: *Farm Shapes*
1961, oil on canvas 30 x 50
[Glenys Ormond Thomas]

XXXIII: *Cockerels and Roses*
1961, oil on board 28 x 36
[Dr and Mrs David Shedden]

XXXIV: *The Road to Gower*
1963, oil on canvas 28 x 36
[Huw Davies and Sian Vaughan]

XXXV: *Landscar*
1964, oil on canvas 30 x 30
[The Artist's Estate]

XXXVI: *Forest Enigma*
1964, oil on canvas 40 x 50
[The Artist's Estate]

XXXVII: *Enigmatic Blossom*
1967, oil on canvas 60 x 60
[The Artist's Estate]

XXXVIII: *Entrance to a Barn*
1967, oil on canvas 28 x 36
[Percy Thomas Partnership]

XXXIX: *Fernhill III: And the sun grew round that very day*
1977, oil on canvas 36 x 48
[University of Wales, Cardiff]

XL: *The Enclosed Balcony*
1980, oil on canvas 28 x 36
[Miss G. Cemlyn Jones]

XLI: *Paddock Bird*
1985, acrylic on paper 21 x 29
[Donald Moore]

XLII: *On the Dyfed Coast*
1987, oil on canvas 36 x 40
[Dr and Mrs David Shedden]

XLIII: *Upland Farm*
1992, oil on canvas 30 x 30
[The Artist's Estate]

XLIV: *September*
1996, oil on canvas 48 x 48
[Dr and Mrs Huw Bevan Jones]

XLV: *The Lonely Servant*
1980–97, oil on canvas 20 x 20
[The Artist's Estate]

Chronology

1916 Born 20th November, Emlyn Mill, Adpar, Newcastle Emlyn, Cardiganshire.

–1930 Adpar County Junior School.

1930–1934 Llandysul County Grammar School.

1935–1937 Carmarthen School of Art. Awarded Prize for Animal Drawing 1934–1935, and the Prize for Figure Drawing 1935–1936.

1937–1938 West of England College of Art, Bristol. Won Royal Exhibition Scholarship in Painting to the R.C.A.

1938–1940 & 1946–1947 Royal College of Art, London. Awarded the Diploma Prize, College Prize for Life Drawing and Rodney Burns awarded a two-guinea prize for a landscape in his Diploma Exhibition.

1940 Objector's Tribunal. Directed to land work, on the forestry and in food production.

1942 First contribution to a National Eisteddfod of Wales exhibition. Commissioned by Paul Matt (designer for the Brynmawr Furniture Company) to design and execute a backcloth for *Meini Gwagedd*, a play by Kitchener Davies.

1947 Worked as a graphic designer in the London offices of J. Walter Thompson.

1948 First exhibited at the Royal Academy. Moved to Portsmouth to take up an appointment as Lecturer in Painting at the College of Art, where he remained until 1953. First correspondence with Winifred Coombe-Tennant who in turn introduced him to David Bell at the Welsh Arts Council.

1949 Began a series of paintings on the theme of Sunday in rural Cardiganshire in the 1920s – chapel going, festivals and funerals. First London exhibition with Jack Wright at the Paul Alexander Gallery.

1951 First of many contributions to the annual 'Pictures for Welsh Schools' exhibitions organised by the Society for Education through Art (S.E.A.), and staged at the National Museum of Wales, Cardiff.

1950–1953 Paintings of the miners and their landscape near Pont-rhyd-y-fen.

1953 Moved to Winchester where he taught at the School of Art. First illustrations for *Radio Times*.

1953–1958 Paintings of farm life in Cardiganshire, many executed for S.E.A. exhibitions.

1956 Awarded 'Gold Medal for Fine Art' at the National Eisteddfod of Wales in Aberdare. Designed dust jacket for Glyn Jones' first novel *The Valley, The City, The Village*, published by J. M. Dent.

1958 Designed and executed sets for a production of Antigone at the National Eisteddfod of Wales, Ebbw Vale.

1959 Adjudicator, Youth Section in Painting and Drawing at the National Eisteddfod of Wales, Caernarfon. First illustrations for Shell County Guides.

1960–1964 Paintings based on the seasons, and on the growth and felling of trees in the Savernake Forest, begin edging their way towards abstraction.

1963 Commissions from Barclays Bank, Glaxo Laboratories and the General Post Office.

1965 Solo exhibition at the Leicester Galleries, London. Invited to become Honorary Member of the Royal Cambrian Academy of Art.

1965–1969 Paintings of seasonal changes in his garden and an examination of the inner structures of blooms and seed pods.

1967 Six lithographs of Welsh landscapes commissioned by The Collectors' Guild, Madison Avenue, New York for a scheme organised by Andrew Purchase and printed by the Curwen Press (zinc plates). The Curwen commissioned two further lithographs of Caernarfon and Harlech castles, printed from the stones by Stanley Jones. John Elwyn produced more lithographs for the American market in 1971 (printed in seven colours at the Curwen in editions of 250).

1968 Invited selector for the 'Pictures for Welsh Schools' exhibition, organised by the Society for Education through Art and the Arts Council for the National Museum of Wales. Second solo exhibition at the Leicester Galleries in November.

1969 The Welsh Arts Council commissioned two paintings of chapels for the *Recording Wales* project.

1970 Married Gillian Butterworth. After ten years of near abstraction returned to a more direct representation of the Cardiganshire landscape.

1976 Fine Art Adjudicator (with Kyffin Williams) at the National Eisteddfod of Wales, Cardigan. Retired from Winchester School of Art.

1979 Elected member of the Royal Institute of Painters in Watercolour.

1981 Lithograph of *Capel Hawen, Rhydlewis* reproduced as a Christmas card for the Commission for the Protection of Rural Wales.

1982 Elected Honorary Member of the Gorsedd, the Bardic Council of the Eisteddfod, adopting the Bardic title *Arlunydd Dyfed* (Painter of Dyfed).

1984 Commissioned portrait of Dr Raymond Edwards, Principal of the University of Wales College of Music and Drama, Cardiff.

1986 Commissioned portrait of Sir Alun Talfan Davies, President of H.T.V. Wales.

1990 In May underwent major surgery at Winchester after it was discovered he was suffering from cancer.

1993 Twenty-nine line drawings illustrating *House of Leaves*, a volume of poems by Dafydd ap Gwilym, published in a limited edition by the Old Stile Press, Llandogo, Gwent.

1996 Honorary D.Litt. awarded by the University of Wales in recognition of his contribution to art in Wales. The National Library of Wales staged a retrospective exhibition of his work to commemorate his eightieth birthday.

1997 Last solo exhibition held at the Martin Tinney Gallery, Cardiff. John Elwyn died at 4.30am on 13th November at the neurological unit of Southampton General Hospital. He was cremated 20th November at Southampton Crematorium, on his 81st birthday.

1998 Ashes interred on 6th April in a plot alongside his family at Parce Cemetery outside Newcastle Emlyn.

1999–2000 Memorial exhibition tours the National Library of Wales, Bell Fine Art in Winchester, Carmarthenshire County Museum, Martin Tinney Gallery in Cardiff and the Royal Cambrian Academy.

2000 Gregynog Press published in book form *The Twelve*, wood engravings illustrating *Dysgyblion yr Iesu* (Disciples of the Jesus) that were cut in 1944, with accompanying extracts from the Bible selected by Dr Glyn Tegai Hughes.

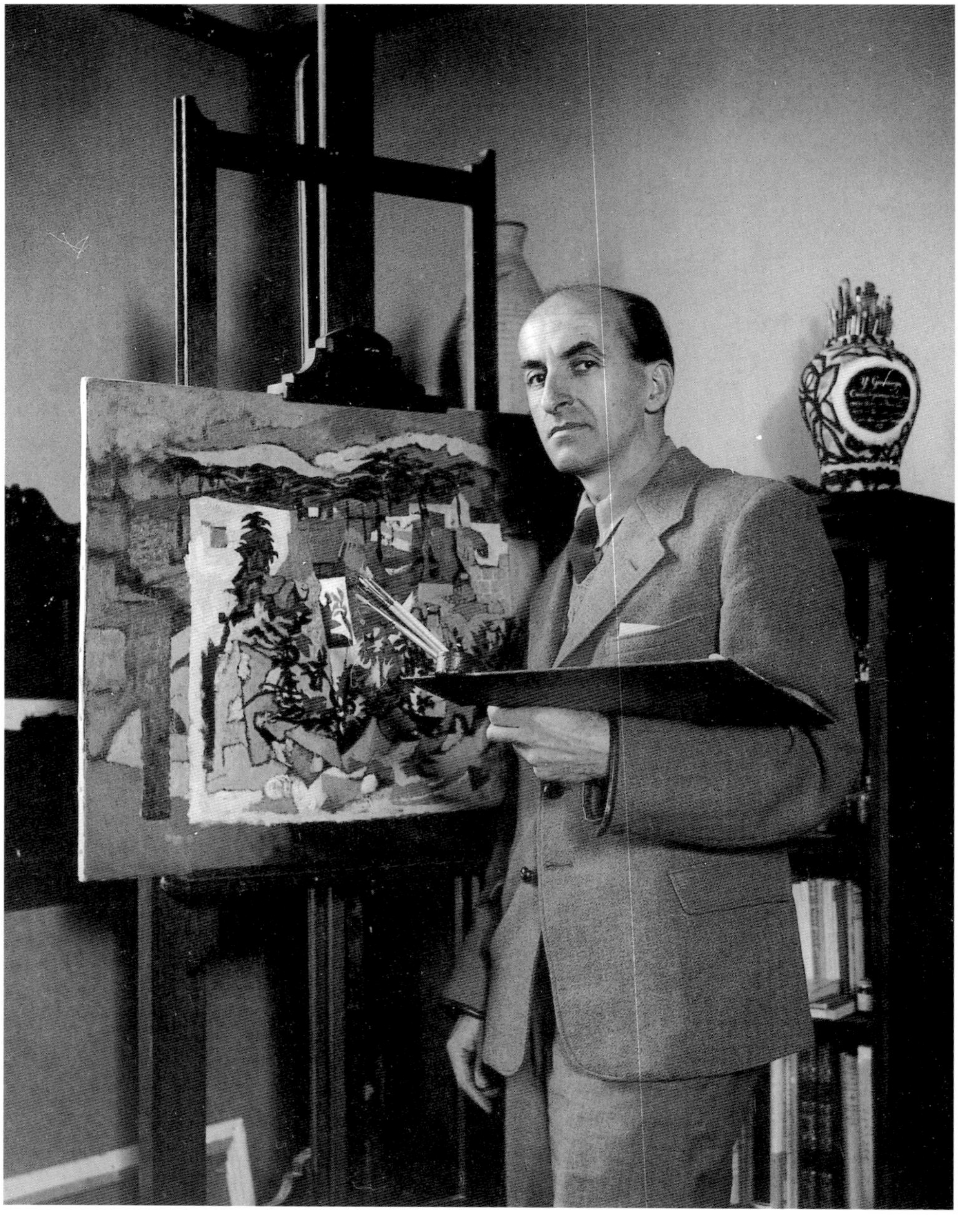

John Elwyn painting
The Derelict Barn,
Winchester 1955

Chapter 1

young and easy under the apple boughs:

a childhood in Wales

JOHN ELWYN was born in the heart of rural west Wales in the small village of Adpar, a close and self-contained community of farmers, weavers and local craftsmen. His childhood memories were happy ones, of playing by the river Teifi, around the leat and in the smallholding that surrounded his father's woollen mill. The remainder of John Elwyn's life seemed to echo those first sensations; these early experiences shaped his art and his attitude towards the landscape and its inhabitants. He often remarked upon his 'rural idyllic village', and recalled memories of childhood days in this staunchly Welsh-speaking and Nonconformist part of the country:

> I was born to the sound of the clickety-clack of the looms, which were the thickness of a stone wall away. I realise that this was a fairy tale situation. A castle, a palace and our home was a mill on the banks of the river Teifi. Across the river and within easy distance was the remains of a castle, and at the back of our mill on high ground facing the castle was the landlord's mansion – owner of the plot of ground we lived on. There were no other buildings within this triangle which was our area of play, either climbing trees or mucking about on the rocks in the river and catching shilgots in jam jars in the summer.[1]

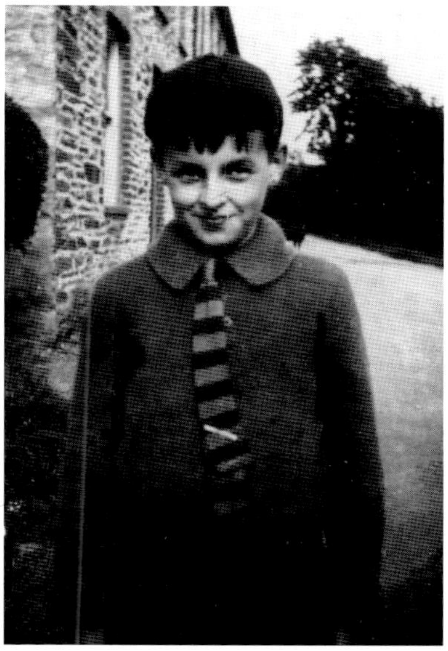

William 'John Elwyn' Davies aged 10 outside Emlyn Factory 1927

Adpar is on the Cardiganshire banks of the river Teifi, discrete from the neighbouring market town of Newcastle Emlyn across the river in Carmarthenshire. In the nineteenth century the textile industry flourished along the Teifi Valley, a predominantly agricultural area characterised by dairy herds on the meadows and sheep grazing on the uplands. By the 1890s factory production had replaced most hand-loom weaving and the Teifi Valley became the principal centre of textile manufacture in Wales. The mill supplied flannel, tweeds, knitting wool and striped shirting-flannel, and made an important contribution to the community. Craftsmen like John Elwyn's father, who used his skills to provide for the needs of others in the locality, were fast disappearing from the Welsh way of life. As a result of industrialisation, mass manufacture, economic competition and the improved transportation of goods, small craft industries in the country were in sharp decline.

William John Elwyn Davies, known at home as 'Elwyn', was born on 20th November 1916, the youngest child of David and Anne Davies, who were then both in their mid forties.[2] In his teens David Davies had been an apprenticed hand-loom weaver at Brondeg Mills in Felindre. In 1902 he rented Emlyn Factory from the Cilgwyn Estate and established his own company, David Davies & Co. Woollen Manufacturers. In 1913 it was rebuilt and enlarged, and although it remained a small-scale operation the term factory was used to distinguish mechanised production from hand-loom manufacture. David Davies generally employed three weavers, a carder and a spinner. In 1916 production was at its peak as manufacturers met Government contracts for angola flannel for soldiers' shirts. The mill was driven by a deep-pit turbine powered by the waters of the Teifi. The leat, a man-made channel cut six feet deep into the rock, directed water from up river into the pit. The weight of the water propelled the turbine blades, moving a vertical spindle connected to large mitred cogs, driving a shaft that entered the mill through a wall. The awesome power generated as the main belt gathered speed and vibrated with the 'hum, chuff and clatter' of the looms, caused the building to vibrate. The family lived to the perpetual rhythm and clickety-click of the weavers' shuttle in the loom, a noise to which John Elwyn fell asleep at night and awoke early next morning. The mill was a place of great fascination and danger for the young boy.

John Elwyn had three older sisters – Sally, Mary and Katie – the first-born child was a son and he had survived just a few days.[3] Perhaps as a consequence of his brother's death in infancy, his mother and sisters were totally devoted to Elwyn.[4] It was an organised and peaceful household and 'a place of joy and refuge' for the children. He wrote:

> I have no recollections of experiencing difficult scenes in our family life. My parents were always peace makers in the community and neighbours sought their advice when in trouble ... my parents were an important formulating factor in my life.[5]

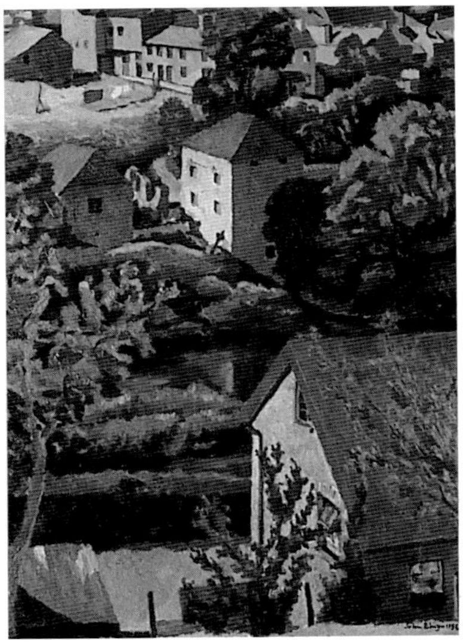

Above the Mill at Adpar
(looking towards Newcastle Emlyn)
1936, oil on board 24 x 18
[The Artist's Estate]

John Elwyn's childhood was spent mostly in the company of older people, including the many visitors, clients and tradesmen who called at the mill and brought news of the outside world. There were few books in the house and no radio, nor was there a town library, so most of his time was spent observing home life and activities around the village.

The Davies family were firmly integrated into the social and economic infrastructure of the village and they seldom travelled beyond south-west Wales. A dyeing class some forty miles away in Aberystwyth was perhaps the furthest David Davies ventured. Yet compared with other villagers, particularly some farming families in the hinterland, this was a cultured and in a small way cosmopolitan family. Each member of the family had an interest and knowledge of music, there were frequent gatherings around the piano at home, and they participated in musical events at local *eisteddfodau*. Katie had a fine contralto voice, sang locally in chapels and was a soloist on radio. Mary was a chapel organist and gave piano lessons in the parlour of the mill. David Davies's profession brought the family into contact with all kinds of outsiders. Trade links with north and south-west England, and the industrialised mining valleys of south Wales, introduced them to a world beyond Newcastle Emlyn. It has been said that the Teifi Valley woollen manufacturers were really quite urbanised and allied themselves more to the industrialised areas of south Wales than to the local farming community.

Emlyn Factory was typical of the smaller woollen mills, in which raw wool was prepared, dyed, spun and woven, then sent to be 'finished' at a fulling mill in Drefach. David and Anne Davies were born and reared in the locality and knew most of the farming families; their business relied principally on local trade. Wool was delivered from the farms by horse-drawn wagons and also purchased from further afield: from Newtown, Welshpool and, during war-time rationing, Bradford. Farmers and their wives travelled miles to deliver consignments of fleeces. It was a rare day away from the farm and they were given special attention at the mill. They spent time in the domestic quarters, over cups of tea 'from the best china and lump sugar', catching up on news of local and national importance. John Elwyn sat absorbing these conversations around the table attempting to unravel and explain the varied activities that centred on the mill and smallholding. When the wool was weighed and a price agreed clients were taken to the stock room where, in exchange for their consignment of wool, they selected items from the display of blankets, rolls of tweed and flannel, and knitting wool in all colours. The *Emlyn Factory Account Book* recorded the value of goods exchanged, but there appears to have been a minimum amount of

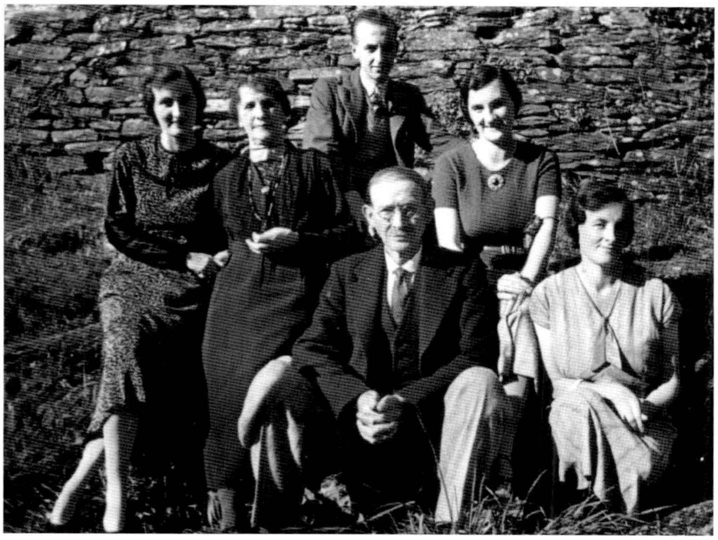

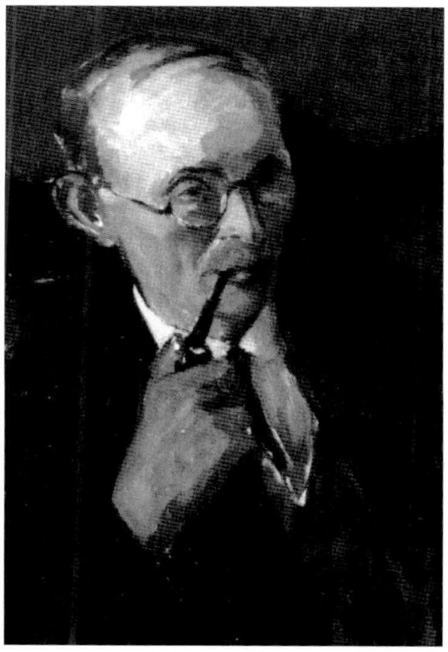

The Artist's Father (detail)
1940, oil on canvas 24 x 20
[National Library of Wales, Aberystwyth]

The Davies Family, September 1936

book keeping; cash was never exchanged since all transactions involved barter in some form or another, and the balance was carried over until the next visit.[6] In exchange for woollen goods arrangements were made with a nearby farmer to put aside rows of potatoes in his field for the mill, or allow the use of a small field for their cow.

David Davies was something of a celebrity at local *eisteddfodau*. He wrote poetry whilst working at the loom, pausing to celebrate a recent event, natural phenomena, or comment on some moral, social or spiritual dilemma. He pencilled stanzas into a variety of pocket diaries, exercise books, and on the backs of old invoices.[7] These are sensitive and keenly observed works by an untrained writer, and some attempted even the strict meter of *cynghanedd*. The poems were refined over several re-writings and subsequently copied in ink onto ruled paper using his neatest hand writing. He read volumes of poetry and would have heard recitations at *eisteddfodau* or the chapel literary society. He also recited his own poetry at local *eisteddfodau* and a few were published in Welsh newspapers such as *Baner ac Amserau Cymru*. In the evenings he read them aloud to his family in the parlour.

The poems give an insight into David Davies's preoccupations, enthusiasms, obsessions and beliefs. Clearly many of these qualities were passed on to his son and contributed to forming the character of the young John Elwyn. The sanctity of the family is solemnized in poems such as *Englyn i'r Fam* (a four line poem in strict meter to Mother), whilst there are several other poems entitled *Cartre* (Home) which describe love in the home. Religious, moral and philosophical issues are explored in stanzas typical of turn-of-the-century poetry concerning the love of God, man's inner strength and the road that leads to sin. John Elwyn recalled:

> Sunday evening discussions around the hearth after a fiery and theatrical sermon was a very common occurrence. The good and the bad set, life and death were recurrent topics for a young child to hear. The Chapel was of great importance and contributed much to my formative years.[8]

David Davies kept a small notebook that summarised the sermons given by visiting preachers at Ebenezer Chapel. Themes such as Death, Truth, Peace and War were also popular with him, and the evils of drinking, smoking and football are observed in *Os wyt am fod yn Ddyn* (If you want to be a Man). He disapproved of football which he believed was keeping the young men from chapel. David Davies was particularly interested in politics, he was an active member of the local council and sat on committees for amenities and various good causes. Like many from his social background who had experienced genuine hardship and poverty, and toiled long and hard to attain some degree of financial stability and respect within the community, he would not tolerate laziness. The poems themselves were the result of his conviction that hard work and meaningfully deployed leisure time led to enlightenment and self-improvement. As a young man at Felindre, he had met with fellow workers in the evenings and written poems to be entered in literary competitions. He also attended the debating group in the chapel vestry. In *Ymgomwest yn y Festri* (Debating Competition in the Vestry) 1935 he expresses his love of:

> food for the pure in mind.
> These meetings are like many a garden
> Working and not lazy ...
> The free lessons dealing with morality,
> They surpass all the schools ...
> Nobody are more contented in the world
> Than the little class in the vestry.

In a poem entitled *Social* (1936) he described Thursday evening gatherings in the vestry of Ebenezer Chapel where he listened to papers presented on different topics. Tea, cakes and animated, often humorous conversation ensued by 'the best debaters in the world'. (Plate IV) Other poems celebrate local events such as *Etholiad Sirol Ceredigion* (Ceredigion's County Elections), *Cwrdd Llenyddol* (The Literary Meeting), *Calan Mai* (The May Fair), *Yr Elor Gerbyd* (The Hearse) and *Nos Sadwrn Pae* (Saturday Pay Night). John Elwyn was to paint similar events and social gatherings for his first solo exhibition in London which included paintings entitled *The Deacon's Dilemma, A Social Tea Party, Whitsun Festival Interval*, and *April Communion.*

Landscape and cycle of the seasons were also themes to which David Davies sang as bard and recur later in his son's paintings – *Y Bryn ar Doriad Gwawr* (The Hill at Dawn) conveys his delight as 'the dawn threw its white mantle over the sky', *Y Gwanwyn* (Spring) when 'sleep disappears from the lap of the valley', and *Afon Ceri* (The Ceri River) 'singing and whispering under the bush ... being lazy on the meadow'. Fields of wheat, harvest-time and 'orchards full of mellow fruits' are described in *Yr Hydref* (Autumn); summer days past in *Cwymp y Dail* (The Fall of the Leaves); June mornings with 'the heather moving like a colourful cloak' on the hills above the Teifi (untitled, undated); and *Dyfodiad yr Hydref* (The Coming of Autumn) with 'The hot sun ripening the corn ... How beautiful are the fields in their gold ... and Autumn warms the leaves and fern'.

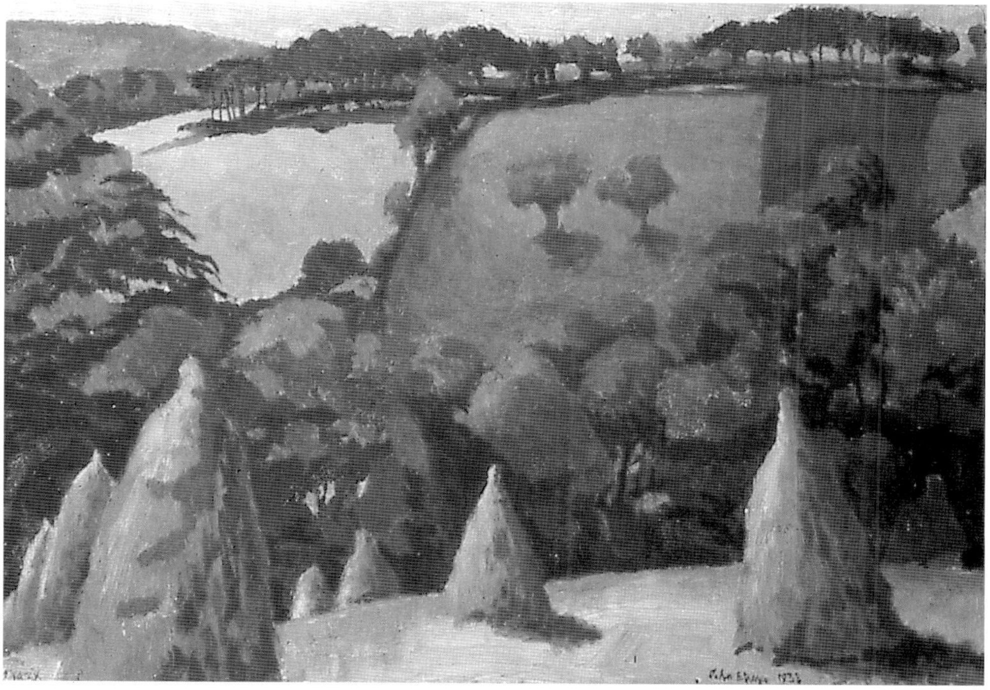

Haystooks in the Meadow above the Mill
1938, oil on board 12 x 18
[The Artist's Estate]

John Elwyn grew more aware of the importance of the seasons as he observed activities around the mill and realised that life revolved with nature's cycle from seed-time to harvest. He soon came to understand the imperatives of the seasons and he never lost that fascination with nature's mystery. It intrigued him why it was that his father dug over the kitchen garden at certain times of the year and not others. There were times when the mill came to a standstill for a day or two, and the looms remained idle as the weavers were re-deployed to help the farmer with hay making, the harvest, or planting seed potatoes. There was some urgency and this work took priority over the mill's routine. Each family member took an active role in the seasonal activities, and it was through his participation in family and community activities that John Elwyn learned as a young boy to be a 'good' person, and embrace Christian attitudes as a way of life, in terms of social awareness and helping family, friends and neighbours.

A close contact with the farm animals was a further source of happiness and intrigue. The first clutch of eggs hatching, the first calf and the arrival of a new piglet from the market were days in the year of special significance. John Elwyn quickly learned the strict pattern to each day, week, month and season. 'I was alive and aware to the reality of life', he wrote, 'in its joy and suffering with the beauty and harshness of nature in the cycle of the seasons.'[9] Life was hard at Emlyn Factory; in addition to the working day at the mill there were the essential daily chores on the smallholding, the produce from which the family depended. There was a cow to provide milk, butter and cheese, a pig was kept for bacon, chicken and ducks for eggs, and bees for honey. The cow grazed in their field on the hill above the factory and in a meadow kept for hay some quarter of a mile away alongside the Teifi. It was John Elwyn's responsibility to fetch the cow from the grazing field twice daily and return it after milking, a trip that took him 'at cow-speed' through the centre of the village. His mother was conversant with the running of the mill and smallholding. She was born and reared in the nearby Ceri Valley where her father had worked a smallholding and mill producing spun yarn.

Each spring his father brought home a piglet from the local mart, kicking and squealing under his arm. It lived at the bottom of the garden in a corrugated tin sty surrounded by laurel bushes and apple trees. Here it was fattened on kitchen slops collected in a wooden drum outside the mill.[10] The pig was usually slaughtered on a fine day during November when the stages of the moon had been consulted in *Saddler's Almanac* to forecast the best weather to cure fresh meat. The day began about 5 a.m. when John Elwyn's sleep was broken by the crackle of burning wood and his father stoking a fire which blazed beneath a large cauldron of boiling water. From his bedroom window on dark winter mornings he observed the spectacle with horror and excitement. When he saw the peripatetic butcher sharpen his steel blade, and heard the pig dragged protesting down the garden path, John Elwyn took sanctuary in the parlour. He hammered on the piano keys to drown the pig's heart-rending squeal as the blade plunged in the unfortunate beast. When silence fell he ventured to the back door where bright red blood was now forming rivulets across the yard. Pails of boiling water were poured over the carcass and the hairs were scraped away with an old tin candlestick. In no time the pig's carcass was hung from a metal bar on the back wall of the mill, a piece of wood between its hind legs secured by the ligaments in each foot. The butcher passed his sharp knife down the belly of the animal and disembowelled it into a barrel. He then left to keep his next appointment and returned in the evening to cut up the carcass. Anne Davies cured or salted the meat for several days on the cool slate slabs of the pantry. Eventually the joints were hung from great hooks in the kitchen ceiling above the heat and smoke of the open fire. Spare ribs and odd cuts of meat were packaged and given to neighbours. The highlight for John Elwyn was the bladder that when blown up made an excellent football and gave many hours of pleasure before it punctured. The sty, washed down in readiness for the next season, was a place for the children to play in the spring and early summer.

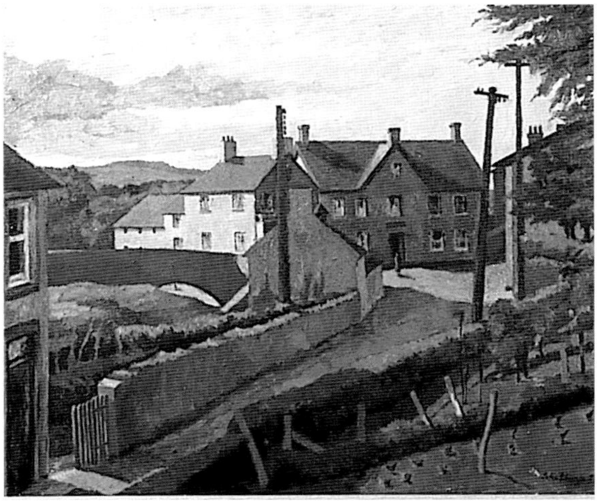

The Lamb Inn, Adpar
1938, oil on board 18 x 22
[The Artist's Estate]

The May Day, September and Christmas Poultry Fairs, where farmers came to buy, sell and exchange livestock and produce, were held in 'the square' outside the Lamb Inn at Adpar, a short distance from the mill. The great horses with plaited manes and tails, and decorated with metres of coloured ribbon in readiness for sale, pranced across the square. The slapping of hands to clinch a sale was acted out with excitement and all the seriousness of play acting, the two parties then moved on to the Lamb Inn to seal the deal. It was also the time in the year for farmers to stock up on clothes, flannel, footwear and turned wooden domestic utensils. The May Day Fair was also the occasion to hire domestic help and farm hands for the season. The fairs were also the occasions for pleasure seeking and there was much drinking when the evening festivities took place over the bridge in Newcastle Emlyn; traders lined its streets with stalls, ballad singers performed, wrestling contests took place, and the swings and roundabouts of the fun fair were set up on the farmers' mart. The show ground at night was a great attraction for John Elwyn who was easily caught up in the variety and excitement of the occasion. In an undated poem his father described four friends visiting such a fair where they saw 'a girl playing a tambourine, a beautiful monkey in a red waistcoat, a man playing the organ together with a blind fiddler, and an Englishman from Ireland showing a giant who had been caught in the forests of Patagonia'.

By the 1930s there was little demand for the tweeds which his father manufactured and no longer a living to be made should John Elwyn have wished to take over the factory. For a number of reasons the industry went into a steady decline after the First World War. In 1921 the Government put its surplus stock of flannel and blankets on to the market at low prices and the wholesale price for wool plummeted.[11] The miners' strike of April and June 1921 had dramatic consequences for the market for woollen goods, and increased competition from knitwear manufacturers in the north of England and Scotland also took its toll. The demand for woven products was hit by the fashion for more comfortable and cheaper cotton flannelette used for drawers, vests, stockings, aprons and bedclothes, until only the market for heavy-duty underwear and shirts for coal miners, iron workers, farmers and drovers survived. The stiff tweed suit fabrics produced by the mills also went out of fashion, and town-based outfitters such as Burtons replaced local tailors. The mills were generally unable to adapt to the changed circumstances; they were inflexible and would not give up traditional methods and materials. With diminishing orders the Davies family frequently existed on the bread line. In February 1930 David Davies set up a 'clothing club', allowing payment for products by weekly instalments, and to supplement income his wife rented a stall in Newcastle Emlyn market selling flannel and tweeds from the roll.

John Elwyn attended Adpar Village School when the economic depression was hitting this small rural community badly, poverty was widespread and illness, particularly tuberculosis, was rife. Schools were under-funded and under-resourced. John Elwyn was one of the few children who passed the 11+ examination. Both his parents had left the village school around the age of twelve with the minimum state education, and although they were unable to help with the school work itself they encouraged their son in every other way possible to continue with his studies. He attended Llandysul County Grammar School between 1930 and 1934, an institution that stressed academic excellence and success at examinations but did not provide the opportunity for him to study his first love, art; it was not taught or encouraged during his time at the school. As a child John Elwyn drew all the time, mostly pencil copies of the ubiquitous photographs which once hung in every chapel school room – among them were *David Lloyd George* (1932), the preachers *Ieuan Gwynedd* (1931) and *Dr Ben Davies of Newcastle Emlyn* (1931), and the Welsh poet *Eifion Wyn* copied from the frontispiece of a volume of his works. There was a tradition at local *eisteddfodau* to hold competitions for young persons and adults to draw pencil sketches copied from photographs of celebrities and local ministers. Many such portraits could be seen in local chapel vestries. To help him with his school work he saved his pocket money and subscribed to buy Arthur Mee's children's encyclopaedia. Amongst the volumes, however, the small black and white reproductions of oil paintings by Paul Cézanne were the greatest revelation. Inspired to try it himself, he saved his penny-a-week pocket money and bought oil paint by mail order.

John Elwyn had heard that there was an art school at Carmarthen, some twenty miles away, but knew nothing about it. In the autumn of 1934 his father took him to visit its Principal, Sidney Morse-Brown, at his house in Carmarthen which he had called 'Brangwyn' after the artist whom he greatly admired. He offered John Elwyn a place to study at Carmarthen School of Art as a fee-paying student and on 21st December 1934, at the end of the first term in Form 5A at Llandysul, he left to go to art school. He took digs in Carmarthen during the week and returned home at weekends.[12] Families generally kept together at that time, and even when offspring married they did not move far from the family home. John Elwyn, the youngest in the family, was the first to leave home and 'break up the nest'.

At Carmarthen he was the only painting student on the two-year diploma course. In January 1935 he joined a small group of about ten full-time students far more experienced than he, who were studying aspects of design, lettering, calligraphy and woodwork. Within a term he passed the drawing examination, was awarded an internal studentship, and in December that year he gained a First Class Certificate from the National Society for Art Masters. Morse-Brown was the only full-time tutor and he was assisted by a part-time staff of local craftsmen and women. John Elwyn received instruction in perspective, design, anatomy, still-life, cast, portrait and life drawing. The few paintings that survive from his time at Carmarthen, like *Construction* painted in 1937, with its decorative pattern-making across a composition crammed with detail, exotic bright colour, and vigorous, some might say slick, application of paint, are indebted to Morse-Brown's enthusiasm for the painter, designer and etcher Sir Frank Brangwyn. The portrait drawings made under Morse-Brown's instruction point towards a training that espoused the 'classical ideal' fused with close observation of the model, an aesthetic ideal that has its origins in Renaissance Italy. Morse-Brown's own techniques were encouraged as the method of drawing. A soft pencil or black chalk, and white chalk for highlights on toned paper, were used in diagonal hatched lines for putting down tones, darkest-dark juxtaposed lightest-light. A strong side-raking light source, and a mirror beneath the face to reflect light on to the underside of the shadow areas, heightened the *chiaroscuro*. The diagonal hatching, however, produced cold and impersonal results; this process of mark-making made it difficult to adapt the technique to describe variations in surface texture. The most enduring lesson that John Elwyn was to learn at Carmarthen was the importance of a good source of light to accentuate the body's form.

In August 1936 John Elwyn visited the 'Exhibition of Contemporary Welsh Art' at the National Eisteddfod in Fishguard. Wales was commonly perceived to be without a strong visual tradition and this travelling exhibition by contemporary artists of Welsh birth had been organised by the Committee of Valiants and the Committee for the Encouragement of Music and the Arts, to demonstrate that Wales could 'do more than raise her voice and sing ... she could, too, lift a brush and paint'.[13] Its aim was to 'illustrate the Welsh contribution to the visual arts ... create interest in the paintings and sculpture of our own day ... and to enable young artists working in Wales today to see and study the best that is being produced by their fellow countrymen'.[14] The

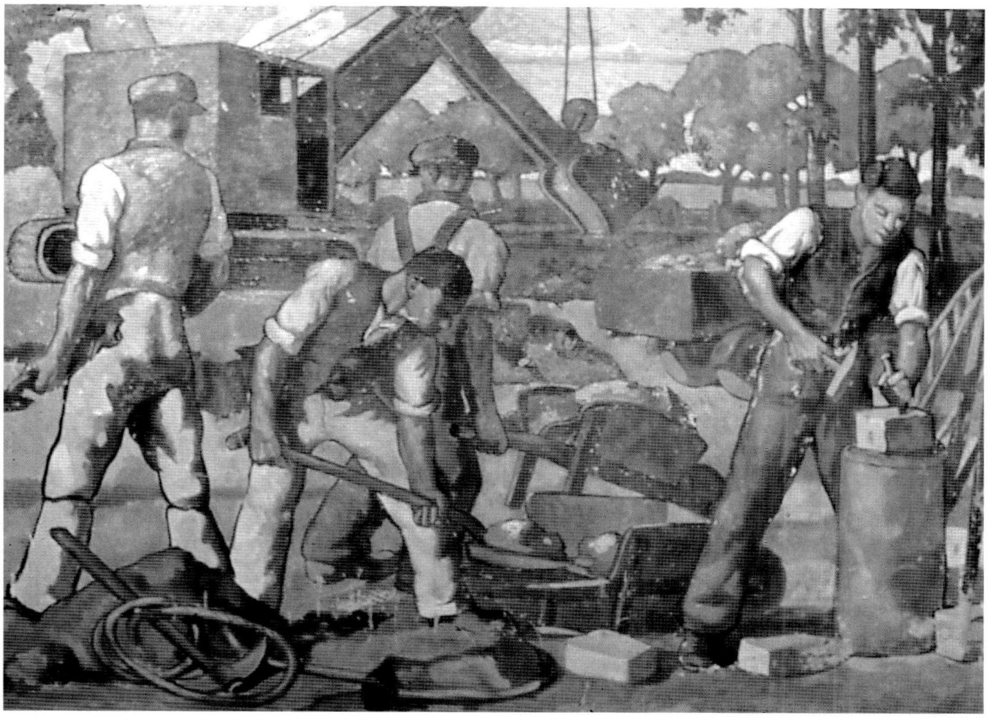

Construction
1936, oil on board 30 x 40
[The Artist's Estate]

paintings by Augustus and Gwen John, J. D. Innes, David Jones, Morland Lewis, Cedric Morris and Evan Walters included in the exhibition had a profound effect on John Elwyn. It was the first time that he had had the opportunity to see original works of art by like-minded individuals from Wales who had achieved success as artists.

In his second year at Carmarthen, a year ahead of schedule, Morse-Brown put John Elwyn's name forward for the South Kensington Board Examination. If he had passed he would in all likelihood have secured a teaching post in a nearby secondary school. Instead, he considered it his great fortune to have failed. It was the turning point in his career; later that summer Morse-Brown suffered a nervous breakdown and recommended that John Elwyn finished his studies at Bristol where he himself had once been a student. In September 1937 John Elwyn enrolled for the final year of his studies at the West of England College of Art in Bristol where Donald Milner was Principal and Evan Charlton had recently been appointed to teach painting. He took lodgings in Bedminster for the first term then moved to the downs at Redland. Away from home for the first time he sought out the Welsh community at the nearby chapel. Under Charlton's instruction, John Elwyn came to realise that there was more to painting and drawing than the formulae he had learnt from Morse-Brown. He believed that he was in danger of becoming too absorbed with 'style' and reliant upon 'slick sketching'; the manner was all too easy and superficial. He felt it necessary to undo his previous training and began to explore alternative means of representation. Few works survive from this period; he discarded much of the work produced during his two terms at Bristol as experimental and of no significance.

For three weeks in June 1938 he worked on the South Kensington Board Examination: a still-life painting in three days, a life painting in the following week, and a sketch for a mural decoration in the next two days, with a further three days to exe-

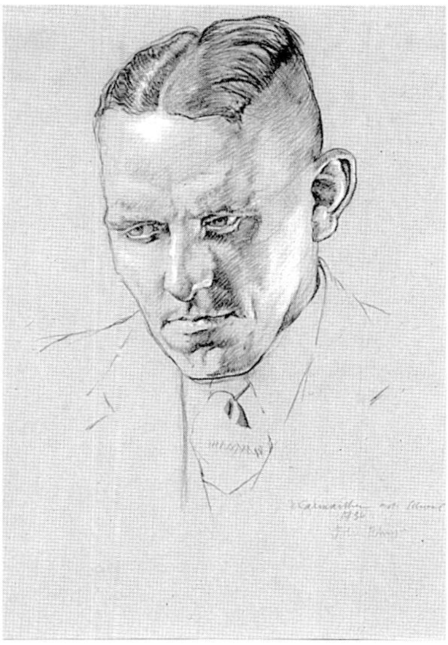

Model, the Portrait Class, Carmarthen School of Art
1936, black and white crayon on toned paper $14^{1}/_{2}$ x 10
[The University of Wales, Aberystwyth]

cute part of the figure composition on canvas. There were written examinations on painting methods and art history. The paintings were crated and sent to the Board of Education for assessment, and he filled in the forms and ticked the requisite boxes as he had been instructed, not realising that he was putting his name forward to be considered for a studentship. To John Elwyn's surprise he was awarded a Royal Exhibition Scholarship to study for three years at the Royal College of Art. There were only six Exhibition scholarships awarded nationally and this was the first time it had been won by a student at Bristol; his fees were paid, he received £150 per annum, and each term he was given a return train ticket home, a few tubes of paint and two canvases.[15] On hearing of his bursary, Morse-Brown sent hearty congratulations:

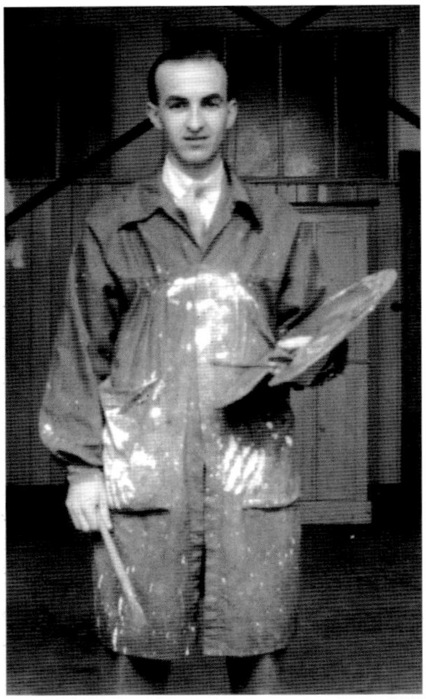

John Elwyn as a student at Bristol, July 1938

> You have justified all my hopes and expectations by winning such a valuable scholarship, and I am very proud of you! ... Go to the College for three years and then come back to help me build up a Welsh 'School' of painters who are content to live and work in Wales ... Stick to *your own* ideas and work hard my lad. There is no profession like ours.[16]

And from Newcastle Emlyn came a poignantly succinct telegram, 'Congratulations on your fine achievement, Mam.'[17]

Two friends and fellow students of painting at Bristol also went up to the Royal College; Denis Reed and Richard MacDonald were both awarded a free entry scholarship.[18] Reed, who had only recently undergone kidney surgery, suggested that they find digs together and share a large studio:

> what do you say, three lads from the west Country. How marvellous it is to be an artist, to see everything in terms of colour, form, rhythm, space and atmosphere, consider how rare a thing it is – it is noble. We live absolutely in another world – how then are we expected to perform duties complying with the rules and regulations of this world.[19]

John Elwyn was evidently not disposed towards the suggestion and he declined the offer. Reed too had a sudden change of heart:

> Dear Elwyn (the Individualist) You are right! About the flat and your work! You know how enthusiastic I was about the idea of a joint studio? Well that idea can be the other side of Hell as far as I'm concerned. I want a place of my own where I can work or rest whenever I please, and I admire you for arriving at this conclusion at the very beginning ... we should not tire of each other's company, as I feel we most certainly would, if we all lived together in an inferno of a studio – breathing the same air, spitting on the same floor board.[20]

In September 1938 John Elwyn moved to London and took lodgings in Earl's Court.

Chapter 2

and fire green as grass:

the war years

IN SPITE OF THE SIGNING of the Munich Agreement on 29th September 1938 which had narrowly averted war, Hitler's threats were being taken very seriously, guns were being set up along the embankment and sandbags were a common sight all over London. John Elwyn's immediate concern was to join a queue for a gas mask. On his first day at the Royal College of Art, he sat before the panel of distinguished staff and asked if he might transfer to the Design School where Denis Reed had just enrolled – although not long afterwards he transferred to the Painting School. However, his scholarship had been for painting and it was not possible for him to change course. Disappointed by their decision, Reed encouraged his friend to:

> Carry on painting, show them how, upset their apple cart ... I have no fear, you are a *good* painter, nobody at the College as good and I prophesy this, in two years time you will have half the "studio" devoted to a review of your paintings.[21]

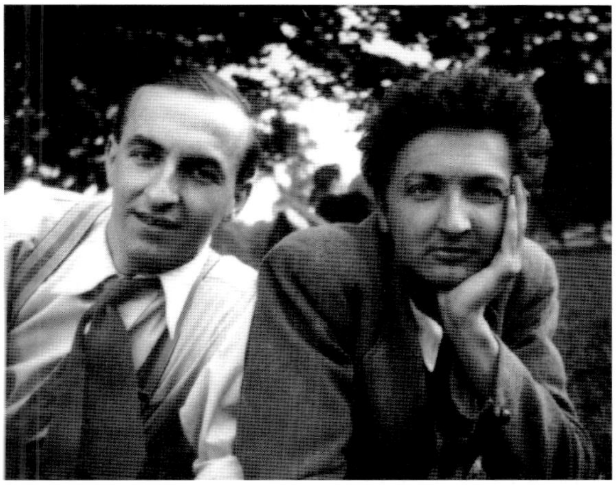

John Elwyn and Denis Reed in Kensington Gardens, June 1940

At the Royal College, Gilbert Spencer was Professor of the School of Drawing and Painting. He was supported by a team of full- and part-time tutors who were also practising artists; they included Vivian Pitchforth, Percy Horton, Francis Helps, Barnett Freedman, Edward Bawden, Alan Sorrell, Rodney Burns and Charles Mahoney.

In the first year students had a rigorous grounding in observational work, with two days a week architectural drawing, one day still-life painting and two days life painting. Attendance was compulsory from 9.30a.m. to 6.00p.m. and there was a register to be signed. John Elwyn was a product of an art school system that still believed that drawing the human figure was the best means to test an artist's powers of observation and expression. In spite of being eroded by modernist tendencies in the twentieth century life drawing continued at the Royal College as an important part of an artist's professional training, a practice requiring strict discipline and sustained effort. Daily, between 2.00 and 6.00 p.m., students from various departments came together for the life class; at that time the male and female students were segregated. Instructors walked around the studio and offered guidance to students. Vivian Pitchforth, for example, encouraged them to describe volume and form in their drawings. He was an advocate of Roger Fry's principles of 'pure form', analysing Cézanne's reduction of the human figure to cylinders, spheres and cones in order to explain the problems students might encounter defining form. Gilbert Spencer held tutorials in his private study and he stressed the importance of accurate proportions. Percy Horton was an enthusiast of Ingres and set the model in strident classical poses, legs akimbo and arms raised to the heavens. He taught John Elwyn to describe volume using a light pencil line and *sfumato* shading, and drew his attention to the stresses, strains and movement of the human figure. Under Horton he acquired a feeling for the body's

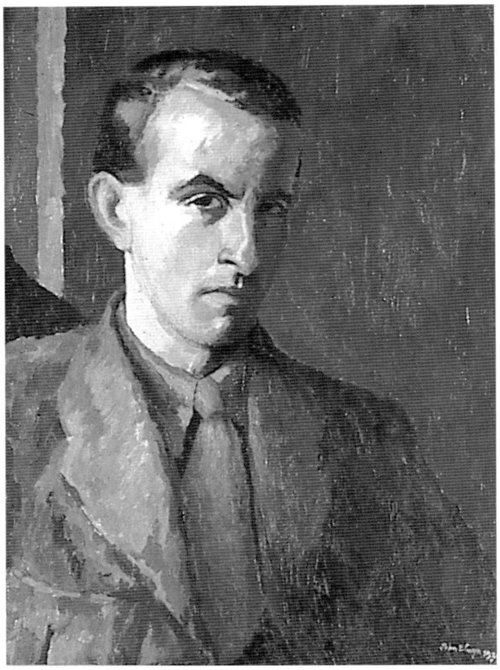

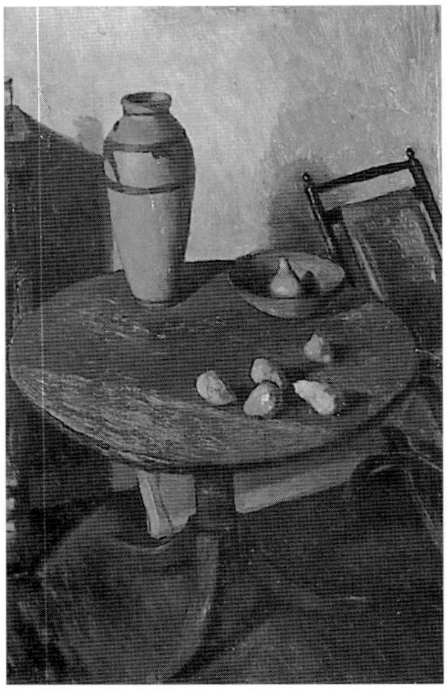

Self Portrait
1939, oil on canvas 20 x 16
[National Library of Wales, Aberystwyth]

Still Life with Stoneware Vase
1947, oil on board 24½ x 16½
[The Artist's Estate]

equilibrium: its balance, distribution of weight and the natural rhythm of the pose.

In the art galleries and museums around London John Elwyn saw for the first time the famous paintings that he had only read about in Carmarthen and Bristol. He was all too conscious of his limited exposure to original art works and lack of awareness of contemporary developments. In the commercial galleries that championed artistic freedom and encouraged experimentation he witnessed more cosmopolitan attitudes, and an easy acceptance of Continental modernism, far removed from the conservatism he had encountered at Carmarthen School of Art. On 22nd April 1939, he visited a centenary exhibition of Cézanne's paintings at Rosenberg and Helft Ltd in Bruton Street, staged in aid of the rebuilding fund of St George's Hospital. He wrote on the back of his copy of the catalogue:

> An excellent collection which proved that Cézanne is a vital force in the modern trend of art. The self portrait appealed to me very much, wonderful colours in it. The landscapes were jewels, full of air and sunlight and yet the shadows did not play a part in the actual rendering of light as might be thought on a sunny day. Landscape No. 20 was a very powerful one – painted by a powerful hand and mind – recession and colour very dominant. Figure comps also a feast of design not so much in colour. Hot spots of the exhibition were the still lifes. Exquisite form and stability with great subtlety in tones. Large canvases kept very fresh throughout. Surprising colours in the shadows. This is the best show I have seen so far in London: only wished it was a permanent one. Cézanne is great.[22]

The influence of Cézanne is evident in much of John Elwyn's student work from his series of self-portraits to the carefully observed interiors and still-lifes; the solid forms of the fruit and slightly aerial viewpoint are reminders of Cézanne's pictorial devices. In 1939 he moved with Denis Reed to lodgings in Kensington and there he painted portraits of Reed within Bonnardesque interiors, and street scenes through the balustrade of their window. They are modest, atmospheric little studies painted in

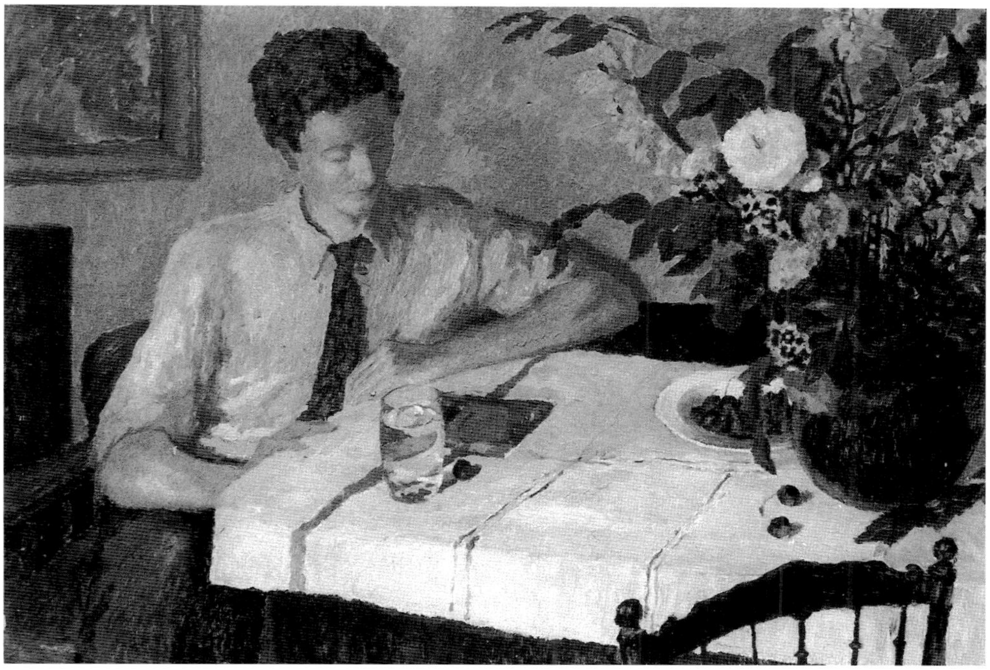

Denis Reed in our Earl's Court Digs
1940, oil on board 24 x 36
[The Artist's Estate]

London's dingy winter light, within a close tonal range of muted colours evocative of the work of William Coldstream, Graham Bell and the painters of the Euston Road School who had all been exhibiting in London in the late 1930s.

John Elwyn was very apprehensive of city life, he felt London was 'a hell of a place and a very lonely place', but at least there was cheer to be found amongst the Welsh community in the London-Welsh Club or packing out the Welsh chapels. On Sunday evenings they congregated in Charing Cross Road, King's Cross Congregational Chapel, and smaller chapels in Flood Street and Waltham Green. Afterwards they went for tea at Fleming's Restaurant in Oxford Street and community hymn singing in Hyde Park in the summer. At the end of his first year in London he returned to Wales and spent the summer of 1939 helping his father at the mill. Joyce Thomas remembers John Elwyn during vacations taking:

> walks on the Cilgwyn Estate. He used to pass my grandparents' house always deep in thought. I knew that he was an artist and wondered what he could see in his mind's eye. If I greeted him, he would look up with a start of surprise. His concentration was complete. He was always neatly dressed – in no way a Bohemian! In the winter especially he would be warmly clad in Welsh tweeds.[23]

During the long summer vacations there was plenty of opportunity to paint portraits of his family, interiors of the mill's domestic quarters, and the local landscape including *Picnic in Cilgwyn Woods* (1940). (Plate 1) He also read a great deal. At school he had been introduced to Welsh poetry and the work of Matthew Arnold, Robert Browning, John Keats and William Wordsworth. He was fascinated by their different attitudes towards life and religion. During his year in London he came to realise that the lifestyle of others could be very different from his own upbringing. In London, he wrote:

> I tried to develop self respect, and respect for people in my new circle of life ... I

> mixed with students from different parts of the country, and was surprised at times at their different ways of seeing and looking at life – I could not understand their moral standards.[24]

This led to more than a passing interest in philosophy and psychology and he read books by Aldous Huxley, T. E. Lawrence, John Macmurray and Olaf Stapledon, who reinforced his pacifist sympathies:

> I read enough to realise that the sum and foundation of everything is that man in relation to his fellow man is the key that brings harmony to life and to the world.[25]

At the beginning of the war John Elwyn discussed his convictions with his parents and they supported his becoming a Conscientious Objector, though it was never discussed afterwards, even when it made news headlines in the local papers. His father especially held strong views on war; his poetry reveals that he believed it was the culmination of 'A proud heart boiling over ... a secret plan lurching in a sinful heart'.[26]

John Elwyn returned to London for the new term in September 1939 as war was declared. The College remained open until the summer term of 1940 when it was forced to send students home after the Fall of France, the Battle of Britain and the heavy bombing of London. Students received letters inviting them to continue their studies at Ambleside in the Lake District, where the College had been evacuated into two grand and fashionable hotels. Few students took the opportunity to continue their studies in Ambleside. Richard MacDonald contemplated the letter:

> I don't know what to say about the R.C.A. I should like to go back – but ... when you have finished the war may still be going strong, then no job ... Reed has passed the A1 and put himself down as a C.O. The best of luck to him and any more C.O.s. Why don't you join their ranks.[27]

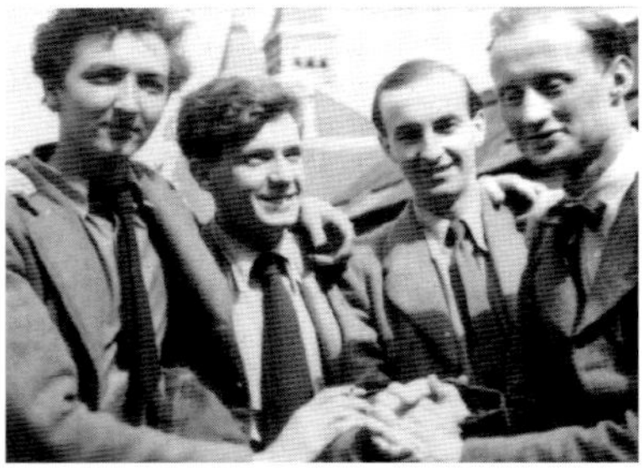

Denis Reed, Richard MacDonald, John Elwyn and Le Fleure, London, July 1940

In April 1940 Reed, MacDonald, John Elwyn and their friends Leonard Renton and Jack Wright were offered camouflage work and they all objected to army service. They faced a Tribunal and were directed to land work; in August 1940 Renton was offered Air Raid Patrol or farming, Jack Wright found land work, and MacDonald became a cow hand at a farm near Dartmouth in Devon. Reed stayed in Bristol where he applied for work with the Auxiliary Fire Services in Somerset, but the authorities refused to give work to C.O.s.[28]

John Elwyn was employed from August 1940 as a forestry worker for four seasons above Pont-Rhyd-y-Fen in the Neath Valley. There was an element of 'sadness' and moments of self-doubt in his decision to become a C.O.; he realised if everyone had taken this course of action the world would be a very different place, but he remained true to his convictions. He was all too aware that he had come into the world at the height of World War I, just two days before the end of the Battle of the Somme in which 600,000 men lost their lives when allied forces staged a series of offensives against German positions. 'It is as if I was born with the smell of blood in my nostrils', he once commented.[29] Life was hard on the forestry working long hours in all weathers on the exposed mountains, the work was heavy and physical and there were long walks to and from his lodgings each day; the experience however toughened his constitution and strengthened his physique. In his letters to John Elwyn, Denis Reed described the devastating effects of the war on Bristol: the air raids, damage to property, and the unnerving consequence of living with the rumble of bombs and the drone of Heinkels by day and night. He speculated at length on the nature and purpose of the war. He believed that the war had been perpetuated throughout Europe to suppress the proletariat, to hold the workers back and re-instate the capitalist class in France and Germany. The letters convey both the exhilaration and terror of modern warfare. He described the Blitz on the evening of 23rd November 1940, which he had witnessed from his window before taking shelter under the stairs with his mother:

> The air raid was the largest, and I believe, the most disastrous, that we have had on Bristol since the beginning of the war, I feel thankful to be alive this morning ... It started about 6.30 p.m. and went on for 6 hours ... a parachute flare that was slowly descending giving me a terrible sense of impending disaster, several more flares illuminated the dock ... and the river reflected the flares like bright pewter. The whole landscape was lit up ... smoke started rising from several points ... and it was not long before the wood yards were blazing furiously ... dense columns of smoke joining into one great cloud which passed steadily overhead, orange, amber, black, grey, red ... Fires now appeared on all sides ... they seemed to be coming over in relays ... some explosions sounded very near ... we crouched with our hands over our ears ... it all seemed so unreal ... but not to the people being sick with heat and fear in the shelters below the burning and tumbling buildings in the centre of the city ... I stood for a long time watching the flames 50 or 60 foot high making cranes on the dockside white hot and the black outlines of sheds and warehouses silhouetted against the inferno. Today I wandered around the ruins ... every large shop in Bristol gone – burnt out ... utterly wrecked, beyond recognition ... smoldering remains, twisted bits of metal, charred wooden beams, bleached walls, soft flowery, barren windows and facades of buildings defaced by bomb splinters ... People had to watch their homes burn, for the A.F.S. could not cope with it all ... crowds of people, seemingly without homes, walking aimlessly ... looking at the havoc wrought in so short a time.[30]

At the Swansea home of Gwilym Thomas, a friend and former pottery student at the Royal College, John Elwyn was invited to join a Quaker community in Cardiff. In September 1941 he moved to Llanishen House where he was involved in food production and market gardening, propagating, planting out, harvesting, ploughing fields and tending to the horses which pulled his cart around Llanishen and Whitchurch. It was a small community of about ten people. The senior member was Miss E. M. Bush, known as E.M. or 'Yem' to her friends. A graduate of the University of London, she was small and physically tired after a life devoted to hard work and the care of others. She was an absolute pacifist and cared for those who stood out against war.[31] Like many pacifists who had objected to the armed services, John Elwyn had found friendship and support amongst The Religious Society of Friends.

John Elwyn's sympathetic and tolerant nature made him an ideal recruit for community living, based on trustful acceptance and caring for each other. In his letters Denis Reed envied him the life he enjoyed in Cardiff, given the support of like-minded individuals for whom Christian attitudes were a way of life. He wrote that he was finding it increasingly difficult to tolerate:

> the weary war background, its nausea and harsh intensity does not go down with you does it? You find it irritating? Or do you shut the whole thing out and still dwell in your Bonnard world of phantasy, innocence, sincerity, purity and simplic-

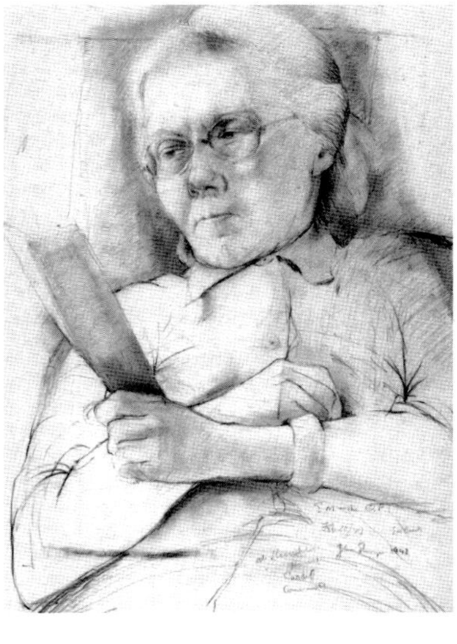

Miss E. M. Bush
1942, pencil on paper 22 x 15
[The Artist's Estate]

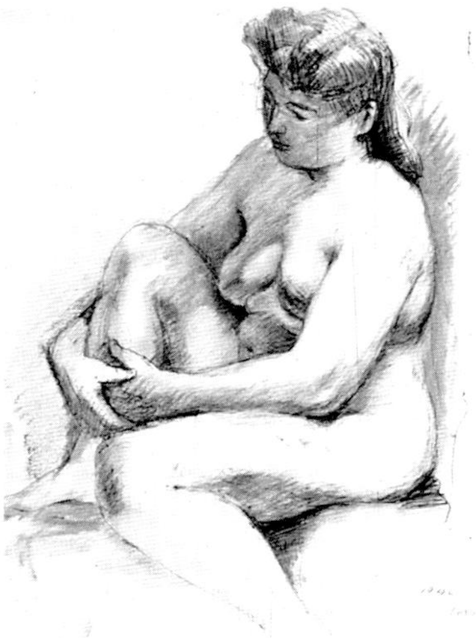

ABOVE AND OPPOSITE
Seated Figures, Cardiff Life Class
1941, pencil and crayon on paper
15 x 11 each
[The University of Wales, Aberystwyth]

> ity – still savouring the wholesome good things in life and shutting both eyes to the wolf breaking in at the back door ... Working long hours alone, day after day, gives the mind ample time for introspection. We are apt to get a little clogged so that everything looks black ... that how is how it has been with me.[32]

Not suited to work on the land, and unhappy with the lifestyle he had experienced as a Conscientious Objector, Reed sought permission of the College authorities to resume his studies in Ambleside. The Board of Education turned down the request and explained that his scholarship would not be renewed during the war, but 'under certain circumstances' may be re-awarded some time after it. He was bitterly disappointed and thought the College had submitted a poor report on his conduct or progress. He believed his career was in jeopardy and feared that employers, and the Government, would be harder on Objectors when the war ended:

> another year of this grind will finish me off – what can I do but join up? That is my intention at the moment. I know what you are going to say – 'escapist', 'turncoat', 'yellow'. Well, to tell you the truth I want security now – I didn't want it when I became a C.O. I had no use for it – but I see how important it is.[33]

John Elwyn responded promptly in a futile attempt to dissuade Reed from signing up. Reed tried to explain himself once more in what was to be their last correspondence during the war:

> If your intention was to make me reconsider, all I can say is that it did, for the thousandth time, and still I find myself standing firmly beside my decision. I assure you it isn't rash – I've thought hard and thought long, to sum it up and be honest, my feelings have undergone a change, a very slow and painful one. Perhaps it has been the people whom I've met and have been influenced by, the turn in the war against Russia, the feeling of being isolated (as a C.O.) or the steady disintegration of my possibly reactionary views when war broke out clouding my then idealistic world. Whatever has brought the change, I have fought it all the way ... now I find myself with fewer ideas on the war than the average layman and impoverished reasons for staying out of it ... It is a foul and disgusting thing to do, to usurp the throne of 'humanitarianism', elementary laws of human conduct and relationship ... When I became a C.O. I did not know fully the whole structure of the implications, it was with me a shot in the dark. I did not bank on being thrown amongst an illiterate mob of people doing drudge work ... If at the end of a year's work in the War Effort I can not get a place in the College – is it not just as likely to inflict the same measure after the war in the chaos of so-called reconstruction – the attitude may be "let those who helped us in destruction – help us in construction – and the isolationists etc. go to the devil – we cannot afford as yet to cater for the needs of all". Such an attitude is quite likely.[34]

Reed subsequently joined the Royal Engineers and served in Wales, Yorkshire and eventually London where, as a result of his ill-health, he became Art Advisor to the London District of Army Education.

In September 1941 John Elwyn met Glyn Jones in the gallery of the Welsh Independent Chapel in Minny Street, Cardiff. Jones wrote poetry, novels, short stories and reviews, and was a key figure amongst the generation of post-war Anglo-Welsh writers that included Rhys Davies, Jack Jones, Alun Lewis, Leslie Norris, John Ormond, Dylan Thomas and Waldo Williams. A close friendship developed and continued until Glyn Jones died in April 1995. (Plate XXVI) Glyn Jones was born in 1905, the son of a collier in Merthyr Tydfil. His forebears were from rural Carmarthenshire, and he regularly visited the area, drawing upon its landscape and people for his subject. He too was a pacifist and Conscientious Objector, and had lost his teaching post in the local grammar school as a result of his convictions. In the 1930s, whilst staying with Dylan and Caitlin Thomas, Dylan had encouraged Jones to write short autobiographical stories about childhood. John Elwyn shared Jones' enthusiasm for story-telling and admired the poetry in which he perceptively commented upon the landscape and indigenous characters that were already so familiar to the painter.[35] He became a regular visitor at 158 Manor Way, the home Jones shared with his wife Doreen. He shared with them the treats that had been sent to him from Newcastle Emlyn – ham, cheese and other difficult to obtain farm produce during war-time rationing. At weekends they sold *Peace News* from a stall in Cardiff market.

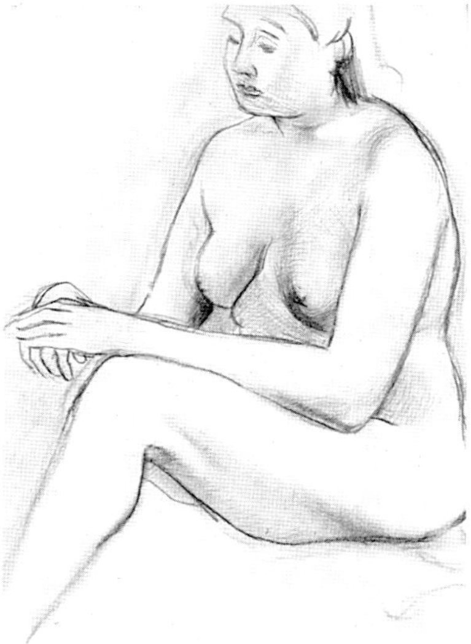

In October 1941 John Elwyn signed up for evening life classes at Cardiff College of Art which were taught by Ceri Richards who was Head of Painting from 1940 to 1944. His influence upon John Elwyn is apparent in the two drawings that survive; their heavy rounded forms, simplified line and tone, and spontaneity of execution were derived from Richards' interest in European modernism, in particular that of Picasso and Matisse. At weekends John Elwyn painted during spare moments: the grounds at Llanishen House, views from the window, figures in interiors, still-life and flower studies. In the evenings he made space on the kitchen table to work on a series of allegorical paintings. The idea evolved after he undertook a commission to illustrate 'Everyman', translated from German into Welsh by Leslie Harries for *Chwe Drama Fer*, a collection of one-act plays published by Gomer Press in 1944. Leslie Harries, who was eight years his senior, taught Welsh and junior Latin at Llandysul County Grammar School. This was a dark period in John Elwyn's life, death seemed always close at hand. Britain had been at war for four years and hundreds of thousands of people had lost their lives. Cardiff and Swansea were heavily bombed, and Denis Reed's horrific descriptions of the bombing of Bristol had left their mark on John Elwyn. Furthermore, his mother developed stomach cancer and died in 1942 after a long illness. The *Chwe Drama Fer* project led him to illustrate further scenes from the medieval mystery play, creating an imaginative, melancholic dream-world in which Death in the form of a skeleton is at the shoulder of Everyman. The tormented figure in *Everyman* (1944), melodramatically holding his hands to his head, screams in anguish. (Plate III) These works are all signed 'John Elwyn'; it was the first time that he had used the name professionally, his family and friends however still knew him as Elwyn Davies.[36] The allegorical paintings that were to follow recall works by his exact contemporaries Michael Ayrton, John Craxton and John Minton whom we now associate with the Neo-Romantic movement that flourished in England during Britain's war-time isolation. Inspired by Graham Sutherland's subjective landscapes made in Pembrokeshire during the 1930s, these painters turned to the Welsh landscape. John Elwyn had also been fascinated by Sutherland's paintings of the gnarled and twisted forms of roots, and dead or dying trees in desecrated landscapes. He had discovered for himself similarly menacing and scarred landscapes whilst working on the forestry. John Elwyn had not been aware of the emerging young Neo-Romantic painters before he left London but he had seen something of Edward Burra's paintings of strange natural objects set against disturbing surrealist landscapes. Like Sutherland his experience of Surrealism, which he had encountered in London before the war, affected his interpretation of natural forms.

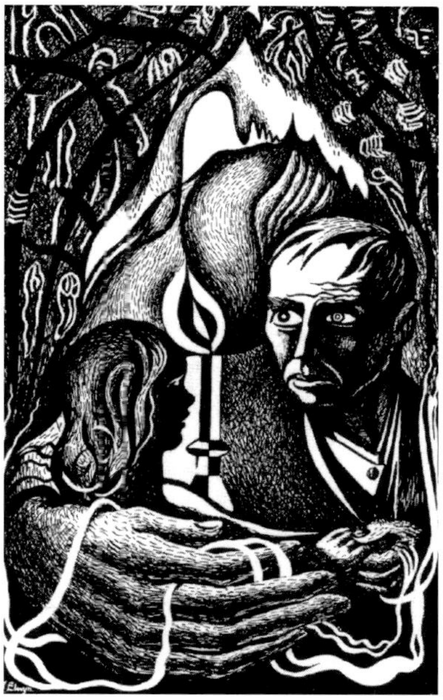

Chwe Drama Fer
1944, ink on paper 5½ x 3½
[The Artist's Estate]

In John Elwyn's landscapes too, the natural elements appear to have a presence beyond the literal, and the atmosphere is heightened by firey blood-red or brilliant green smoke-laden skies; their theatricality to a certain degree was influenced by the set and backcloths of the ballet he had seen just before the war. In *The Stillness of the Roots* (1944) a lone figure sleeps amidst a claustrophobic landscape of tangled vegetation much in the spirit of John Craxton's haunting nocturnal landscapes, in particular the ink and wash drawings *Poet in a Landscape* (1941) and *Dreamer in a*

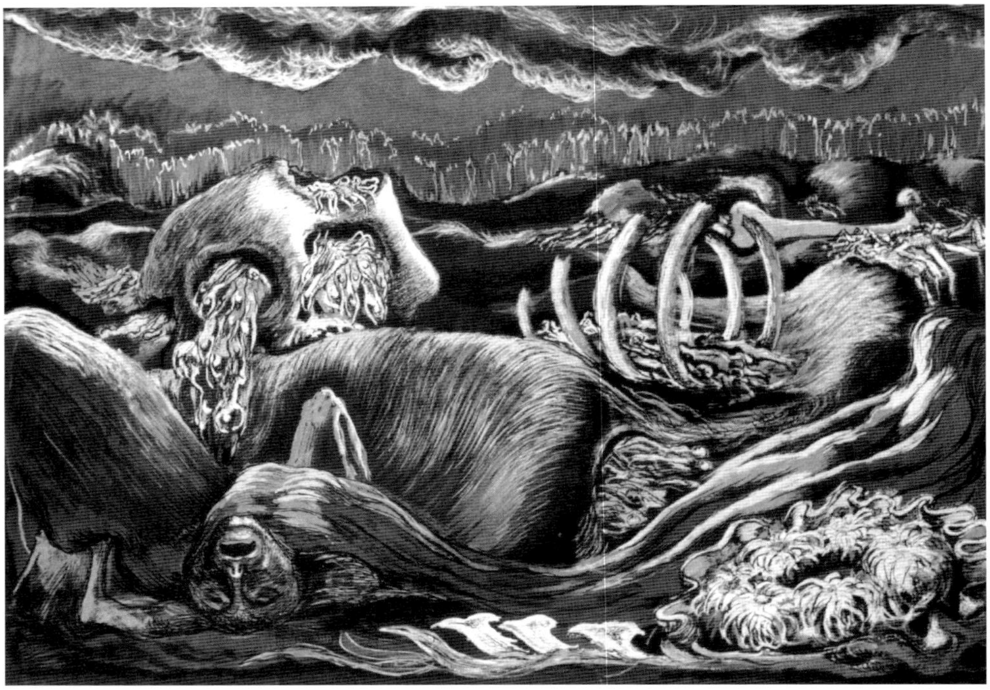

Aftermath
1945, ink, gouache and chalk on paper 15 x 22
[Peter Wakelin]

Landscape (1942), now in the Tate Gallery. (Plate II) Watercolour, ink, gouache, pencil and crayon all lent themselves to the spontaneous effect John Elwyn sought. The Aftermath paintings that followed in 1945 depict surreal scenes of chaos and destruction that reveal the artist's doubts and anxieties about the violent and destructive power of war, and his horror at the atrocities committed at Belsen. The production of these works was undoubtedly a cathartic experience for the artist.

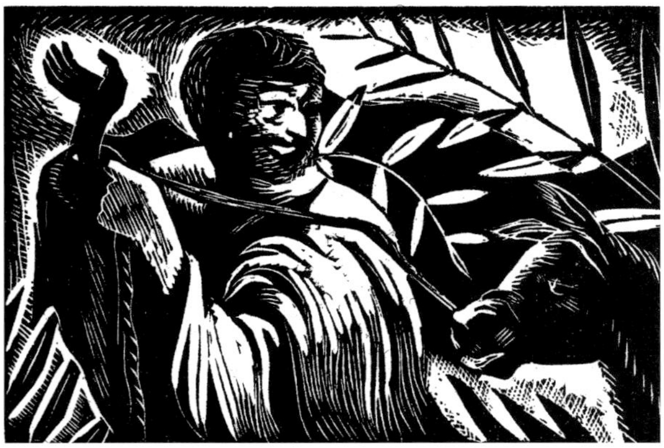

Simon y Canaanead
1944, wood engraving on paper 3 x 2
[The Artist's Estate]

John Elwyn created a similar dark and tormented world in the wood-engraved illustrations for *Disgyblion yr Iesu* (Disciples of Jesus) in *Tywysydd y Plant*, a monthly religious magazine in Welsh for children and young people published by *Undeb yr Annibynwyr Cymraeg* (Society of Welsh Independent Churches). In 1944 he cut twelve boxwood blocks to illustrate stanzas by Leslie Harris describing tales of the disciples. These were insensitively printed on economy-issue paper in monthly instalments during 1946. The origin of this particular strain of Romanticism can be found in William Blake's seventeen visionary wood engravings for Robert John Thornton's third schoolbook edition of Ambrose Philip's *Imitation of Virgil's First Eclogue* (*The Pastorals of Virgil*) published in 1821. The Virgil illustrations have been a seminal force for generations of British Romantic artists. The *Disgyblion* engravings share

Blake's intimate scale and intensity; both are illustrative and at the same time allegorical, suggesting as they do the struggle between good and evil. Like Blake, John Elwyn chose expressive cutting to capture the action and emotions of the disciples rather than adopt a more populist approach based upon precision and the outward signs of good craftsmanship. The *Disgyblion* engravings are highly charged Romantic images in which observation is subsidiary to the manifestation of religious and spiritual ideals; the atmosphere is overwhelmingly tense and anxious. There is a distinct dream-like quality in the strange and claustrophobic settings; the mood and character of the disciples is amplified by the dramatic moonlight.

When the war ended John Elwyn continued to work on the land until the summer of 1946 when he was taken ill with appendicitis. His release was issued in August that year and in September he returned to London to finish his course at the Royal College of Art, taking lodgings at 162 Earl's Court Road, SW5. Back in Wales his sister Mary gave piano lessons in the parlour of the mill and sent the money she earned to help with his expenses. Denis Reed had enrolled in January 1946 and was awarded a Diploma of Associateship after one year. The College had been badly damaged, its windows were blown out early in the war, and in May 1944 its roof collapsed after a direct hit by a flying bomb. John Elwyn came to realise how much his own attitudes had changed and that it was not possible for him to pick up where he had left off. He explained (writing about himself in the third person) that during his years on the land:

> he was able to draft his ideals and re-inforce his opinions and arguments about life in general, at the same time having a direct contact with the soil which appealed to him greatly. The contentment and unobtrusive ways of Nature enlarged his vision generally and enabled him to see much further into the heart of things that matter than he was able to do hitherto. So that when the war ended this young man possessed a new awareness of living which he took back once again to the giant anthill that is London.[37]

Whilst some private galleries such as Zwemmer, Lefevre and the Leicester Galleries had remained open during the war, many were now re-opening in Cork Street and Bond Street to stage exhibitions by young contemporaries as well as more established figures. Mainly English work was shown as it was still difficult to obtain the work of Continental artists. The West End galleries provided a focus for the work of the young English Neo-Romantics – Ayrton, Craxton, Minton, Robert Colquhoun, Robert MacBryde and Keith Vaughan. John Elwyn followed their development with interest, not at that time appreciating the extent to which their work shared similar concerns to his own. Regularly visiting the galleries to keep abreast of recent developments of the English school, as well as studying paintings by his favourite French artists – Bonnard, Cézanne and Vuillard – he saw as an important part of his training:

> I tried to emulate some of these painters – the ones that attracted my attention and creative sensibility in order to cultivate some kind of style. This worked very well for some time but it was not long before I became dissatisfied and disillusioned – this was quite natural in order to master enough technique to get underway. But outside this I needed some point, some purpose to put down statements which were meaningful to me, however small-minded they seemed to be at the time.

> Current styles and fashion for its own sake did not appeal to me. I wanted to discover an area that would preoccupy me in a visual and possibly a literary sense, of my own choice – in other words I was searching for a reason for painting.[38]

He felt that he had mastered the craft of painting, and developed his observational skills, but deciding what to paint presented difficulties. He did not want to imitate others' styles, that came too easily and gave him no satisfaction. The London art scene was a melting pot of modernist tendencies from Surrealism to Abstraction, as well as the more traditional genres of the Euston Road realists. In 1937 the Euston Road painters William Coldstream and Graham Bell published a manifesto called *Plan for Artists* which recommended to students 'the exploration and expression in paint, by actual experience, of the natural world'. Following this advice John Elwyn painted still-lifes, portraits, figures in interiors and street scenes in the Euston Road manner, after those painters described by Kenneth Clark as 'artists with a pinch of earth'. Their subjects derived from the direct and searching observation of everyday life, rendered in a low-key Sickertian palette within close tonal harmonies. John Elwyn took his sketch book into Kensington Gardens and along the Thames in search of subjects. He was commited to a realist style, he knew that he was never going to be at the cutting edge of contemporary art, and realised that he did not possess 'the desire or the ability to push the frontiers of creative thought and activity, to discover new and exciting areas of possibility'.[39]

John Elwyn's paintings of the 1950s shared many of the stylistic conventions and a preoccupation with landscape of the better-known Neo-Romantic painters, but they lack that air of melancholy we associate with their paintings. There are obvious parallels between John Elwyn's works and paintings by Minton, Vaughan, Craxton, Ayrton and later Sutherland. It is in the paintings which he produced in Cardiff during the war, however, that he came closest to the 'kindred spirit' that was the bond between Neo-Romantic painters of his generation, particularly when Neo-Romanticism allied itself to Surrealism and the landscape became a vehicle for the expression of emotional and religious ideals. During the war years he was at his most insecure and vulnerable, but generally he was much more easy going and optimistic than the Neo-Romantic painters who each seemed to possess a much darker outlook on the world. Once asked if he possessed a darker side to his character, or had been prone to melancholia or depression, he responded:

> I am very grateful for possessing the qualities you say I have – like easy going, relaxed, unruffled, taking it all in my stride ... If anything, my main problem in general is exercising too much conscience which at times is a hinderance to the achievement of many things in life.[40]

Ayrton, Colquhoun, Craxton, MacBryde, Minton and Vaughan had all known each other and benefited from being part of a small community. They enjoyed the support of influential patrons during their formative years in war-time London. John Elwyn's personality was very different from theirs: he did not socialise in Fitzrovia and the Soho clubs, nor share their interest in alcohol and drugs, which was a very significant factor in their lives:

> I was a closed book really for most people. You see it's a matter of committing yourself. If you're in a pub and it's "drinks all round, come on lads" ... Oh, I couldn't do that. Conversation starts sometimes and you find yourself talking about things which nobody else has heard, about yourself, which I don't like.[41]

He could never understand why people were inclined to:

> create a stir or draw attention to oneself. That was the last thing I wished to do. As a student I felt very inadequate in London, to take the initiative or impose on anybody. It must start with the genes I suppose, and I am grateful for my parents of what qualities they passed on to me ... One realises that the habits of the home are important factors that builds one's attitude in life towards good and bad, and respect for life.[42]

John Elwyn lacked confidence in his own ideas and was conscious that his values were not those of city-born students who had already spent time in the London art schools:

> If I started to say "I believe this ...", or "I think this is right ...", it would be taken out of context, because of being in London from the country. I didn't have the straightness of thought.[43]

Vera Adie was a student at the Royal College and remembers John Elwyn as 'quiet and reserved and kept very much to himself' perhaps because he was older than his peer group at College.[44] John Ward, who graduated from the Royal College in 1939, was another friend whom John Elwyn visited after the war at the apartment he shared with Jehan Daly. Ward thought: 'He was one of those people one was always on the look-out for, and hoping to meet ... he was ever a respected person ... one loved him for his gentle quiet determination.'[45]

The exhibition for the Diploma of Associateship – the A.R.C.A. – took place in June 1947 at the Imperial Institute. Each student was allocated a cubicle to paint the set examination piece after which they arranged a representative display of course work for the examiners.[46] His final composition on the theme of *Family Life* was derived from sketchbook drawings done at Llanishen House during the war. John

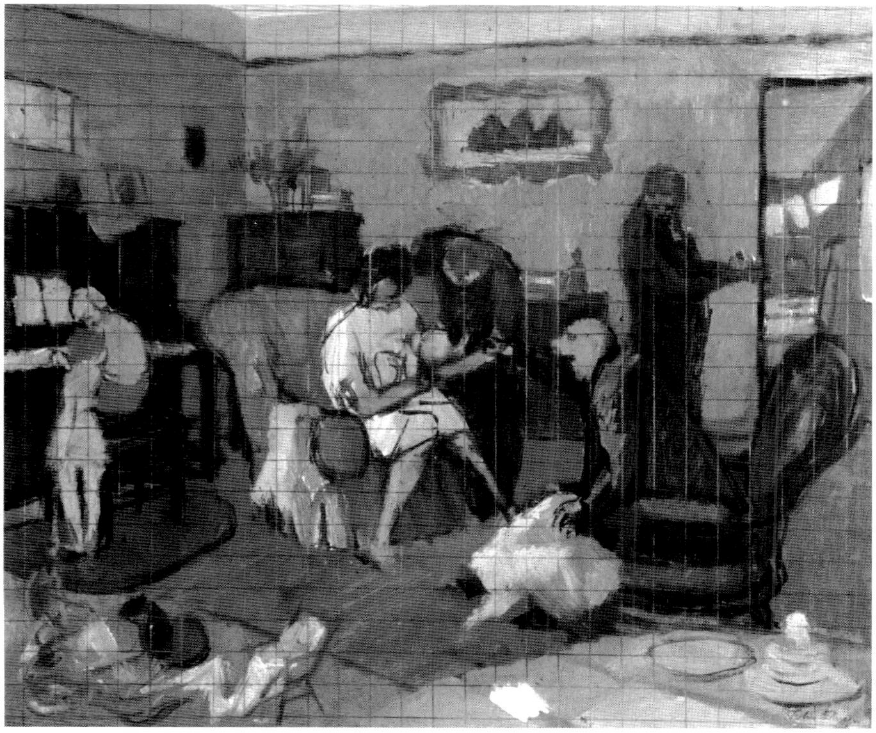

Family Life
(Study for the R.C.A. Diploma piece)
1947, oil on paper 12 x 14½
[Robert Meyrick]

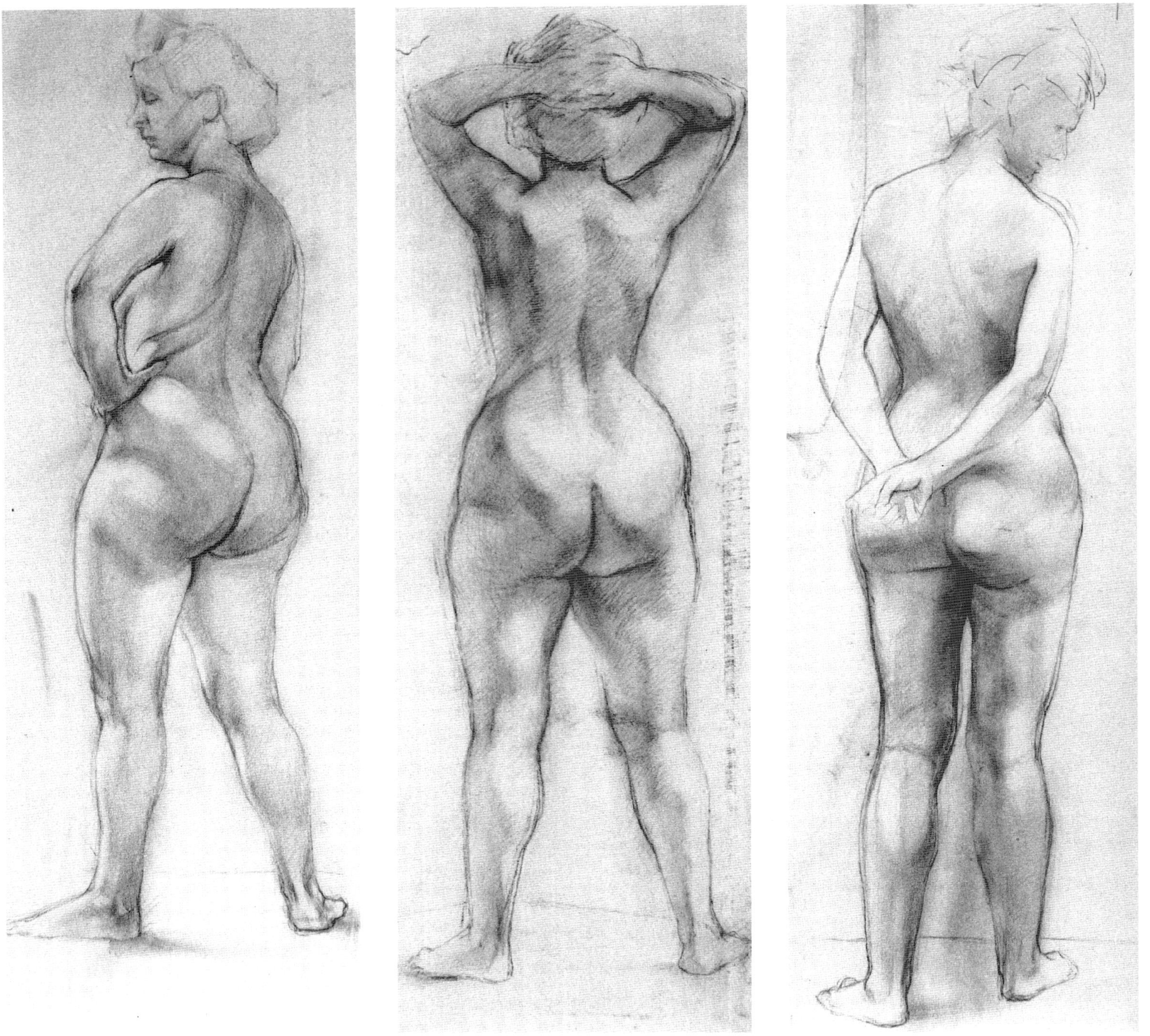

The Life Class,
Royal College of Art
1947, pencil on paper 18 x 7 each
[The University of Wales, Aberystwyth]

Elwyn's figure drawing attracted considerable attention. Gilbert Spencer described him as 'one of the best draughtsmen I have had. He is an objective artist of promise'.[47] In their testimonials the staff unanimously recognised John Elwyn's achievements and agreed that he had been their most able and gifted draughtsman. Percy Hague Jowett, the Principal, wrote 'I have formed a high opinion of his abilities and character ... he has produced painting and drawing during his final year which is of a high standard. He was awarded the Prize for drawing from life this year with a set of drawings which were excellent'.[48] Charles Mahoney remarked that 'His work is of consistent good quality and I must comment on the unusual variety and resourcefulness of his thoughtful, imaginative drawings ... He is a searching sensitive draughtsman from the life and able to cope with the more delicate problems of form'.[49] Percy Horton commented that he had been 'an extremely good student and has shown real ability as a painter and draughtsman. The excellence of his well constructed drawings was recognised by the award of the College Prize for Life-Drawing ... In fact all his work is thorough in aim and execution ... Sincerity of character is apparent in all he has done ... I believe he will do good work as an artist, and he would be a very useful teacher – whose influence could only be beneficial to his students'.[50] High praise indeed for a young graduate about to embark upon a professional career as an artist, ultimately working for thirty years in art education and all that time closely involved with the life class.

The diploma exhibition remained open to the public for four days and this was an occasion when Principals from provincial art schools came to scout for young talent to teach at their institutions. In the immediate post-war years there was a shortage of teachers for art schools and there were countless opportunities for young artists to teach. When John Elwyn was offered a teaching position by Leslie Gaydon, the Principal of Portsmouth he turned it down, explaining that he would prefer to stay in London for a while. The following morning in the National Gallery with two friends from the R.C.A., Gaydon tapped him on the shoulder and asked if he would reconsider. John Elwyn declined once more suggesting that Gaydon interview his colleagues. They too had begun their course at the R.C.A. before the war and were graduating that summer. One of them, the London-born painter Alan Jefferson (b. 1918), was duly offered a position and he taught at Portsmouth until his retirement. The other painter, Paul Bullard (1918–1997) went on to teach at Woolwich and Camberwell. In the summer vacation he declined the offer of a trip to Italy with his R.C.A. friends and instead accompanied Leslie Harris to Prague.

Chapter 3

and the sabbath rang slowly:

chapel days remembered

AFTER THE DIPLOMA EXHIBITION John Elwyn was anxious to secure a part-time teaching post in London where he foresaw the possibility of making a living as a painter. Ceri Richards encouraged him to:

> contemplate remaining in London if possible ... it is natural to want to continue with our creative talent until that time when we find that our fundamental backgrounds don't any more coincide with our achievements ... when I know of a vacancy for the post which you'd like I will remember you.[51]

Richards put him in touch with various galleries and alerted him of opportunities to exhibit, such as the exhibition of Welsh Contemporary Painting at the St George's Gallery in September 1947 to which John Elwyn contributed a picture.[52] The London-Welsh fraternity have a long tradition of looking after their own; for example, in early October 1939 he had made the acquaintance of Carmarthen-born artist Edward Morland Lewis, a pupil of Sickert and a painter John Elwyn admired. Lewis invited him to visit his Fulham Road address to discuss art and see how he might be of help to John Elwyn, but war was declared and they were never able to meet up. Lewis died in Tunisia in 1943 aged forty.[53]

In September John Elwyn was offered a position at the American advertising agency J. Walter Thompson at 40 Berkeley Square where George Butler, head of its art department, was always keen to take on trained painters. He found himself making routine enlargements and reductions of designs for £6 a week. After three months he resigned, because of the intensive eye strain of tracing, and returned to Wales to work at the woollen mill. His father had died earlier in the year and his two sisters were running Emlyn Factory. In February 1948 John Elwyn received the first of fifty letters, written over the next seven years, from the wealthy landowner and enthusiastic supporter of young Welsh artists, Winifred Coombe-Tennant. 'Mistress of the Gorsedd Robes', commonly known by her Bardic title 'Mam o Nedd' (Mother of Neath), she had amassed an important collection of contemporary Welsh art at her home in Cottesmore Gardens, Kensington. She was to establish numerous contacts on John Elwyn's behalf with galleries, picture dealers and museum curators.[54] 'As a family', she wrote to John Elwyn, 'we have lived in the young painters' world, and at Cadoxton Lodge, our home in the Vale of Neath, they came in relays each summer to paint – to talk – to think – and to be welcome yet absolutely free.'[55]

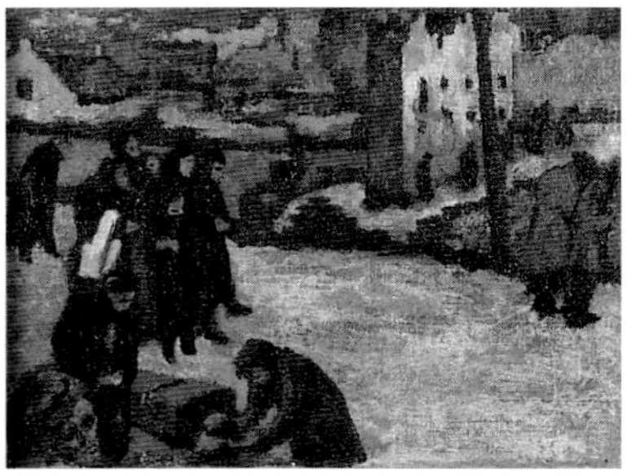

In the Valley (Refugees)
1947, oil on canvas 8 x 10
[Glynn Vivian Art Gallery, Swansea]

On 15th January Coombe-Tennant had chaired the opening of the 'Exhibition of Paintings by Welsh Artists' at the Mansard Gallery in Heals on Tottenham Court Road. John Elwyn had contributed a small painting, *In the Valley* (*Refugees*), which had attracted her attention sufficiently to write requesting to see more of his work and elicit information about himself. 'I am in touch with various art circles in Wales', she wrote, 'and I think I might be of use to you – it having been the custom of our family for the past thirty years to "lend a hand" to young painters.'[56] In less than a week she had contacted William Grant Murray, Director of Swansea Art Galleries and formerly Curator of the Glynn Vivian Art Gallery, to alert him to John Elwyn's work. Murray had made an important contribution to art in Wales as Principal of Swansea School of Art between the wars. He went specially to see the exhibition during its tour and purchased *In the Valley* (*Refugees*) for the Glynn Vivian. Grant Murray wrote to thank Mrs Coombe-Tennant for drawing his attention to John Elwyn's work. He endorsed her good judgement and agreed with her that John Elwyn possessed a rare facility for small-scale figure compositions. He was, they thought, a modern day Breughel.

In her letters she emphasised her experience of young Welsh painters and the lessons to be learned from following their careers, especially those who had been drawn into a web of 'corruption and jealousy' in the London studios, and whose talent had become 'extinguished by stimulating friendships and rivalries'. Her unequivocal advice was to get closer to nature. She recommended he stay in Wales and work at the mill in a job separate from his individual creativity. This would allow him, she wrote, to paint in the evenings 'as the spirit moved him' regardless of the market, and to preserve his 'own very individual vision. It is because I know, after seeing only one of your pictures, that you can become a painter of worth'.[57] Time and again her letters stressed the importance of individual vision, drawing from direct experience and using the Welsh landscape as a subject.

Not long afterwards John Elwyn received a letter from Leslie Gaydon who had heard that he had left London. Once more he offered him a post teaching drawing and painting at the Southern College of Art, Portsmouth. On this occasion he

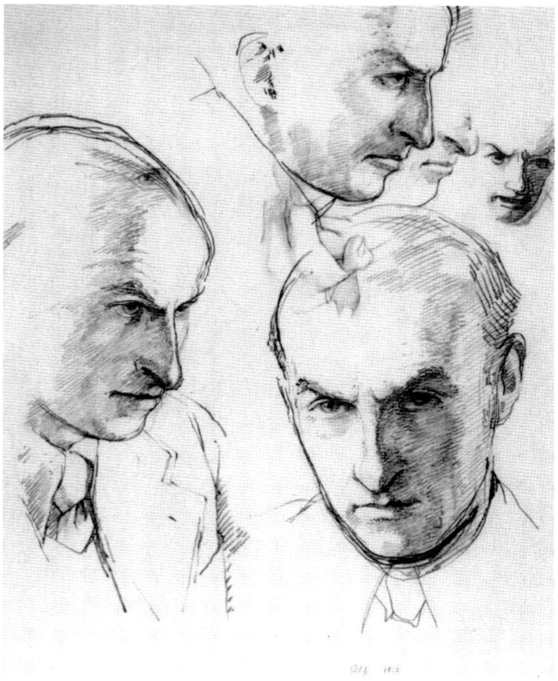

Self Portrait Studies, Portsmouth
1950, pencil on paper 21 x 15
[The University of Wales, Aberystwyth]

accepted the invitation and moved to Hampshire in April 1948. He took lodgings firstly at 18 Villiers Road, Southsea and within a year he moved into 5 St Ursula Road where there was a room for him to paint. He shared with Anthony Eyton who also taught at the art school.[58] They saw a great deal of each other at meal times and had long and lively discussions about painting, music, literature, commented on each others' work, and John Elwyn painted a small portrait of Eyton. 'He seemed to see the best in people', wrote Eyton, 'he was a very kind and modest man, very serious about his painting and easy to talk to.'[59] In 1951 Eyton was awarded an Abbey Major Scholarship and moved to Rome. John Elwyn's small circle of friends were mostly colleagues at the art school and he became particularly close to the Head of Painting David Pare and his wife. Their daughter Vivian recalled his:

> delightful sense of humour, and infectious laugh, he was an avuncular figure in our house ... It was later when he taught me at the Art School where my father was Principal that he demonstrated great kindness, thoughtfulness, and skill when it came to communicating with young people. His class always had everybody's full attention.[60]

John Elwyn was increasingly conscious of his bachelor status, and envied the family life enjoyed by his colleagues, and he appears to have channelled his energies into painting, embarking upon a professional career as an artist. With war-time shortages, however, art materials were scarce and he was limited to painting on off-cuts of board and small panels salvaged from old furniture. He cycled down to the docks to collect free Scandinavian wood from packing crates and loaded his bicycle with timber. In the bedroom of his digs he nailed them together to make crates to send paintings off by rail to exhibitions in London and Wales. By the end of the 1940s John Elwyn was exhibiting regularly at the Royal Academy, the New English Art Club, and at exhibitions arranged by the National Eisteddfod of Wales and the Welsh Committee of the Arts Council.

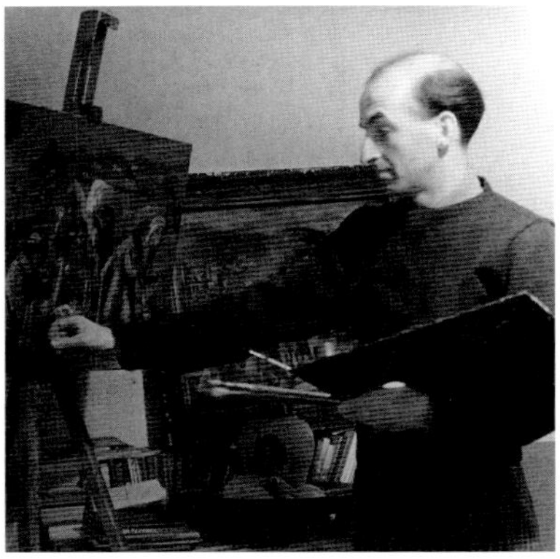

John Elwyn painting *The Wool Dyers,* Portsmouth January 1950

His first paintings in Portsmouth were small, quiet studies concerned with sailors and the sea like *Afterglow at Portsmouth* and *The Front, Southsea* which he exhibited at the New English Art Club in 1948. Concurrently he began to explore the possibilities of anecdotal paintings based upon his childhood recollections of Newcastle Emlyn. It was during his final months at college that he had first begun to consider producing oil paintings based on his memories of the rituals and festivals associated with chapel-going in the late 1920s. In his quest for meaningful subject matter he soon came to realise that he knew more about himself than anything else. The idea of illustrating his experiences and writing stories about his childhood in paint provided his first reason for painting. He later recalled:

> I had a very happy childhood in the country, nurtured by a very caring family. At the centre was the mill, making cloth. Around that was a small-holding, very busy at times with sufficient livestock to keep the family going all the year round. That was the inner circle, so to speak. Outside that, in a larger circle, was the village community and social activities, and at the centre of that was the chapel. Nearly everything ultimately centred on that. These gatherings at the religious centre provided me with many ideas for composing small anecdotal pictures. As a ten year old I absorbed much of this activity.[61]

At first he relied on studies made direct from nature but in time he abandoned these to invent or paraphrase characteristic incidents and situations from memory. In his boarding house in Southsea the fond recollections of a happy childhood in rural Cardiganshire offered a degree of comfort as he recalled the comings and goings outside Emlyn Mill on a warm Sunday evening in the summer. 'I was not the kind of person to attempt to push back the frontiers of modern art,' he wrote, 'there in the centre of "the Great Wen" I realised that my umbilical cord had not been severed.'[62]

In the wake of a devastating war it is perhaps not surprising that John Elwyn, like so many artists of his generation, found security in the past. A fond nostalgia and his yearning for the homeland that the Welsh call 'hiraeth', manifested itself in a remarkable series of paintings which drew upon episodes of his life as a young teenager.

As a boy his family had been stalwarts of Ebenezer Welsh Congregational Chapel in Newcastle Emlyn, attending three times every Sunday. David and Anne Davies were devoted chapel-goers and their children were disciplined to take an active part in the meetings and varied social activities. Sundays were very sober occasions, the mill's looms shut down and chapel was the focus of the family's attention. Its festivals and services were a focal point for the community. The annual Sunday School Outing brought Newcastle Emlyn's four places of worship together for a trip to the

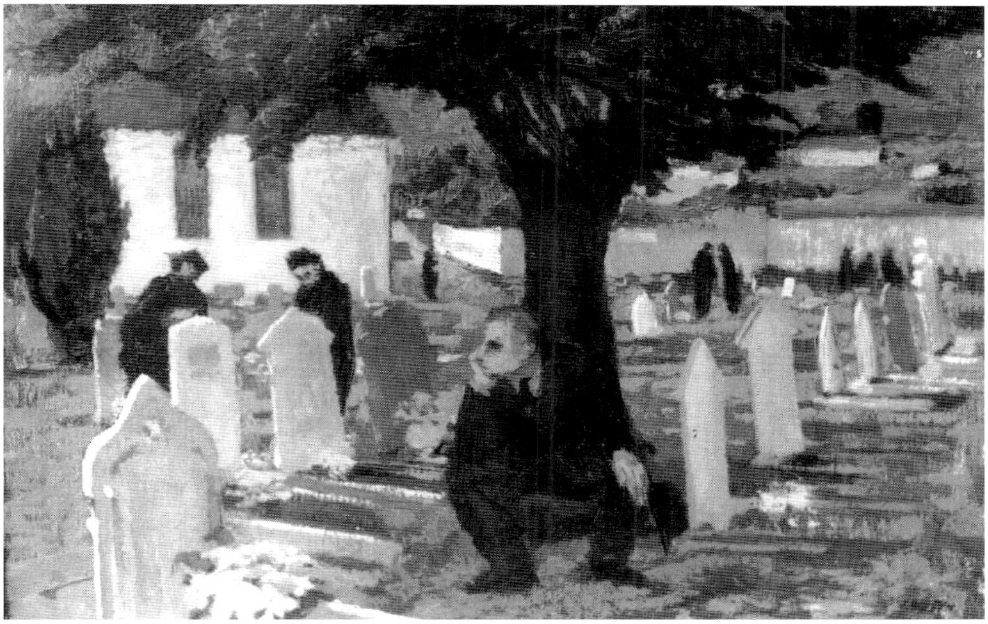

Palm Sunday
1949, oil on board 13 x 19
[Alexander Coombe-Tennant]

seaside by train. On the mile-long walk to the station friends and their families joined the procession; weeks of excitement and expectation culminated with 'an extra-special bath, clean boots and bags of sandwiches'. John Elwyn's recollections of *Palm Sunday, April Communion* and *November Thanksgiving* were fertile subjects for paintings.

The sophisticated use of rich tonal values and strong local colour, the softened rounded forms painted in mellow light, short dabbed brushstrokes and decorative use of broken planes of colour recall paintings by Pierre Bonnard (1867–1947) and Edouard Vuillard (1868–1940) whose paintings he had admired so much and emulated as a student at the Royal College of Art. Many of these compositions, such as the two women dressed in their Sunday-best acquiring *Up to Date News before the Meeting* (1949), centre on groups of people standing around in animated conversation. For these he gained inspiration from Honoré Daumier's paintings of law courts and those commenting on life and manners in nineteenth-century Paris, particularly the way in which Daumier was able to distil the individual peculiarities of a face and capture the essence of a character. Sketch-book drawings after Daumier explored the potential of composition. Talkativeness and the love of debate is perceived to be a

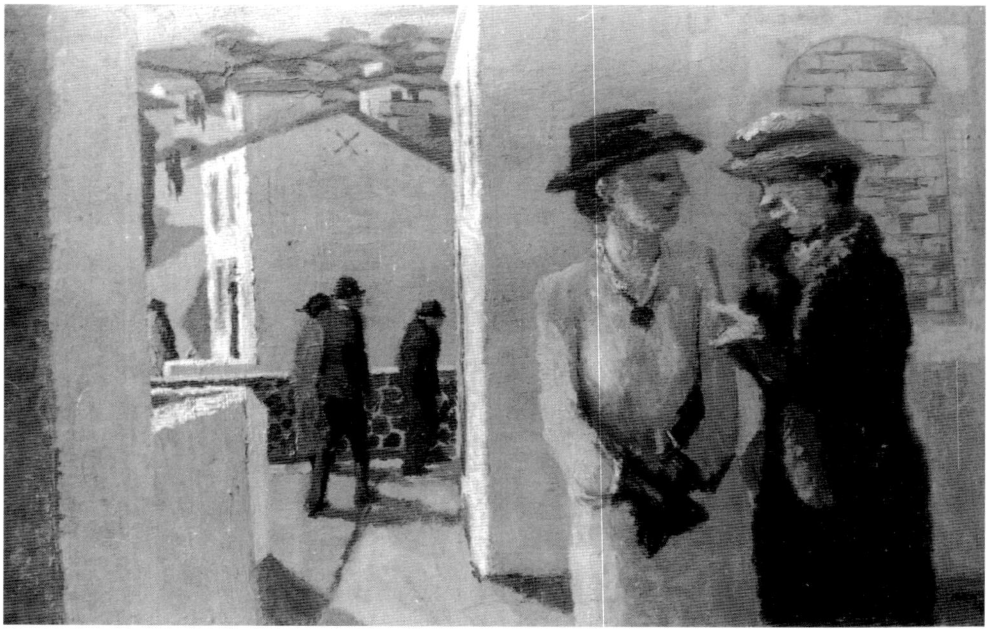

Up to Date News before the Meeting
1949, oil on board 13½ x 22
[The University of Wales, Aberystwyth]

national trait in the Welsh; two people, he said, and you have a conversation, three and you have an argument. *The Hymn Critics, A Debatable Point* and *Settling a Small Point over a Hymn Tune* reflect not only John Elwyn's memories of such gatherings, and the wonderful characters he knew as a child, but the warmth of his character and his own love of conversation. (Plate v) He recalled:

> sunny Sunday mornings with bowler-hatted farmers and small businessmen in their starched collars and dark tweed suits for their weekly outing, some of the material had actually been woven on my father's looms and had been tailored by my uncle. I had on many occasions followed my parents to chapel, passing other villagers going to their chosen chapel – we would pass them every Sunday more or less exactly at the same place and exchange the same remarks in all weathers. Congregating outside the chapel doors after the service was a must for everybody to exchange some gossip or some remarks about the sermon just delivered – sometimes it would develop into an argument about some aspect of belief.[63]

He also began to read short stories by Anglo-Welsh writers to reinforce the characters that were already so familiar to him – especially short stories by Glyn Jones who was a keen observer of human behaviour. *Merthyr* is a long poem in rhyming couplets which particularly appealed to John Elwyn for its perceptive and witty recollections of a boyhood in the mining valleys:

> But far more than the scene, the legendary
> Walkers and actors on it, the memory
> Of neighbours, worthies, friends and relatives ...
> My grandfather's fantastic friends, Old Sion
> O Ferthyr, occultist, meddler in the unknown ...
> My undersized great granny, that devout
> Calvinist, with mind and tongue like knives

Jones described himself as 'a regional writer' and like John Elwyn he drew his subjects only from the landscape and inhabitants of his native country. He created such mischievous and affectionate characterisations as Bopa Lloyd, his school-friend's mother in *An Afternoon at Uncle Shad's*, a short story told from the child's perspective:

> Presently Bopa Lloyd came out of the kitchen to throw some potato peelings over the fence ... She was a fat woman wearing a black flannel bodice with grey pin-stripes and a wet sack apron that hurt you when she wiped your nose with it. On her forehead she had lines across like you use for music, and her grey hair was coming down out of her combs like the feathers of an untidy hen. Her nostrils were black and big enough for her to put her thumbs up them ... "Shad," she shouted, "come from by there now and wash yourself for dinner." [64]

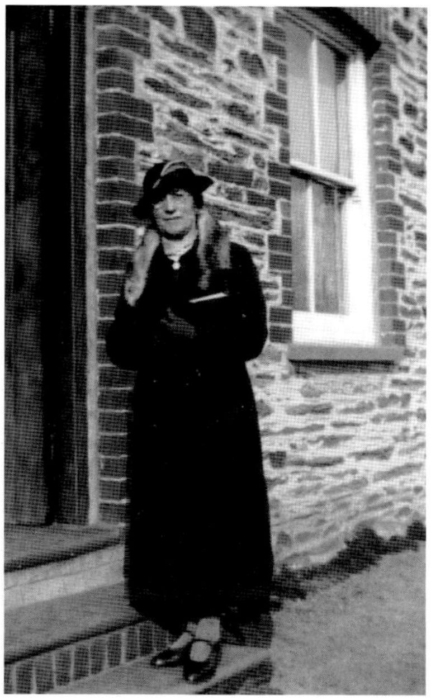

Anne Davies, John Elwyn's mother on her way to chapel, early 1930s

The older women members of the community also play a significant role in John Elwyn's paintings, hardly surprising for the only son in a household with three older sisters. At chapel the women came together from distant parts and for them the occasion was the place to catch up on the local news. They were actively involved in the chapel community – for many the Sunday services, weekday prayer meetings, *gymanfa ganu*, Sunday School anniversaries and other festivals were their only social life and source of entertainment. No respectable woman would be seen in the public house. In working class industrial and rural communities, particularly during the austere years of depression, the 'Mam' was very much the controlling factor at home, often uniting the community as well as the family, offering friendship and support to neighbours. In his paintings we see them at work or at rest, in conversation in the village or over the garden wall to catch up with *Yesterday's Gossip* (1949), but especially we see them outside the chapel before and after the evening service. Chapel was a place of public display, the only occasion women had to wear their Sunday-best and reaffirm their standing in the community. In small communities such as this judgements were easily passed on appearances and cleanliness: in spite of poverty these were the criteria of standing and respect. In the 'chapel' series of paintings John Elwyn captured their dignity, restraint, dress, posture and gestures with great affection. The new hat, fur collar, handbag hung over the forearm and the family hymnal clutched in a begloved hand are observed and recorded with great integrity. (Plate v)

The moral gravity and ceremony of the chapel ritual is more evident in his depiction of the chapel deacons and male members of the congregation. *A Funeral Gathering on a Welsh Hill Farm* (1949), for example, is not a pious representation but one full of humour, warmth and respect. *A Funeral Gathering in the Snow* (1949) represents a line of mourners dressed in black, walking through deep snow at a rural funeral. It is painted with all the poignancy of the French nineteenth-century realist painter Gustave Courbet. The powerful influence of the chapel on the rural community contributed enormously to forming the character and behaviour of its inhabitants. The strict code of dress, the black suit and bowler hat against the green landscape and the simple geometry of white-washed chapels provided a striking visual contrast for the artist. He recalled the origin of *The Hymn Critics* (1949):

> On the walk home from chapel there might be that special hymn that had been sung that morning, and this would be the reason for two black-bowlered hymn enthusiasts to stop during an argument and sing – *sotto voce* – in the middle of the road, fingering the red or gold edged pages of their hymn book.[65]

The Whitsun Singing Festival was an occasion when the Congregational or Indepen-

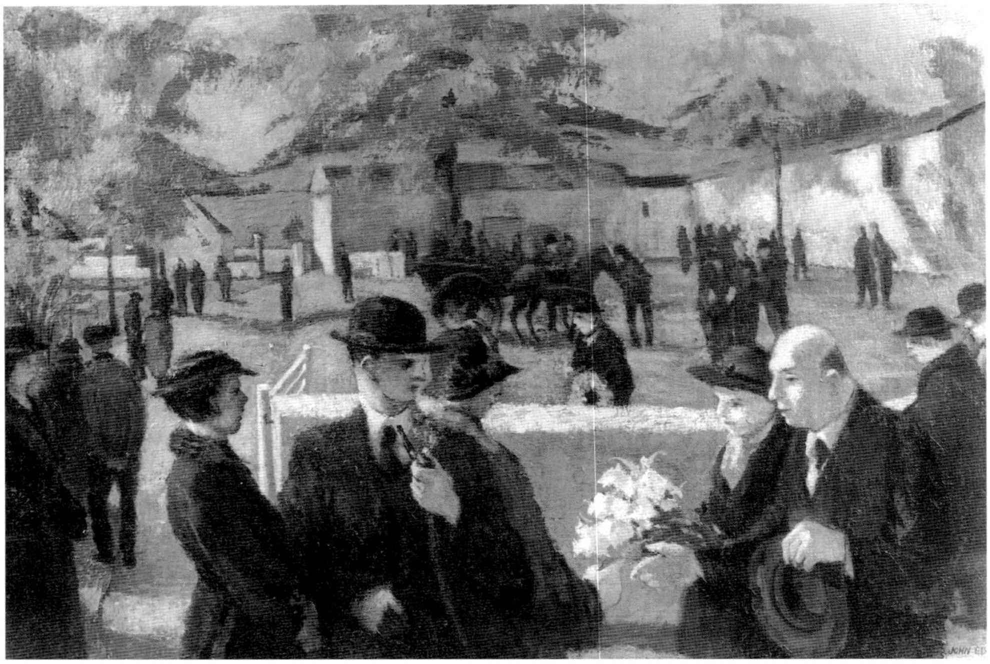

Funeral Gathering on a Welsh Hill Farm
1949, oil on canvas 20 x 30
[Contemporary Art Society for Wales/Powys Fine Art Association]

dent chapels in the area converged on Ebenezer for a grand *gymanfa ganu*. There were three sessions during the day and during the intervals everybody congregated on the castle grounds. It was *the* meeting place for young men and women of the community.

Despite the narrow range of his subject, the closely observed details of the landscape, chapels, deacons and the congregation in his native south Cardiganshire the paintings have come to represent aspects of all such chapels in rural communities throughout Britain, taking on a relevance beyond the regional. He later recalled that the challenge was to:

> re-create situations which were something more than mere recording. This is not necessarily inspiration, but a creative shiver of excitement which compels one to express or project one's feelings and make a visual statement for its own sake, irrespective of any demands from elsewhere. In themselves they were comments with no particular significance outside my own world, in a regional or parochial sense; at the same time they had a kind of universal connotation for me.[66]

As well as the 'chapel' paintings John Elwyn drew on other experiences in Wales such as the woollen industry or farmers and weavers at Newcastle Emlyn mart discussing wool or livestock prices. Each painting provided an opportunity to depict individuals in close physical proximity, in conversation or debate. Sunday meetings, Market and Fair days were things that he had observed, but he also put into paint episodes that were outside his direct experience – stories that had been related over the hearth by a neighbour or visiting client from south Wales who came with news of a recent accident at the colliery. In *Rumours of a Pit Disaster in the Next Valley* (1949) the villagers run over the fields at dawn towards the colliery, united at a time of adversity. Glyn Jones had also drawn from such experiences. In the short story 'Explosion' from *The Water Music* published in 1944, he tells how news of a disaster at the local colliery affected one of his school friends. These are records of commu-

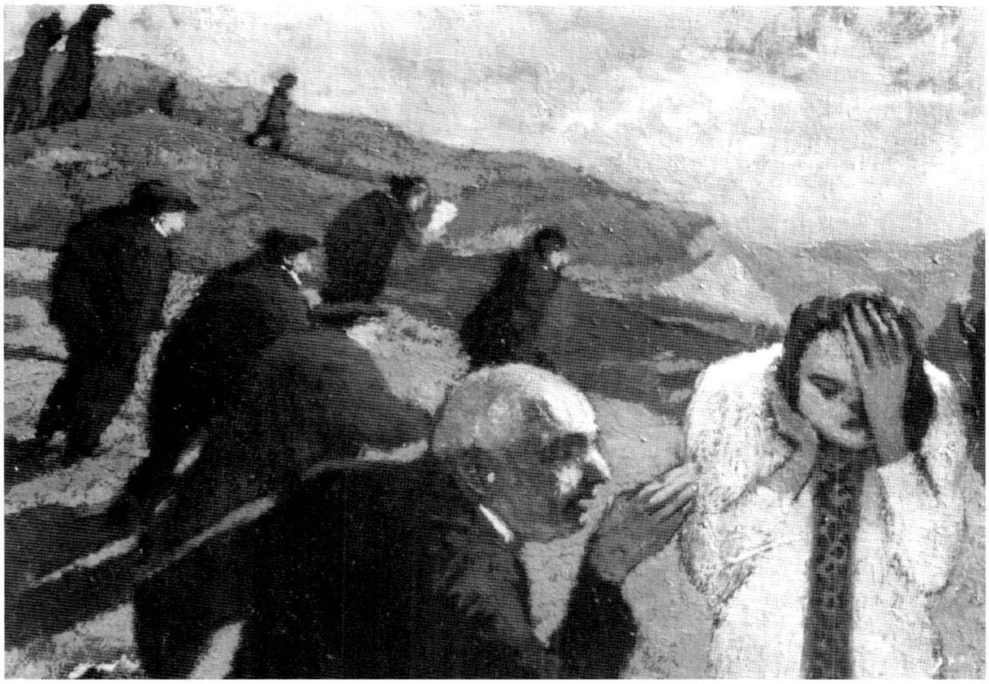

Rumours of a Pit Disaster in the Next Valley
1949, oil
[Dimensions and present whereabouts unknown]

nity spirit which is nowadays under threat. 'All this had nothing to do with esoteric modern art but simply autobiographical illustration', John Elwyn wrote, 'I have a parochial mind – sometimes today it's called regional. I agree with Benjamin Britten when he says "the important things are the local things".'[67]

The satisfaction for John Elwyn in making these paintings came in the knowledge that this was not something anyone else had done. 'I rejoice to hear you are painting', wrote Mrs Coombe-Tennant, 'painting after your own inspiration ... Wales has undisclosed wonders to show the world ... in my thoughts I see you as *the* interpreter.'[68] Contemporary writers had worked on similar themes, the eccentric local character, life in the rural village or mining town, and the chapel, but literary critics thought it was 'a rather tired genre', particularly since the authors were inclined to over-do the 'Welshness'.

Twenty-four of the 'chapel' paintings were exhibited at John Elwyn's first exhibition, with the Sheffield-born painter Jack Wright, at the Paul Alexander Gallery in Kensington Church Street, Notting Hill. A fellow painting student Penelope Salmond had written to John Elwyn in January 1949 inviting him to show at the gallery with Dick MacDonald in April, or Jack Wright in June. Wright was then living in Christchurch, Hampshire and teaching at the Southern College of Art at Bournemouth. John Elwyn chose to exhibit with Wright and the exhibition was opened on 28th June by Carel Weight whom they came to know when he joined the R.C.A. staff after the war. All the works had been painted since November 1948. Mrs Coombe-Tennant took it upon herself to publicise the exhibition and further his interests by sending catalogues to newspapers and 'people who know good work and buy it'.

> Now that you are moving forward in the ranks of painters of the first order men who express themselves in their own idiom – and are not derivative – paint what "belongs" to their own experience, paint the life they know ... You have made

your mark as a painter of Wales, with figures in landscape ... and for the next five years you should *adhere to that* line ... until you are firmly rooted in the public mind as a painter of *that*.[69]

The Tredegar Workmen's Institute made the first purchase with a fund established from the profits of its cinema to buy original works of art. Coombe-Tennant praised his work to the wealthy Swansea businessman J. T. Morgan who had family and business connections at Newcastle Emlyn. He agreed:

what you write of him and his work makes me very happy too. His sojourn in England has left him a true Welshman with his heart in Cardiganshire – and your interest in him will hearten him and encourage him I know. I would like you to meet him some day. He is a very civilised and well-mannered young man, never self-assertive or cocksure (the vices of so many of the young to-day!).[70]

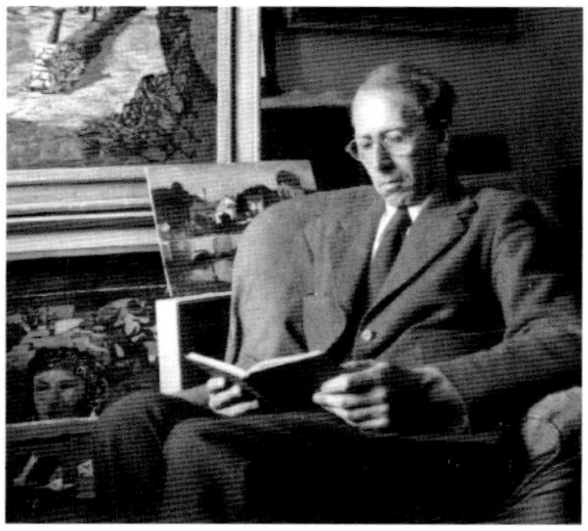

David Bell in John Elwyn's studio, Winchester 1954

On the advice of Mrs Coombe-Tennant the collector Dr Iorwerth Hughes Jones from Swansea bought a painting, and John Steegman, Keeper of Art at the National Museum of Wales paid a long and enthusiastic visit to the exhibition. Ralph Edwards from the Victoria and Albert Museum visited the exhibition and wrote to Steegman in Cardiff suggesting he consider buying *The Hub of the Village* for the museum. Mrs Coombe-Tennant also sent an invitation and letter introducing John Elwyn to David Bell.

David Bell (1915–1959) was a painter, art historian, and from June 1946 Assistant Director of the Regional Office in Cardiff of the Arts Council of Great Britain, who did much to further the cause of fine art in Wales after the war. He had trained under William Rothenstein and Gilbert Spencer at the Royal College of Art and during the 1930s he exhibited with the N.E.A.C. and at the R.A. During the war he joined the historical office of the War Cabinet Office. With his father Sir Idris Bell he translated a selection of works by the medieval poet Dafydd ap Gwilym. In February 1951 he was appointed Curator of the Glynn Vivian Art Gallery in Swansea and was responsible for numerous Arts Council touring exhibitions promoting the work of contemporary Welsh artists. He was author of *The Language of Pictures* (1954) and *The Artist in Wales* (1957) which for many years was the only historical overview of the subject. He was to become a close friend and advocate of John Elwyn – together with Mrs Coombe-Tennant he played a significant role in encouraging the artist and establishing contacts on his behalf.

The 'chapel' paintings are remarkable examples of social observation; the two largest and most fully worked paintings, *Suliau Mebyd* (Sundays of my Youth) and *Bore Sul* (Sunday Morning), were both painted in 1950 and exhibited at the National Eisteddfod that year. (Plate VII) Winifred Coombe-Tennant saw the exhibition and thought the paintings were over-worked. John Elwyn agreed:

I can tell you in one word what is wrong with them – laboured. I spent too much time on them and was well aware of it long before they were finished. It is alright possibly to spend an appreciable time on a portrait or a group but when the motif is a purely imaginary one – it should be executed rapidly. Having learnt my lesson I believe it was worthwhile to experience the results.[71]

Bore Sul was purchased by the Contemporary Art Society for Wales. When it was exhibited at the National Museum in Cardiff on the fiftieth anniversary of the Society, the poet and broadcaster John Ormond wrote:

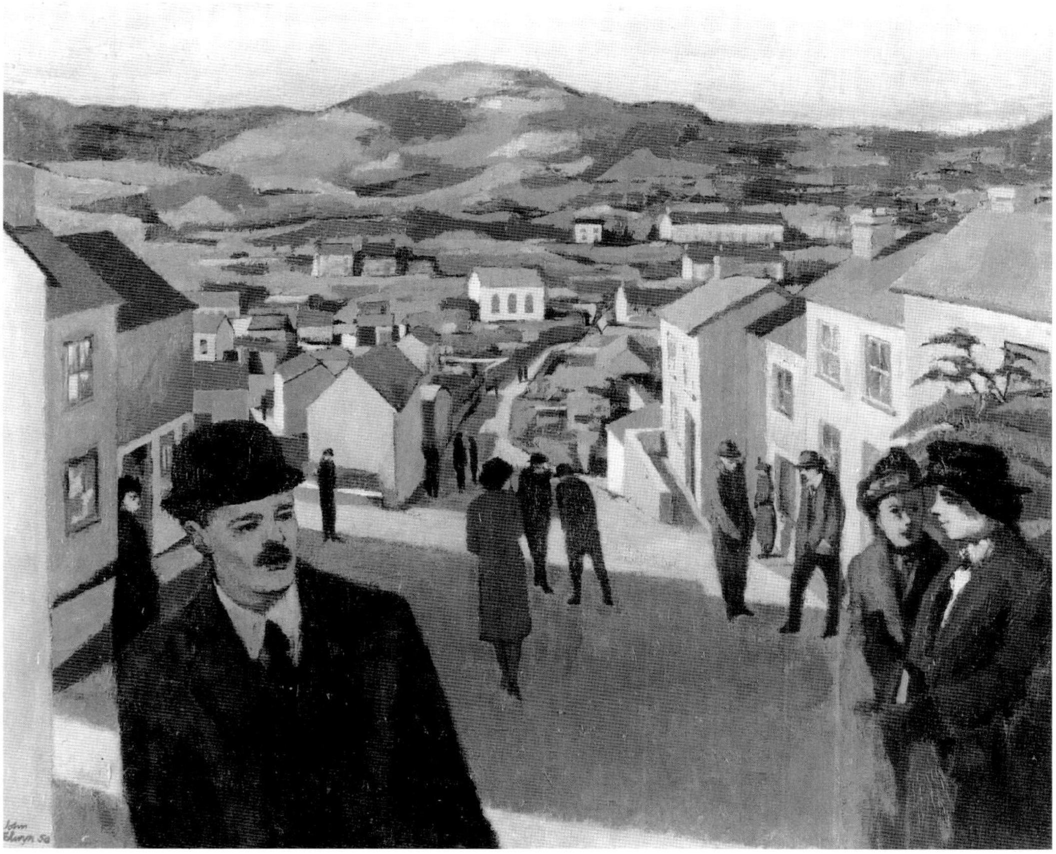

Bore Sul (Sunday Morning)
1950, oil on canvas 20 x 24
[Contemporary Art Society for Wales / National Museum and Gallery of Wales, Cardiff]

> I recognised my Uncle Willie Beynon with his bowler and heavy moustache in the foreground. A lovely picture, calm, rural peace, the smell of Sunday gravy coming out of the keyholes and back doors to arise (as in the Bisto Kids) to whet the appetites of the deacon and drunkard on the hungry, salad-serving clouds of heaven.[72]

Motivated by the success of his first exhibition, John Elwyn began to explore further the possibilities of working from recollection and experience. On 15th September 1949 he wrote to Mrs Coombe-Tennant to tell her he was working on new compositions dealing with 'the primitive way we use in Cardiganshire to dye wool and yarn in the open air'. (Plate XI) His father dyed the wool himself during the summer months. As a boy John Elwyn had been spell-bound by the coloured skeins of hand-dyed wool drying in the sunshine on the hedges outside the mill. David Davies spent hours on his colourful experiments, mixing the wool on a primitive machine called the 'devil' or 'wild willey', disentangling the fibres of the wool and re-mixing colours in different quantities like paints on a palette. The creative process surely helped kindle his son's creativity and love of colour. Regular visits to Wales fired his enthusiasm to paint:

> now that the Spring is here one feels more like work, or perhaps I should say creative work, especially after a walk in the country when one becomes aware of the great feeling of expectancy and urgency in nature about and around me ... refurbishing myself for further adventures and excursions in paint on my return over the border. It is strange perhaps but I can paint imaginative compositions better

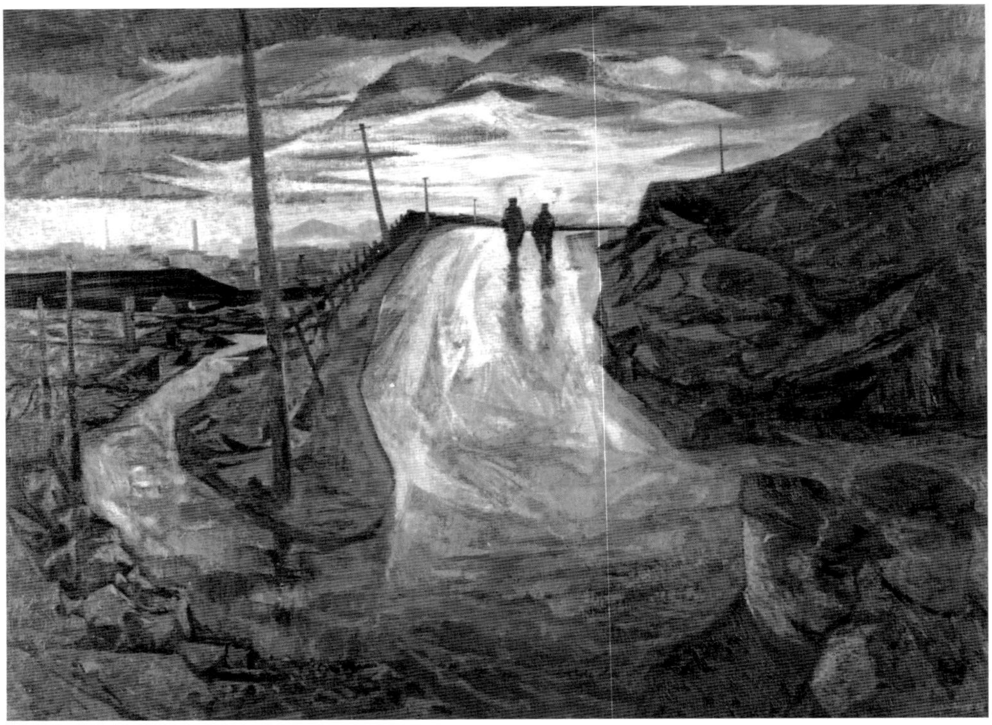

Miners Returning Home on a Wet Evening III
1953, oil on canvas 30 x 40
[The Arts Council of Wales]

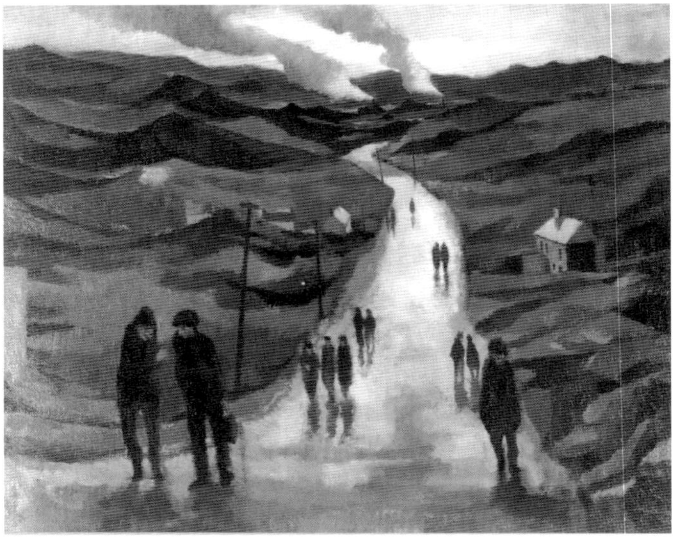

Miners Returning Home on a Wet Evening II
1951, oil on canvas 20 x 24
[Present whereabouts unknown]

when I am removed from the object of interest. This may be because one can select essential things easier and quicker when one has to rely on memory work.[73]

He next went on to paint a series based on miners and their landscape near Pont-Rhyd-y-Fen where he had lived when working on the forestry during the war:

Having experienced a cycle of seasons working on the forestry slopes above Dyffryn Coalmine in the Afan Valley, I had been stimulated enough to explore a new subject. Recalling the blue-scarred white temples and the staccato speech of the hard-working miner in his home, talking to the miner and his family brought

> home the ever present element of danger and perpetual concern with the forces of nature. To recall gazing into a sulphurous sunset and seeing the rows of small silhouetted figures of miners like insects with shadows and reflections scribbled on the wet roads making their way homewards to their tin baths in front of the kitchen fire, was a visual experience of the first order.[74]

The visual drama of the industrialised landscape in the gloaming, with the setting sun through the smog-laden sky, provided an exciting contrast to the tranquillity of the chapel paintings. Across an open wasteland, scarred by industry, the miners descend a road in pouring rain, walking in single file, their long reflections cast in the wet tarmacadam. They are in stark silhouette against the sulphurous sky into which distant chimneys at Port Talbot belch their waste. The picturesque urban romanticism of *Wet Day Miners* (1950) and *Miners Returning Home over Waste Ground* (1951) was a rare departure from the concerns of mainstream British painting; few artists were recording the industrialised landscape, the 'miners' series pre-date George Chapman's paintings of the Rhondda and other south Wales coal-mining communities of the mid 1950s. (Plate XIII)

There are also a number of paintings of *The Mothers*, depicting the women of the mining community standing in an urban landscape and nursing their babies. (Plate XX) They are swaddled 'Welsh fashion' in a fringed nursing shawl, the sort produced at Emlyn Factory and a familiar sight in the valleys until the 1960s. In 1952 he painted a series of views from windows, among them *The Frightened Goldfish* in the glass bowl on the windowsill, its swirling orange forms interwoven with the refracted colours of a landscape of white-washed cottages, stone walls, vegetation, a harbour jetty and brilliant blue sea. The view through the window of *Baner ac Amserau Cymru* looks over a small hamlet in the foreground and along a winding country road in the Neath valley towards the chimneys of Port Talbot steel works on the horizon. The young woman seated on the right is cropped by the picture plane; something John Elwyn learned from looking at Bonnard. The colour and patterning of the woman's dress, curtains, tablecloth, vase of flowers, and the newspaper from which the painting gets its title, is echoed in the landscape. In *After the Rain (Gosport)* he employed flattened forms and a close tonal range of muted colours to compress spatial recession. (Plate X) The vista across the wet pavement, through tall buildings towards the sea is ambiguous. This uncertain relationship between the inside and outside world is controlled to best advantage in his farmyard scene *The Egg* painted in 1952. (Plate XIV)

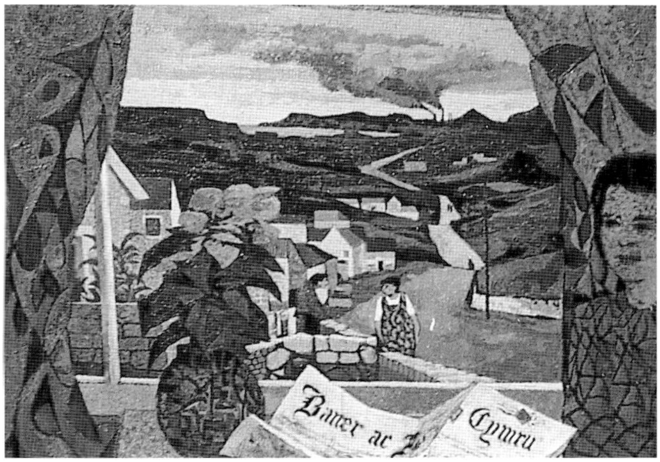

Baner ac Amserau Cymru
1952, oil on canvas
[Dimensions and present whereabouts unknown]

The paintings based on Portsmouth and Southsea by comparison came less naturally to him. These have the detachment of an outsider looking on: their warmth derives solely from his astute observation of human behaviour. In July 1951 he wrote to Winifred Coombe-Tennant to tell her that he was working on some local subjects like *Southsea Front* and *Family Outing, Southsea* for exhibitions in Portsmouth and Southampton, 'they are rather pretty paintings of street and park scenes with marines in their white caps and vermilion bands'.[75] (Plates VIII & IX) The sketch-book drawings from which these were painted are made in outline with copious annotations describing colour schemes, relative tones and reflections. At weekends and on

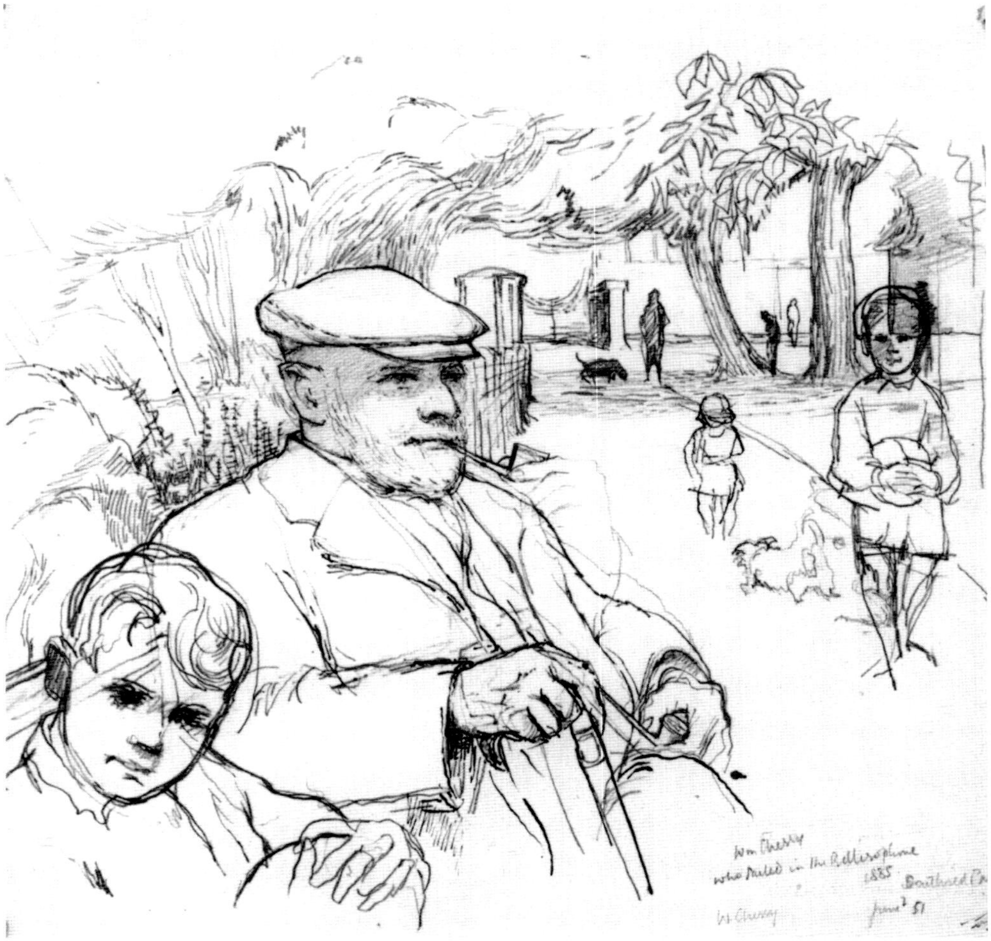

Mr Cherry, who sailed in the Bellerophone
1951, pencil and ink on paper
10½ x 12
[Robert Meyrick]

summer evenings he took his drawing materials on to the promenade, into the parks and tree-lined squares of Southsea, or walked to Portsmouth harbour where he made careful pencil drawings of the water-front, ships in dock, and sailors loading and unloading vessels like *The Pompeii Light* berthed in Portsmouth (1951). *Mr Cherry who sailed in the Bellerophone 1885* (2nd June 1951) was drawn in Southsea Park. John Elwyn sat alongside Mr Cherry who was resting on a bench in the sunshine smoking a pipe, the child seated with the old man looks with curiosity at the artist. The swirling leafy canopy and colonnade of tree trunks create a tunnel around the footpath which recedes into the distance, and alternating patches of strong sunlight and shadow intersecting the path. This drawing is amongst the earliest of his works to concern itself with the same pictorial devices which he was to employ throughout much of his professional career as a landscape painter.

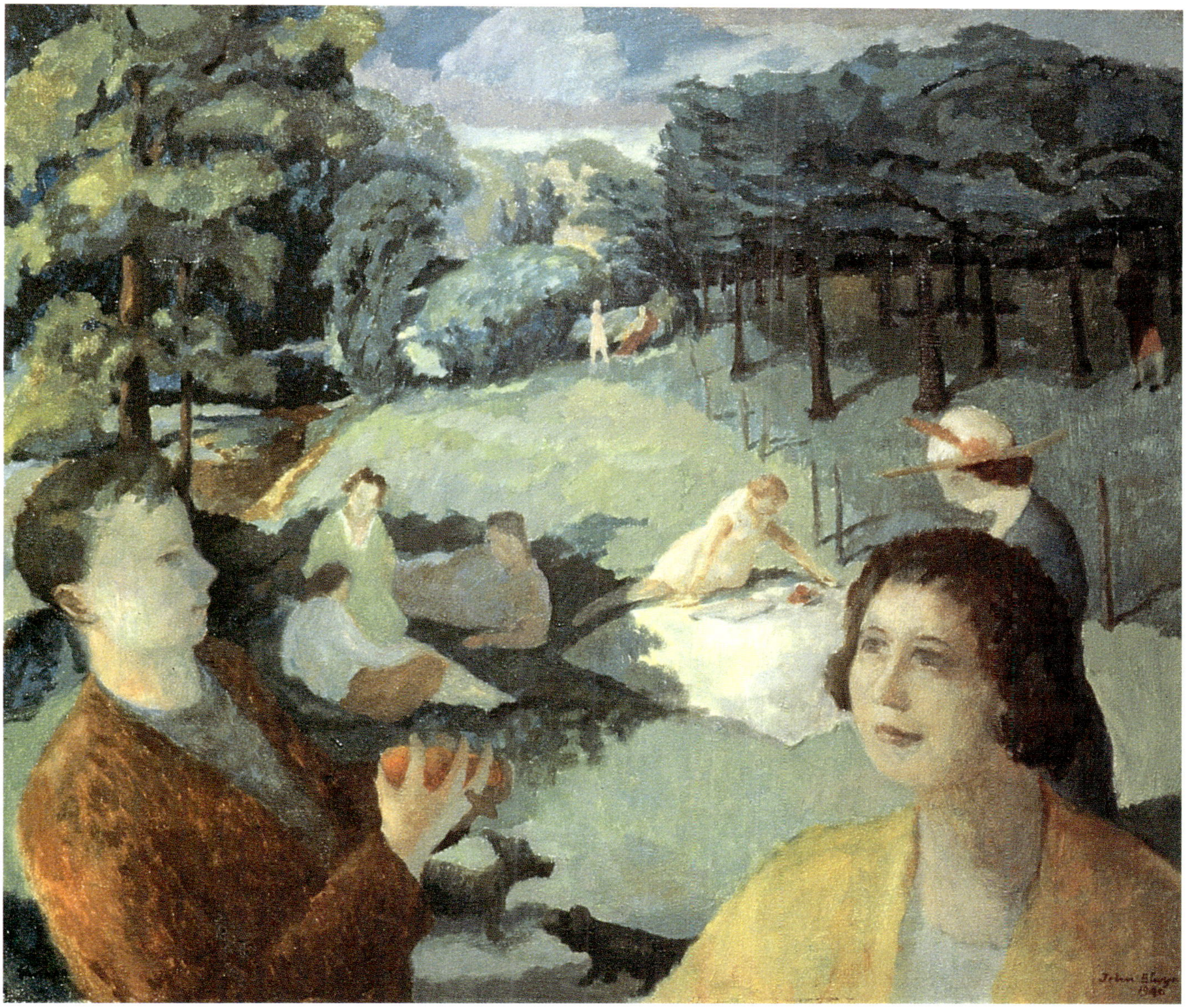

1: *Picnic in Cilgwyn Woods*
1940, oil on canvas, 16 x 20
[Professor and Mrs Derec Llwyd Morgan]

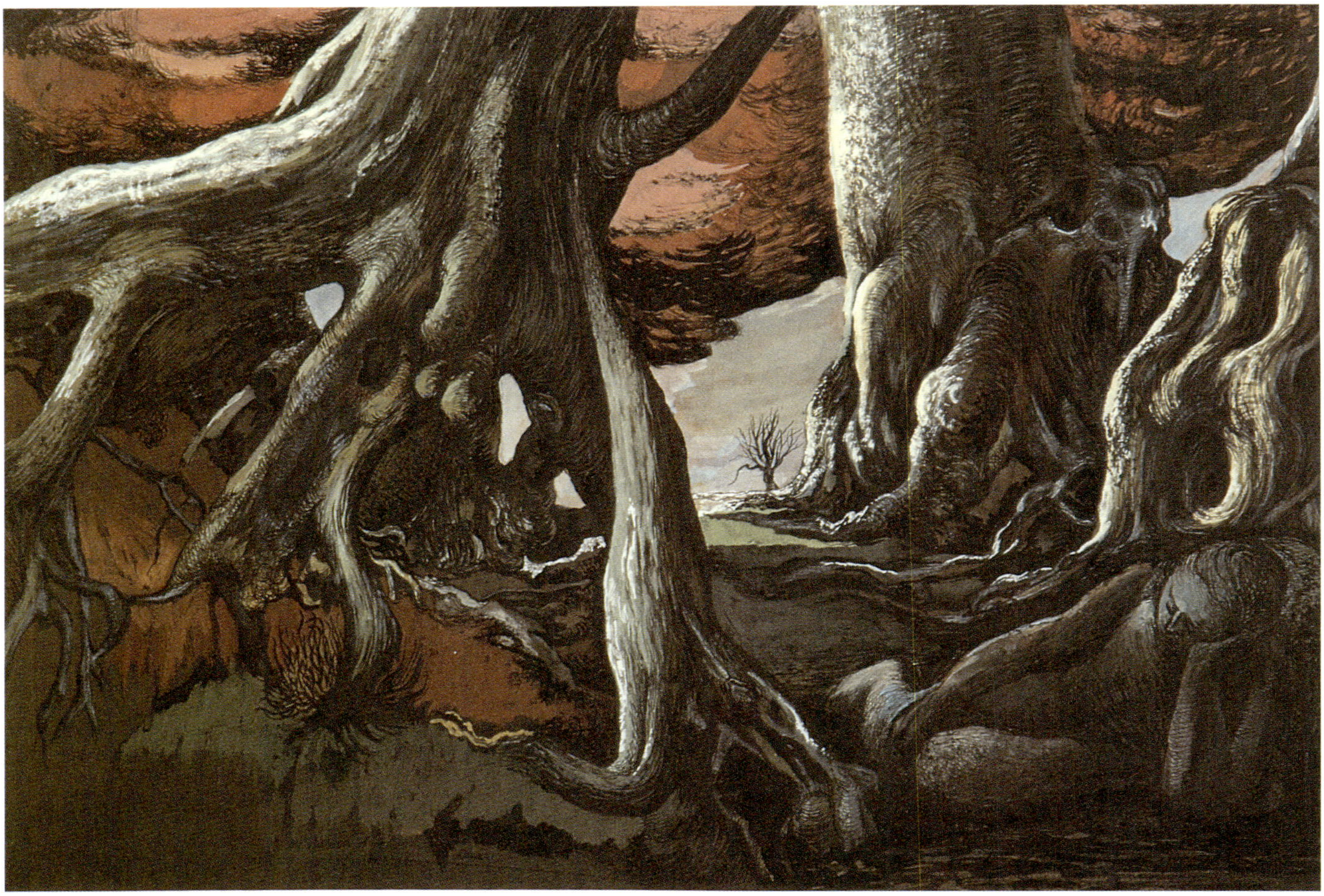

II: *The Stillness of the Roots*
1944, ink and watercolour on paper, 14½ x 22½
[Peter Wakelin]

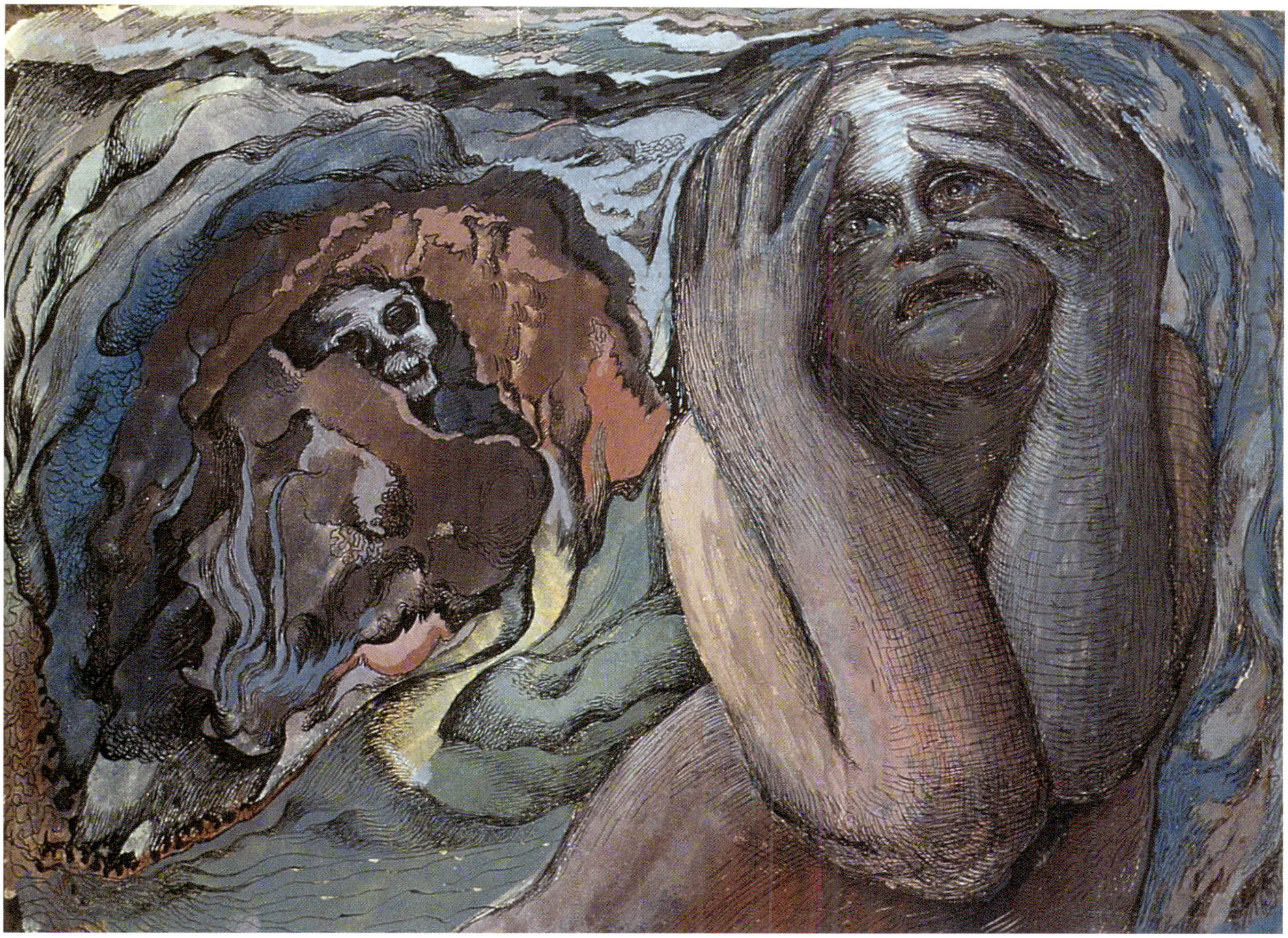

III: *Everyman*
1944, ink and watercolour on paper, 11 x 15
[Robert Meyrick]

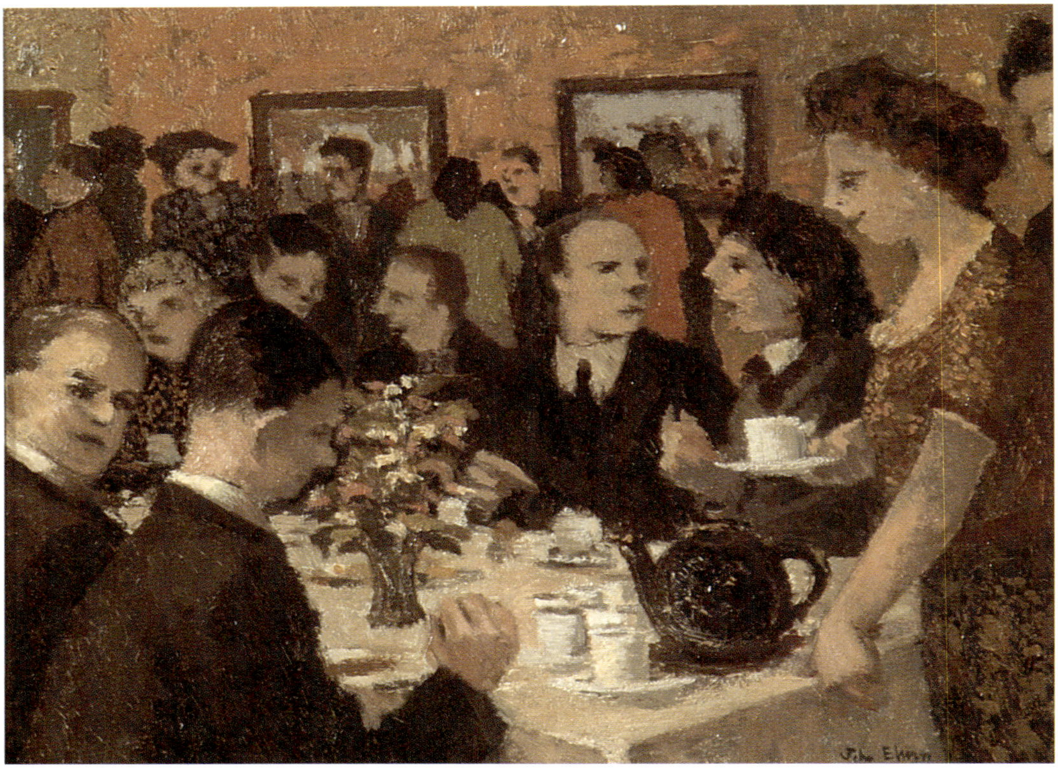

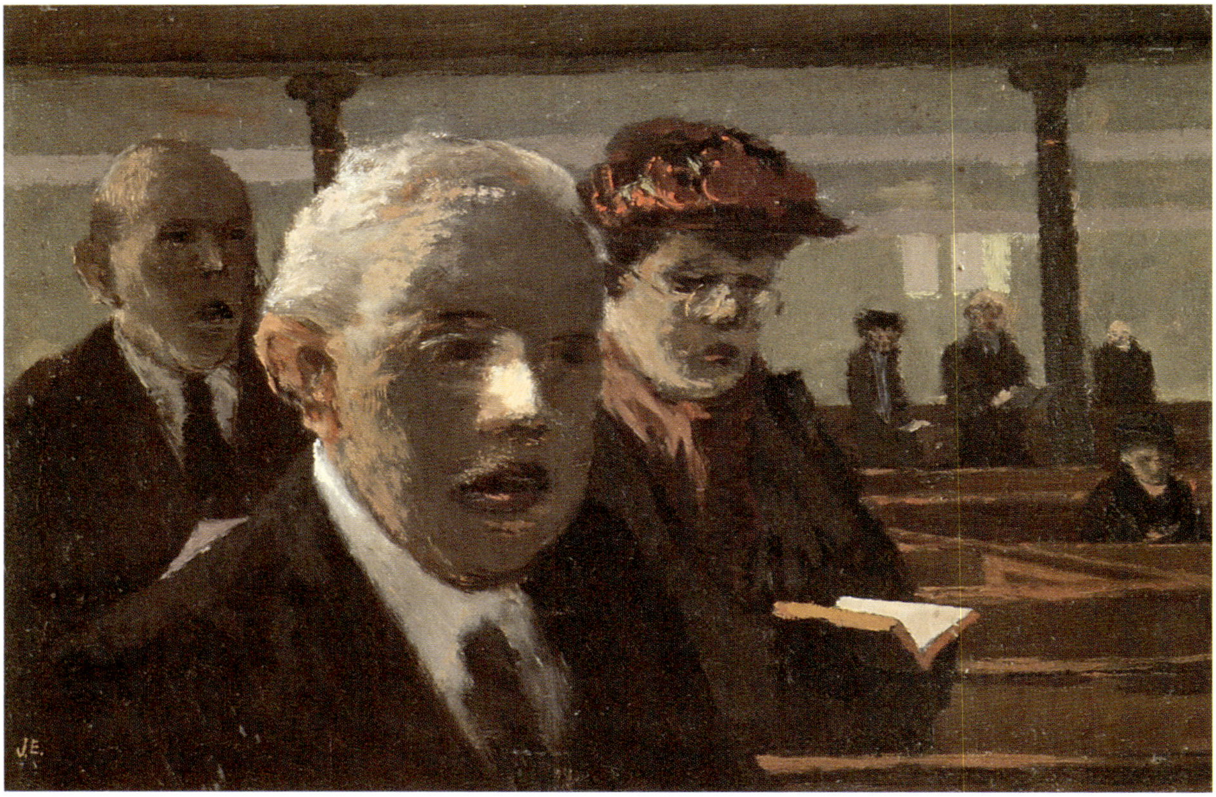
J.E.

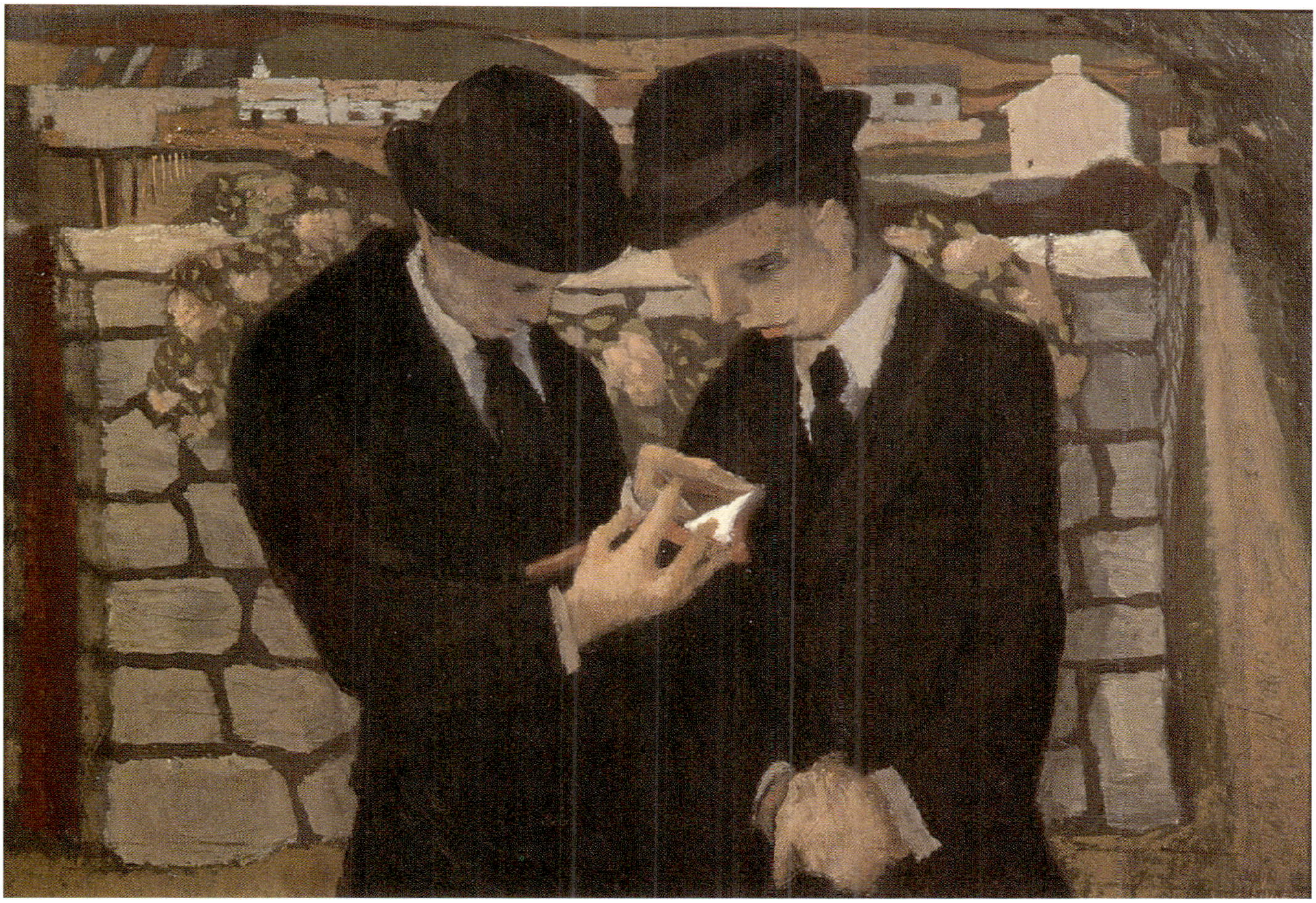

VI: *The Hymn Critics*
1949, oil on board, 13 x 19
[The Artist's Estate]

IV: *A Social Tea Party*
1949, oil on board, $10\frac{1}{2}$ x 14
[The Artist's Estate]

V: *The Faithful Few*
1949, oil on board, $11\frac{1}{2}$ x $18\frac{1}{2}$
[National Library of Wales, Aberystwyth]

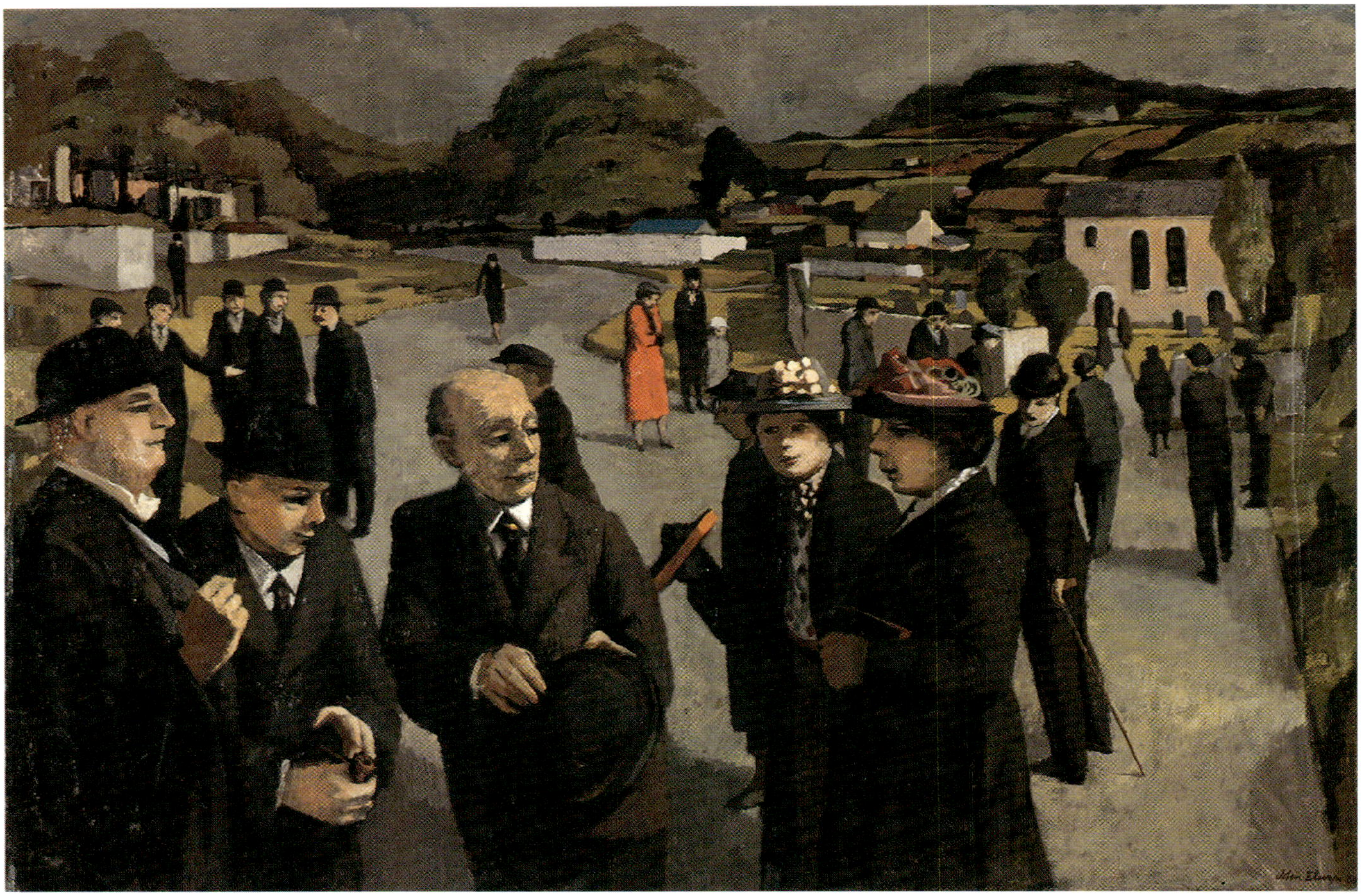

VII: *Suliau Mebyd*, (Sundays of my Youth) a.k.a. *Before the Meeting*
1950, oil on board, 23 x 35
[National Library of Wales, Aberystwyth]

VIII: *Southsea Front*
1951, oil on board, 18½ x 24½
[Frances and Nicolas McDowall]

IX: *Family Outing, Southsea*
1951, oil on canvas, 20 x 30
[Homer Sykes]

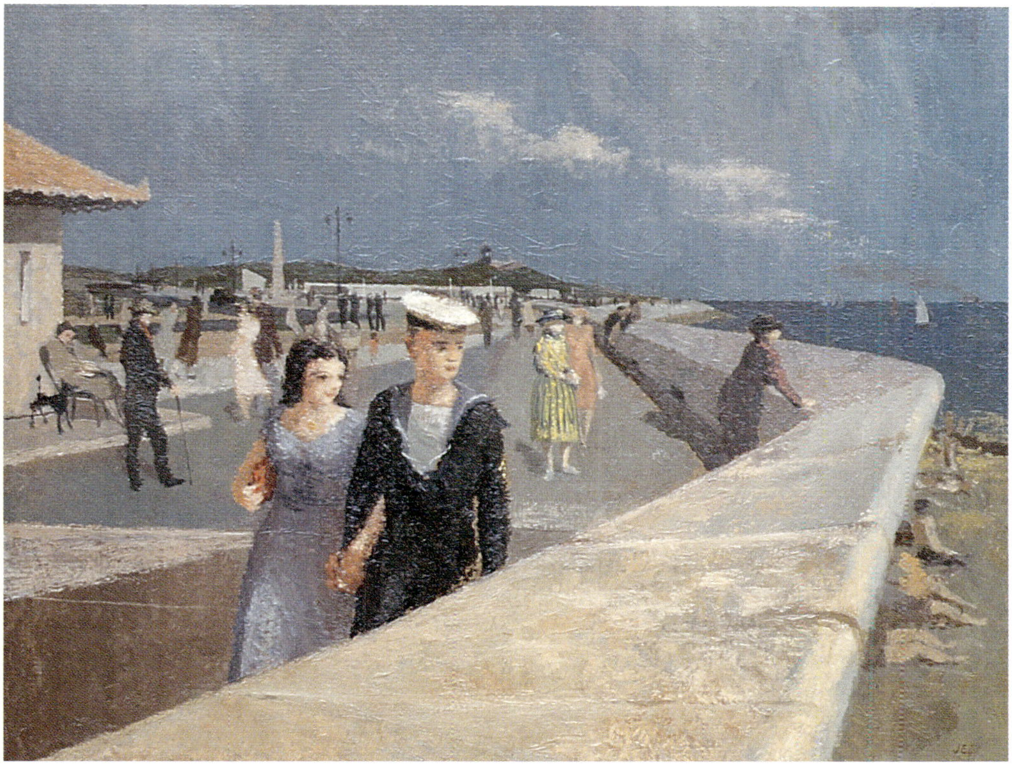

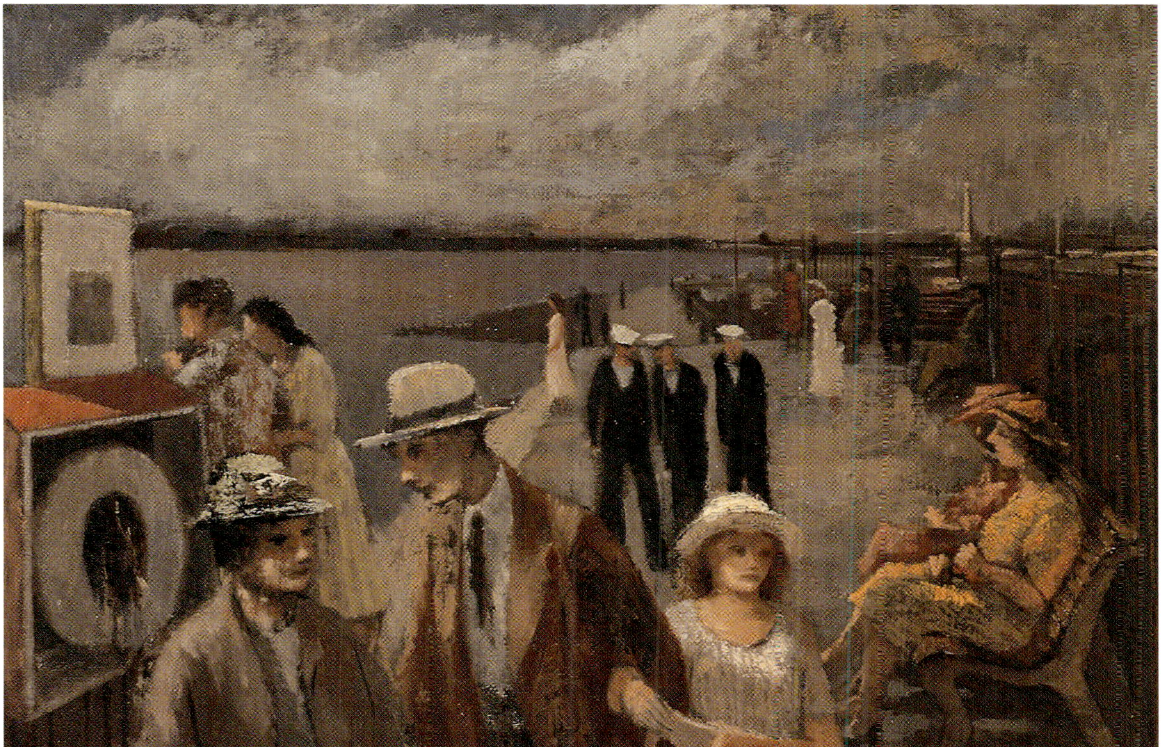

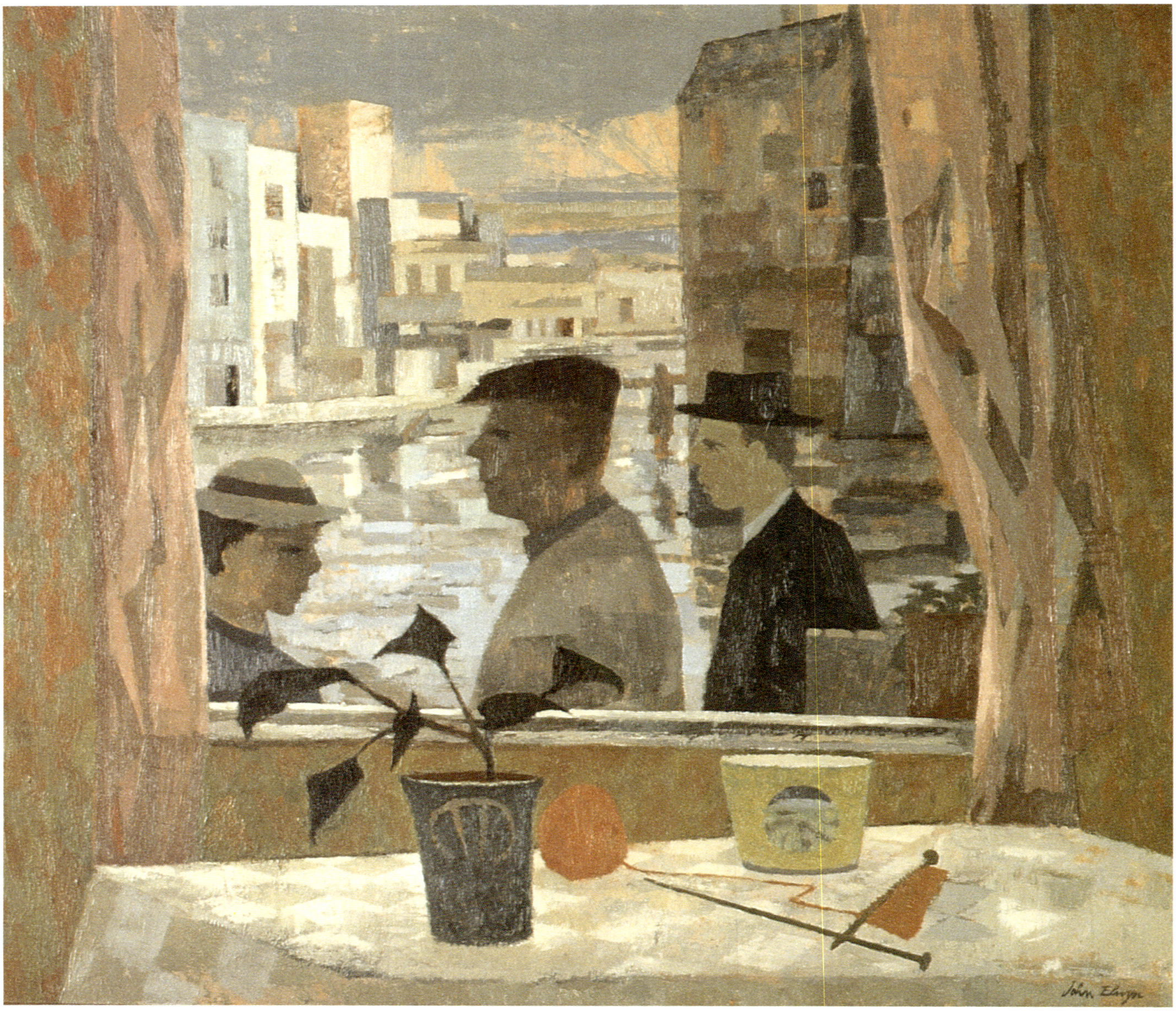

x: *After the Rain (Gosport)*
1952, oil on board, 20 x 24
[Robert Meyrick]

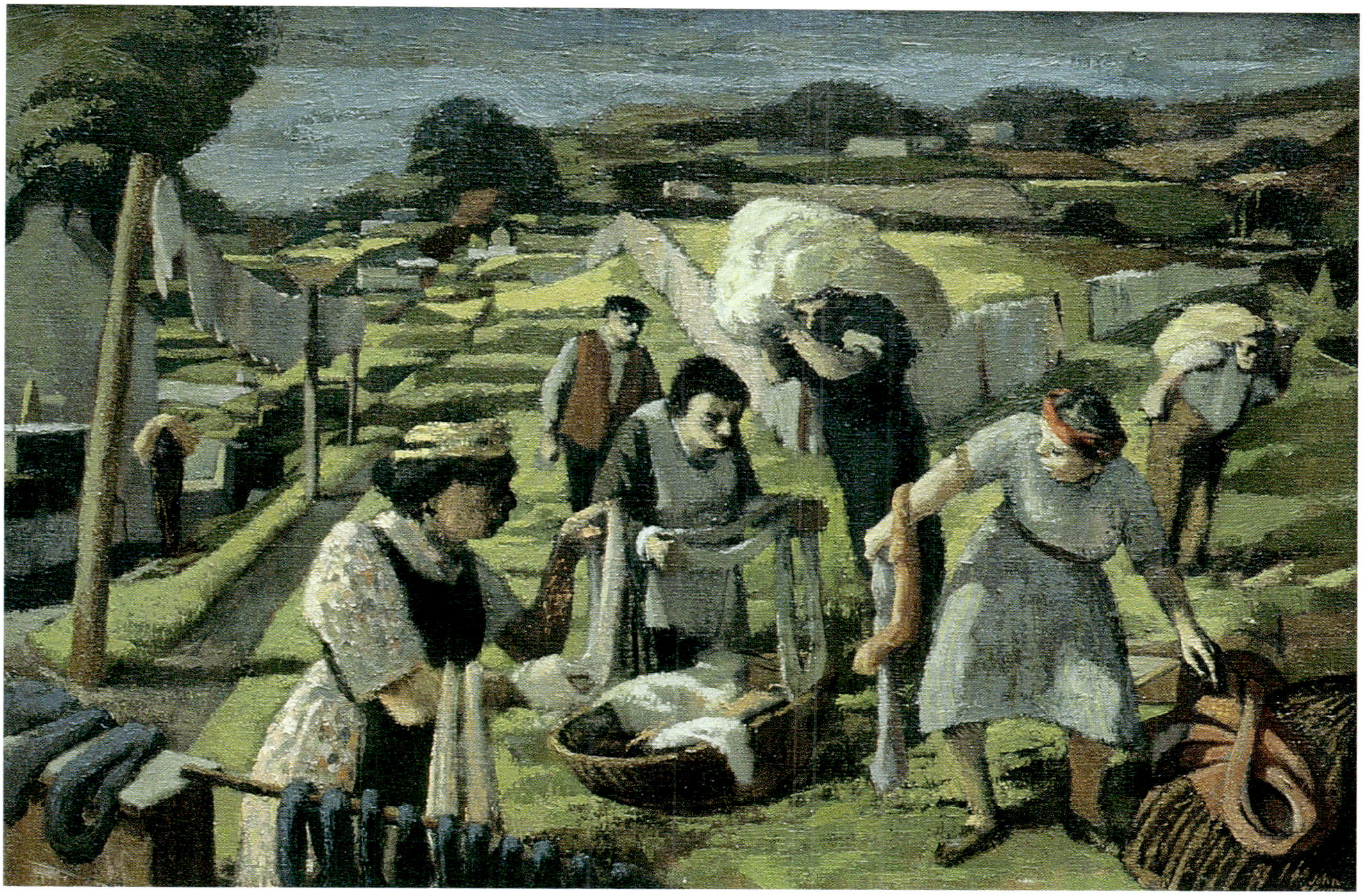

XI: *Wool Dyers*
1950, oil on canvas, 20 x 30
[Gillian Arthur]

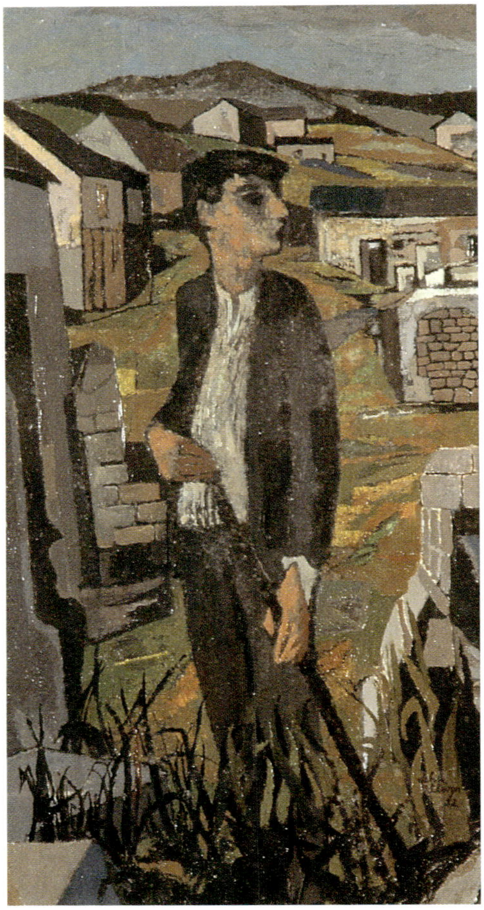

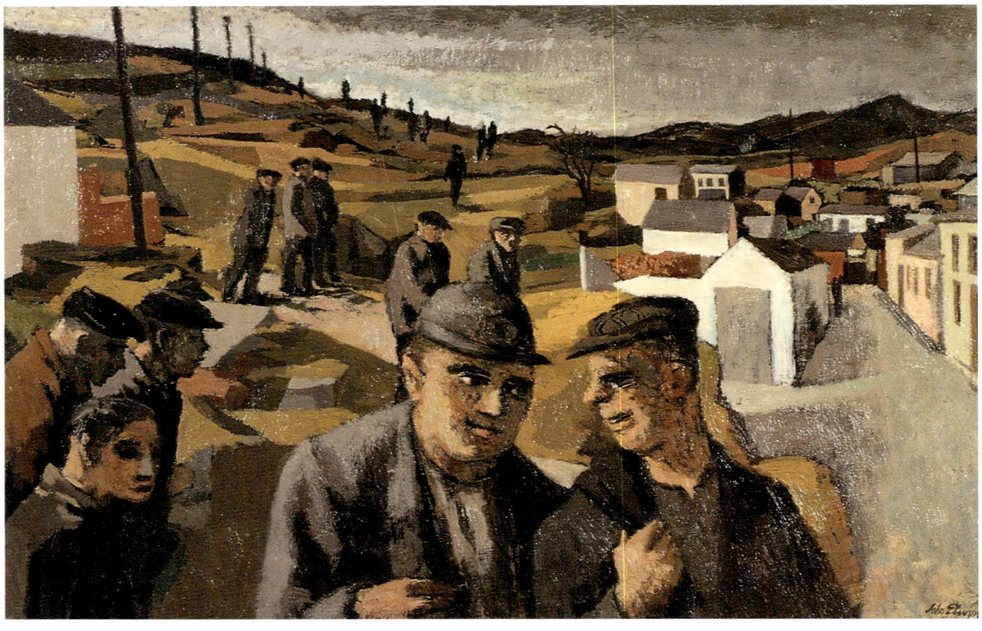

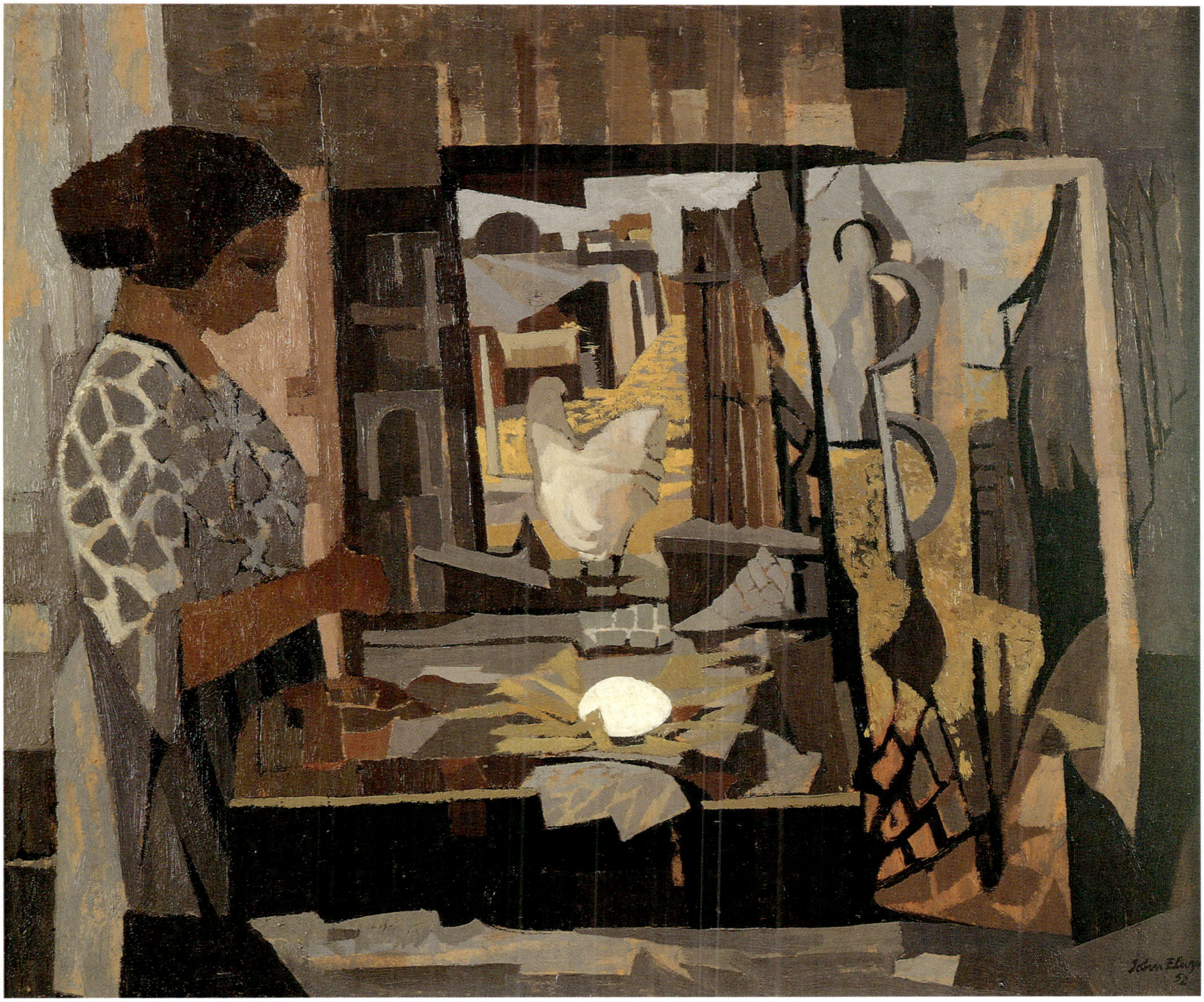

XIV: *The Egg*
1952, oil on board, 20 x 24
[Frances and Nicolas McDowall]

XII: *The Sweeper*
1952, oil on board, 20 x 11
[Frances and Nicolas McDowall]

XIII: *Miners Returning Home over Waste Ground*
1951, oil on board, 14 x 20
[The Arts Council of Wales]

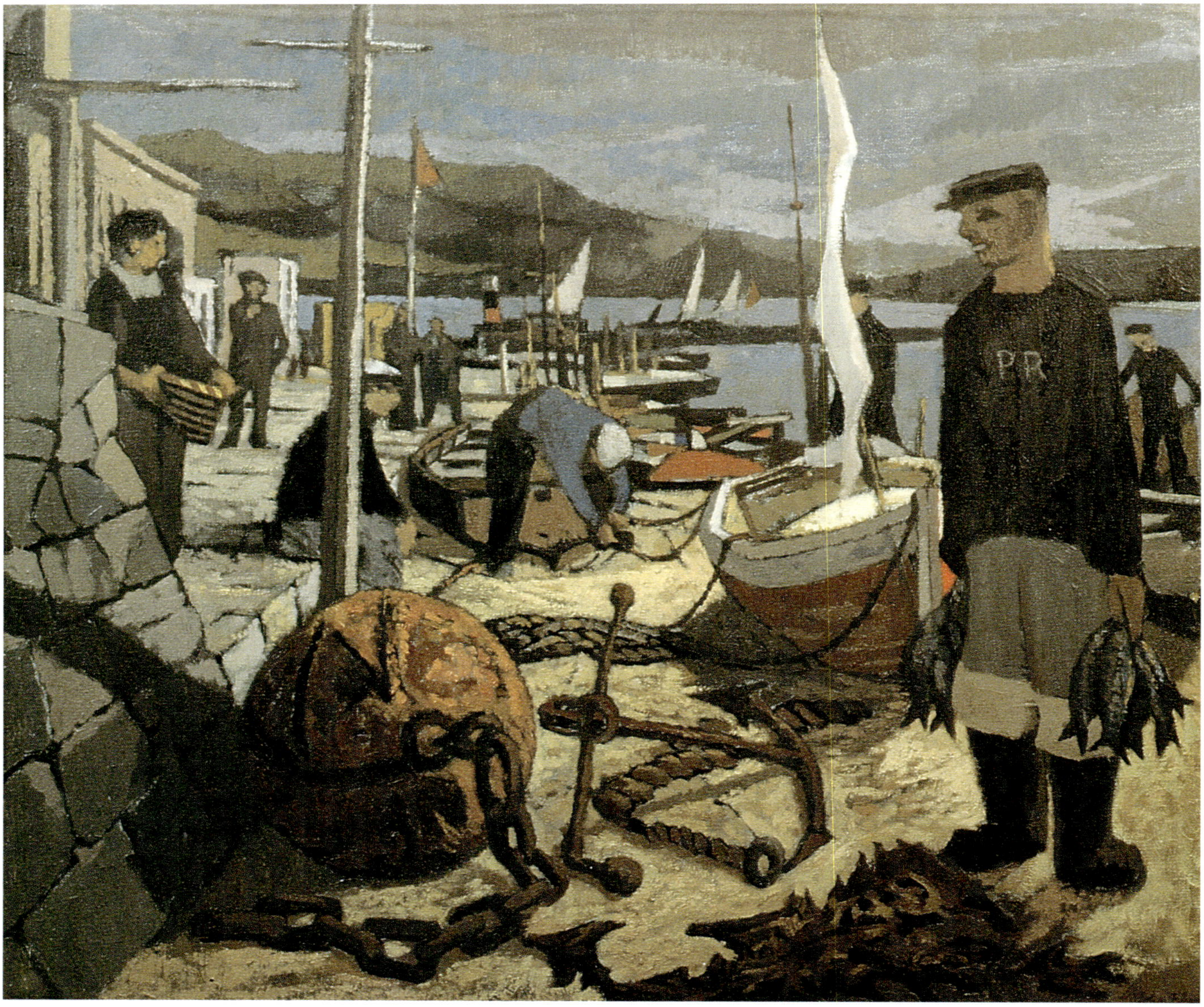

XV: *The Sailor's Return*
1952, oil on canvas, 20 x 24
[Martin Tinney Gallery]

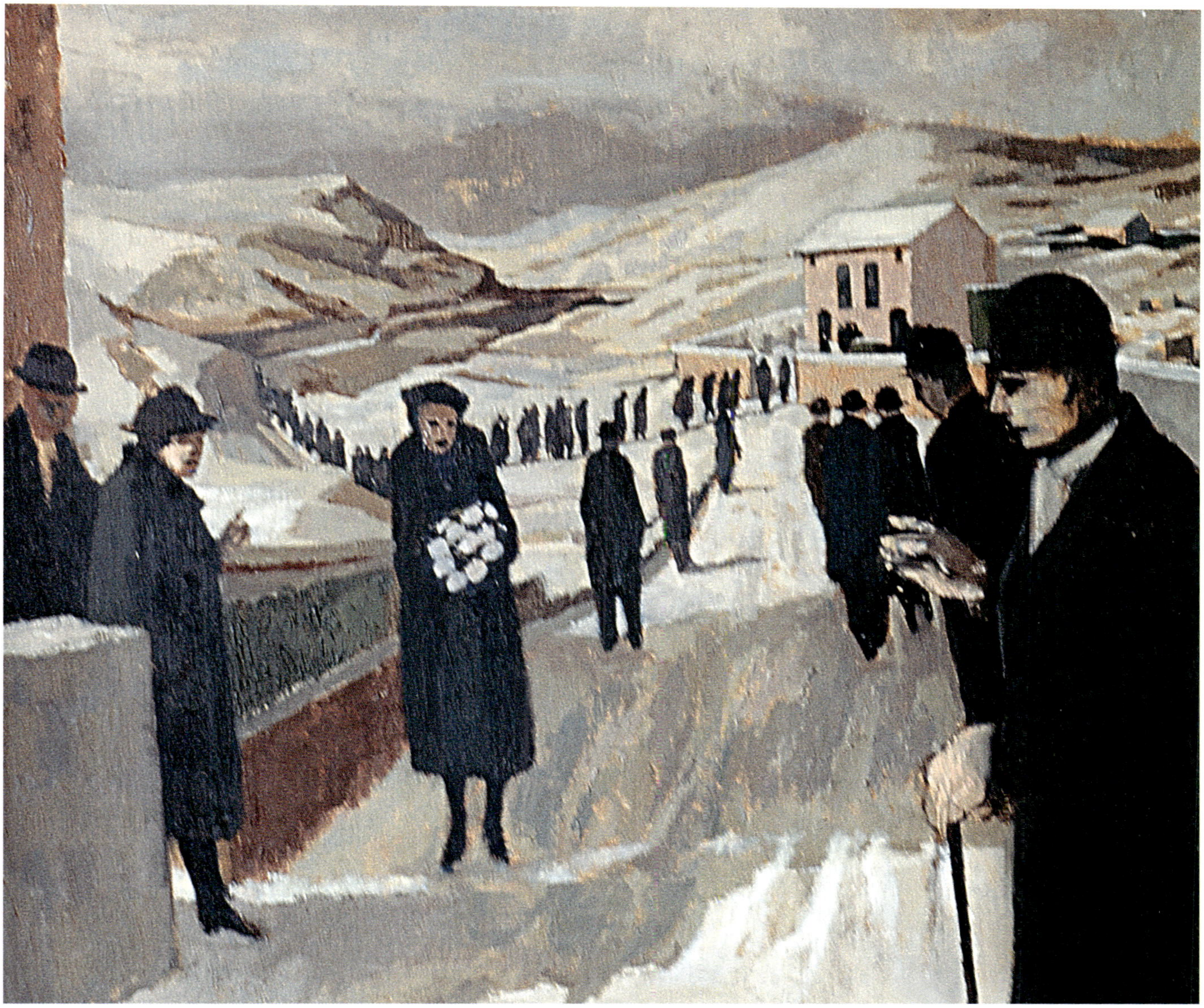

XVI: *Funeral in the Snow*
1953, oil on canvas, 20 x 24
[Present whereabouts unknown]

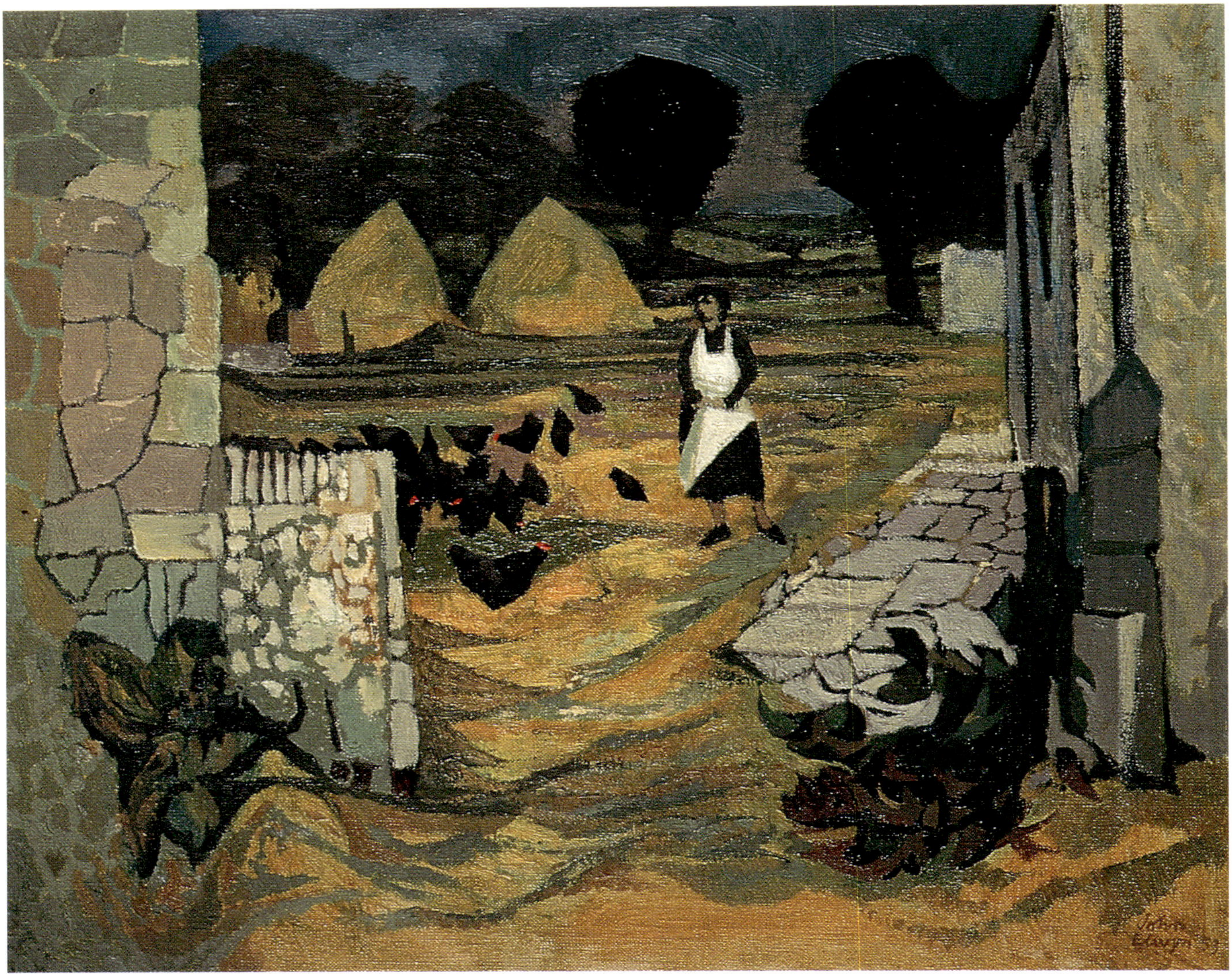

XVII: *The Farmer's Wife*
1953, oil on canvas, 16 x 20
[Robert Meyrick]

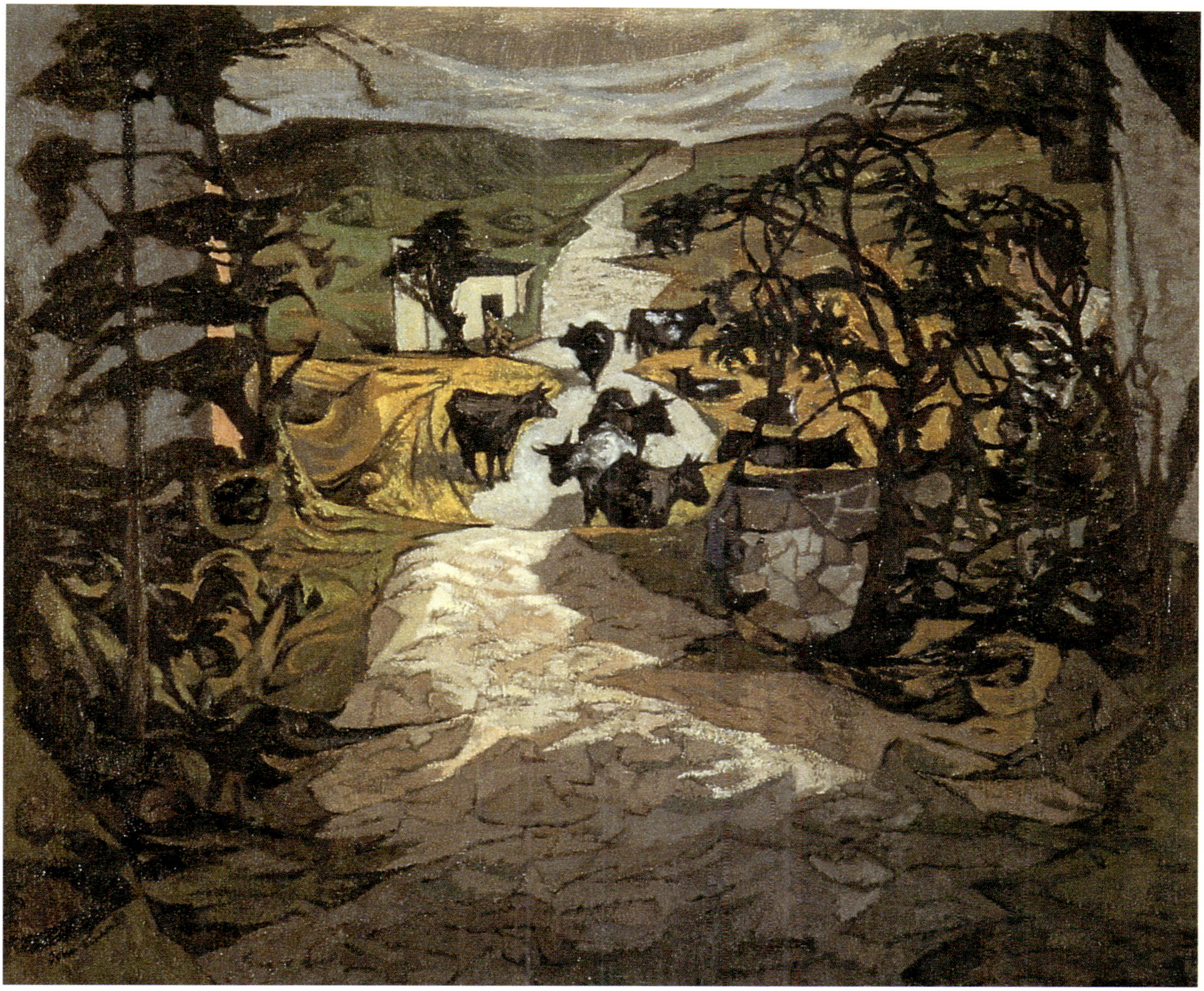

XVIII: *The Milky Way*
1953, oil on canvas, 20 x 24
[National Museum and Art Gallery of Wales, Cardiff]

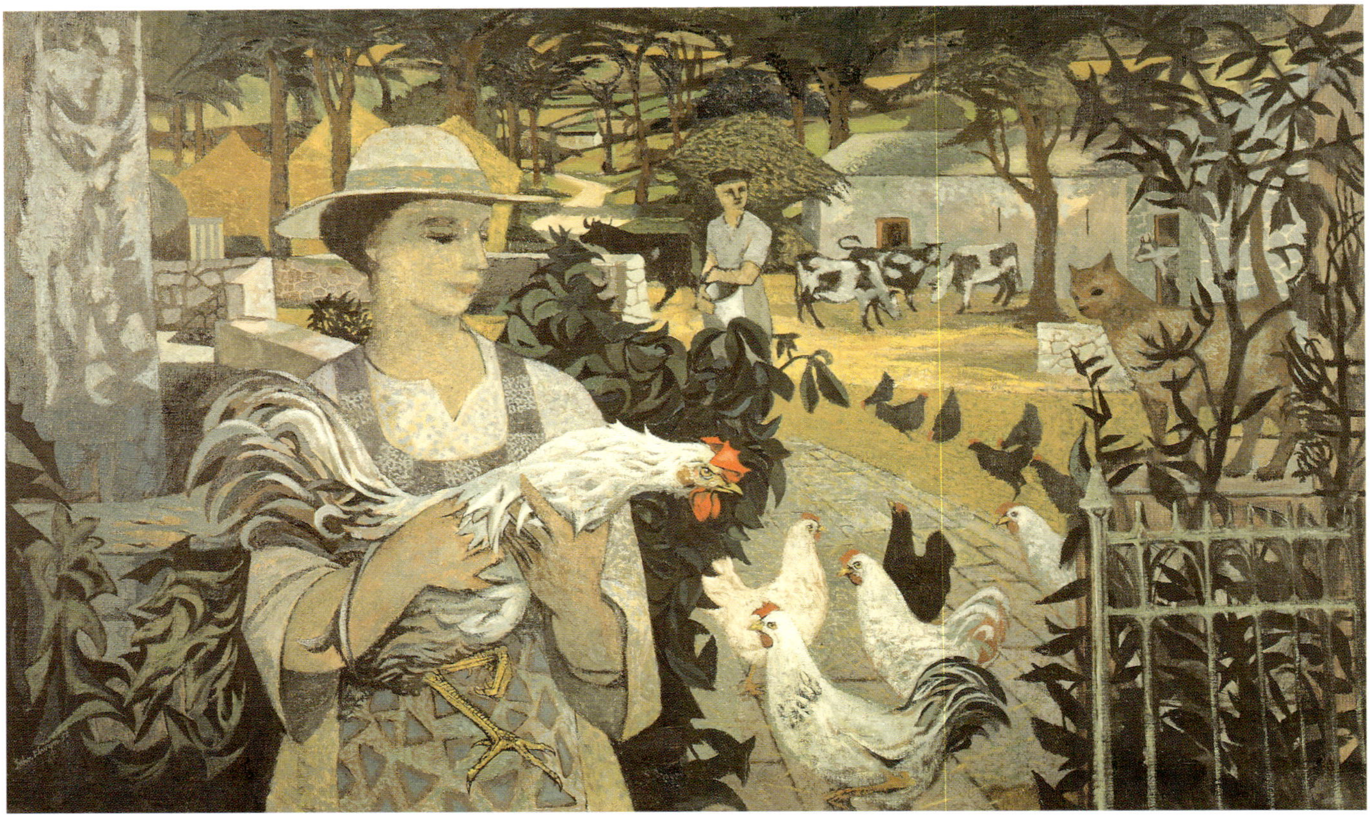

XIX: *The Pet Cockerel*
1953, oil on canvas, 30 x 50
[Powys Education Authority]

Chapter 4

famous among the barns:

establishing a reputation

JOHN ELWYN'S PAINTINGS were widely acclaimed by the early 1950s, particularly in Wales where the opportunities for artists to exhibit had improved considerably due to the endeavours of the Regional Office of the Arts Council of Great Britain under the direction of David Bell.[76] Arts Council catalogues frequently celebrated Welsh achievements 'with the pen and the voice in a land of song and chapels' but perpetuated the notion that Wales had never had a tradition of the visual arts. This view has been called to question in recent years as art historians reassess the rich and diverse visual culture of Wales.[77] In 1947 writing for *The Welsh Review*, Gwyn Jones warmly commended the intelligent and enthusiastic work of the Arts Council in promoting exhibitions, but launched a piercing attack on Welsh parochialism and complacency:

> Heaven knows Wales needs exhibitions of good paintings, if only that as a people we may at last realise there are standards in the arts higher than those of the Cwmscwt eisteddfod ... for never was there a people more ready to take the third-rate for the best, and to compliment itself on the mediocre as though it were the superb.[78]

The Arts Council, the National Eisteddfod, the National Museum of Wales' Art Department, the Society for Education through Art, and the Contemporary Art Society for Wales were all active from the late 1940s staging touring exhibitions of contemporary art. It was hoped that their combined efforts would improve the cultural climate for artists, to initiate and nurture an artistic community, and ultimately a 'Welsh School of Painting'. In 1951 the Arts Council staged an exhibition of 'Contemporary Welsh Painting' to celebrate the Festival of Britain and 'give some idea of the diversity and vitality of painting in Wales today'.[79] It toured to venues, large and small, throughout Wales. Its object was twofold: 'to serve as a stimulus to the increasing practice of the art in Wales by giving artists of Welsh extraction or living and working in Wales an opportunity to put their work before a wider public than the current exhibitions in Wales can command; and secondly to provide that public with an introduction to the art of its country and countrymen'.[80]

In the Festival year a sum of money was allocated by the Arts Council for the purchase of paintings to start a collection, selected by an independent panel of practising artists. In February 1951, John Elwyn exhibited *Miners Returning from the Pit on a Wet Day* at the Mansard Gallery in Heal's. Winifred Coombe-Tennant saw the painting and suggested that he arrange to have it delivered to her in order that she might 'show it to the right people'. She hung it in a prominent position in the sitting room, invited David Bell to tea and waited for him to ask 'who painted that picture?'. In March she wrote to inform John Elwyn that Bell intended to buy it for the Arts Council's Welsh Collection from its new fund for the purchase of pictures from exhibitions in Wales. She added that she would be pleased to keep other paintings at her home that he might 'want people in London to see'.[81]

John Elwyn had made his first contribution to a National Eisteddfod exhibition at Cardigan in 1942. He was a devoted 'eisteddfodwr' and rarely missed a festival, but on this occasion he did not attend because his mother had recently died. The National Eisteddfod of Wales exhibitions are potentially the most important annual showcases for Welsh art. Their audience is far larger and more geographically diverse than any other museum or gallery in Wales could ever hope to attract. Since their introduction into the festival the exhibitions have provided a focus for debate on art produced in Wales. The profile of the Arts and Crafts Exhibition at the Eisteddfod in the early 1950s was of major concern and attempts were made to redefine its role. To counteract widespread criticism of the low standard of the art and craft pavillion, 'artists of standing' were encouraged to contribute work to an exhibition selected by a committee. In 1950 the small monetary prizes for the open competition were abolished. John Elwyn thought the new scheme was a good one:

> and certainly a step in the right direction. It has possibilities and maybe the beginning of a Welsh School of Painting or at least a Welsh Group. If the National Eisteddfod week becomes the meeting place of painters as well as bards and songsters then surely the new venture will have achieved a great deal.[82]

To enhance the exhibition's reputation, invitations were made to artists whose work it was believed represented 'the highest achievements of Welsh painting'. John Elwyn was invited and he exhibited *Bore Sul* and *Suliau Mebyd* in Caerphilly that year. In the following year the Gold Medal for Fine Art was introduced, and awarded by the panel for one piece in the exhibition. It was awarded to John Elwyn at the National Eisteddfod in Aberdare in 1956.

Such initiatives on behalf of artists in Wales continued to gain momentum. In 1951, the Welsh Committee of the Arts Council, with the support of the Welsh Joint Education Committee, invited the Society for Education through Art (S.E.A.) to arrange 'Pictures for Welsh Schools', the first exhibition of its kind in Wales. The S.E.A. had been established in London in 1947 to arrange annual exhibitions of 'Pictures for Schools', but the venture was short-lived in England. Local Education Authorities in Wales were encouraged to send representatives to the exhibitions at the National Museum in Cardiff and other venues in Wales to purchase works for distribution amongst its schools. Eight local authorities acquired works in the first year, as well as the National Museum School's Service and some private collectors. John Elwyn sold twenty-three paintings to local authorities in Wales and England between 1950 and 1968.

Artists submitted works before a panel that considered their suitability for children as well as their merits as works of art. They were encouraged to paint modestly-priced narrative pictures to encourage written projects and discussion between teachers and the school children. Arguably, paintings such as *The Sailor's Return* (1952) and *The Pet Cockerel* (1953) are among John Elwyn's most confident and resolved achievements as a painter. (Plate XV) At a time when he felt it necessary to adopt a more modern approach to painting, and explore form and colour independent of story-telling, the 'Pictures for Schools' scheme provided him with a good reason to work in the narrative genre he enjoyed, and in which he was most accomplished. David Bell observed in his introduction to the catalogue in 1951:

> though our children are learning to exercise their sensibilities by visual expression, the experience and enjoyment of mature painting, which is rather a different thing

> from the drawings of children, is still unknown in many parts of Wales. It is the main purpose of this exhibition to put within the reach of children the genuine and profound pleasure which works of art can give.[83]

The venture was primarily restricted to Wales and was a great success. Paintings could be reserved by authorities outside Wales and acquired if a Welsh buyer was not found. In addition to their educational objectives, the organisers hoped that the exhibitions would provide a market for paintings by Welsh artists in Wales and therefore stimulate a 'lively artistic tradition'. John Petts optimistically observed in 1952 that 'in a land famed for its song, we are learning to hear with our eyes'.[84]

In 1952 the National Library of Wales at Aberystwyth staged *The Artist in Wales*, 'to give a broad view of the position of Welsh contemporary painting'. The exhibition included the work of Charles Burton, Brenda Chamberlain, Evan Charlton, Joseph Herman, Ceri Richards, Ernest Zobole and John Elwyn whose 'studies of village life in Wales will be recognised for their quiet sincerity,' wrote John Petts. 'We are fortunate in having at least one true genre painter.'[85] After the exhibition John Petts, who had succeeded David Bell at the Arts Council, invited John Elwyn to exhibit with the newly formed North Wales Group. As a guest exhibitor, his contribution as 'one of six important painters working in Wales', would, he wrote, 'help forward the excellent objectives of the Group and assist us in our efforts to raise the standards of art appreciation and execution in Wales'.[86] The Contemporary Art Society for Wales, founded in 1937, played an ever increasing role in helping Welsh artists, heightening public awareness of contemporary Welsh painting by purchasing paintings to be presented to public institutions throughout Wales. The Society have purchased five paintings by John Elwyn for their collection: *Funeral Gathering on a Welsh Hill Farm* in 1949, *Bore Sul* in 1950, *The Mothers* in 1954, *Windfalls* in 1956 and *Wet Summer II* in 1985.

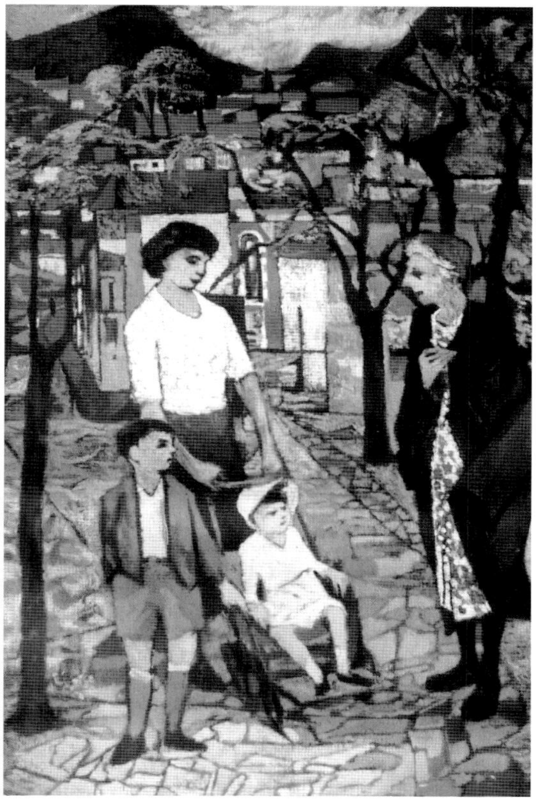

Three Generations
1953, oil on canvas
[Dimensions and present whereabouts unknown]

In October 1953 the Welsh Committee of Arts Council of Great Britain organised an open exhibition of Welsh painting and sculpture for the National Museum of Wales. It provided an opportunity for artists to exhibit and aimed to introduce the public to the appreciation and purchase of contemporary art. It also endeavoured to persuade public bodies and industry to purchase works of art. The panel of selectors, John Piper, Carel Weight and David Bell, were greatly impressed by the quality of works:

> A feeling is conveyed in many of the pictures of love and compassion for humanity and a consciousness of the relations of men and women to nature, buildings, and everyday life in Wales. This concern with the environment seems to auger well for the future of a Welsh School of Painting.[87]

A further selection was made to form an exhibition for the Arts Council's gallery in St James's Square, London. 'Thirty Welsh Paintings of Today' later toured around Wales and Scotland. John Elwyn's *Harvest Yellow* and *Miners Returning Home on a Wet Evening III* were chosen; the latter was reproduced on the catalogue cover and subsequently purchased for the Arts Council's Welsh Collection. At the same time the Arts Council paid John Elwyn £12 to hire *Sun and Snow*, a painting he had entered for an open exhibition of 'Football and the Arts' in 1953. The exhibition was sponsored by the Football Association and travelled all over the north of England and the Midlands during 1954. *Sun and Snow* did not win a prize but was reproduced on the

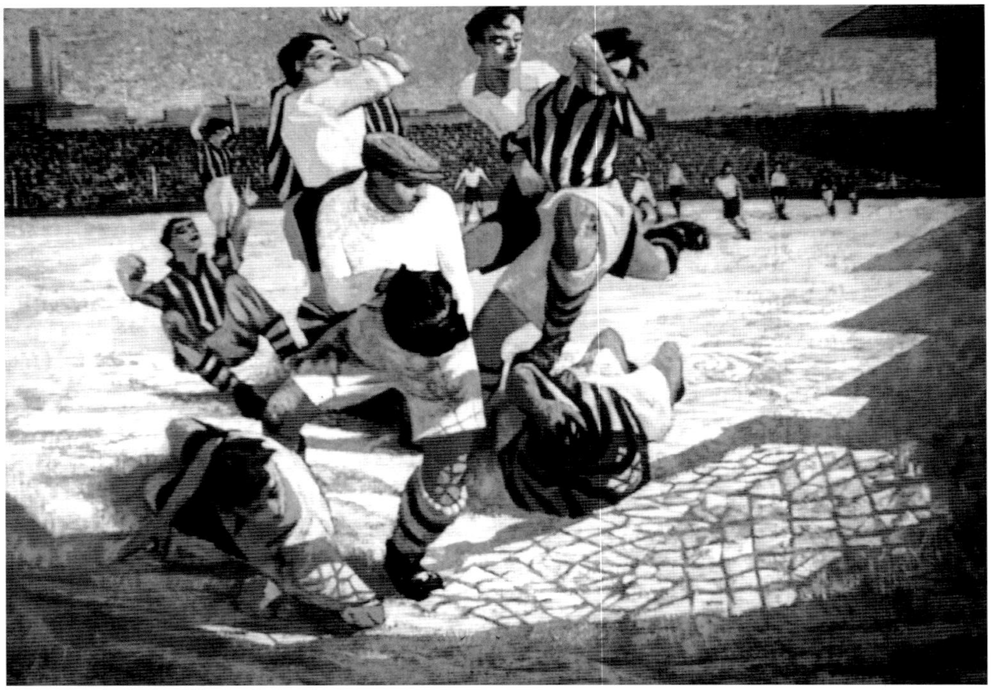

Sun and Snow
1953, oil on board 47 x 55
[Present whereabouts unknown]

cover of the catalogue. As the title suggests the painting was as much about the decorative pattern of the goal nets, the climatic conditions and the way in which bright sunlight transforms the subject, as it was concerned with the scramble of players and drama of the tackle. It was exhibited once more at Manchester City Art Gallery in 1966 in an exhibition to celebrate football in the World Cup year.

All the mixed exhibitions of contemporary Welsh art that took place during these years failed to establish a Welsh National School, but for the individual artists, native or immigrant, living and working in isolation throughout Wales they provided a focus and an outlet. It was apparent, however, that whilst no native school *per se* had emerged many artists had become increasingly dependent upon Welsh landscape and life. Attempts were made to identify and define the Welshness of Welsh art and in many ways John Elwyn's paintings of industrial and rural communities like *Funeral in the Snow* (1953) conformed to the anticipated character of a Welsh national style.[88] (Plate XVI) At a time when many artists in Wales were beginning to explore the possibilities of abstraction, and their paintings became more diverse and international, concentrating on formal values rather than narrative in painting, the Eisteddfod exhibitions championed those who made 'pictures which are sincere comments on the contemporary scene'. These artists were generally the recipients of the Gold Medal Awards: Charles Burton for *Back from the Club, Rhondda* (1954), D. C. Roberts for *Wrth y Ddaear* (1955), John Elwyn for *The Meadow* (1956), and George Chapman for his *View in Merthyr Tydfil* (1958).[89]

In 1952 John Elwyn's friend and Head of Painting at Portsmouth David Pare (1911–1996) left to become Principal of Winchester School of Arts and Crafts. He advertised for additional teaching staff and John Elwyn was amongst forty-one candidates interviewed for a post. In January 1953 he was appointed to teach painting, illustration and life drawing and took up the post on 1st May that year. He took board and lodgings at 18 St Thomas Street in Winchester with the Bannisters – a canon in the cathedral, his Russian wife and their three young children. John Elwyn occupied a ground floor room large enough to paint and sleep in, and there was a kitchen and store in the basement for his use. He ate meals with the family and had no use for the kitchen. His needs were few and his pleasures simple; he took holidays with his spinster sisters Katie and Mary, and day trips with sister Sally and brother-in-law David John – to north Wales, Pembrokeshire, or along the Cardiganshire coast. The wood engraver Garrick Palmer was a colleague at the Art School. For a time he had been a student of John Elwyn at Portsmouth before he left to undertake postgraduate studies at the Royal Academy Schools. He started teaching part time at Winchester whilst still a student at the R.A., became full time in 1962 and ultimately Head of Foundation Studies. He and John Elwyn became close friends; at Winchester they ritually had lunch together followed by a long walk around the historic parts of the town. When Palmer told John Elwyn that he had no personal experience of the Wales represented in his paintings, he took it upon himself to rectify this and Palmer was taken on a vacation to Cardiff and the valley towns. They travelled many miles around the mining communities in John Elwyn's A30 car, met with his friends, and he imparted his vast knowledge and enthusiasm for the locality.

John Elwyn went to Brittany with David Pare and his wife, and he joined Glyn and Doreen Jones on holidays to Cornwall, north and west Wales, Llansteffan (particularly in latter years), and in 1955 to the Edinburgh Festival. Their house in Cardiff became a second home to John Elwyn, who stayed there whilst on business in the capital or passing through on his way to west Wales. The return journeys to 'the old country' increased after he passed his driving test in April 1955. However, there is a hint of concern in his letters to Glyn Jones that there was still not a girlfriend in his life. Earlier he had written, 'I am now writing on a profound theme – to be published shortly on "How to remain a bachelor"'.[90] At the end of each academic term he packed up immediately and left for Wales where he remained for the vacation; the School closed at noon on Fridays and he was in Cardiff by evening. Usually he took David Bell on a painting expeditions to south-west Wales in the summer. Bell had suffered from multiple sclerosis for over thirty years and was becoming increasingly disabled. On their trip together in 1958 Bell did his last painting. He died on 21st April 1959 aged 43, from pneumonia contracted after a successful operation to improve his mobility. Rollo Charles, Keeper of Art at the National Museum, in a tribute to Bell wrote: 'certainly it is to him more than anyone else that is due the new and wide interest in pictures that has arisen in Wales since the war.'[91]

In 1953 John Elwyn renewed his friendship with Edwin la Dell (1914–1970) who had graduated from the Royal College in the year John Elwyn enrolled. La Dell had succeeded Robert Austin as Professor of Engraving, and John Elwyn asked if he might use his free time to practise lithography. For some months he travelled up to London where he sat in on demonstrations and received practical instruction from la Dell and Anthony Gross. One of these early lithographs *The Canal*, with its weary miners walking alongside the canal after work, was made after an earlier painting of the same title. Since John Elwyn was employed to teach illustration he felt it necessary to be seen to be active in the genre. (Appendix 7) In December 1953 he received a letter from Ralph Usherwood, Art Editor of the *Radio Times*, who had been shown John Elwyn's work by Rowland Lucas, BBC Publicity Officer (Wales). Usherwood maintained the tradition of inviting painters to illustrate for *Radio Times*, which had the largest readership of any weekly magazine.

As television output increased in the late 1950s, however, fewer artists were commissioned to illustrate for radio programming. He wanted John Elwyn to consider

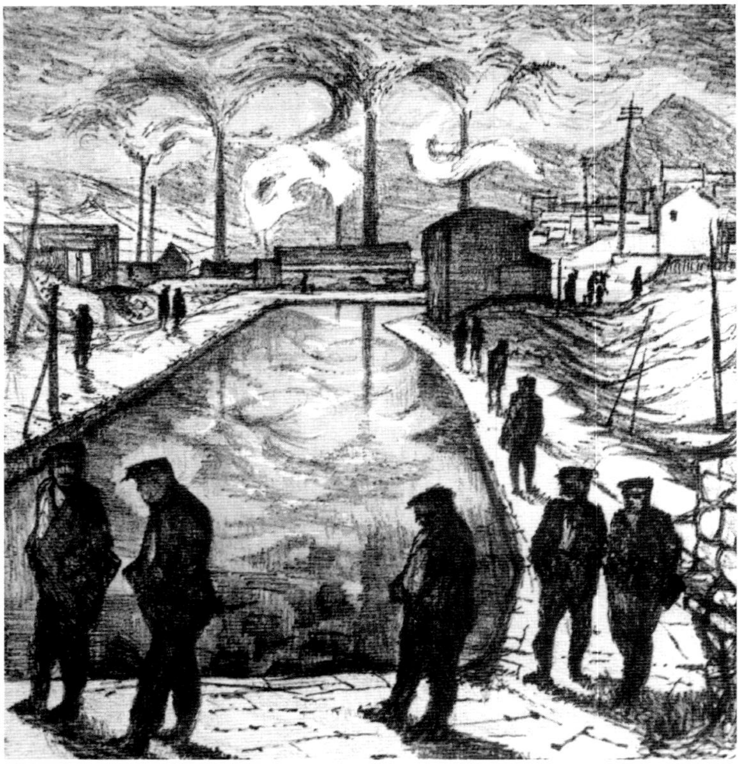

The Canal
1953, lithograph on paper
$12^{3}/_{4}$ x $12^{1}/_{2}$
[The University of Wales, Aberystwyth]

working for the *Radio Times*. He explained that there was generally a five day turnaround and he would need to be at the end of a telephone as programme details were only made available one week before going to press. The *Radio Times* bought full copyright, and 8 guineas was paid for all commissioned work that fulfilled the Art Editor's brief, whether published or not. John Elwyn's first commission was for the radio play *The Country of the Blind* adapted from H. G. Wells, featuring Laurence Olivier, and broadcast on 2nd February 1954. His next illustration was for *Y Corff*, a play by the late Dewi Emrys which was broadcast on 9th February 1954. John Griffiths, the Features and Drama Producer who prepared the script for radio, suggested an early scene when the two old brothers Tomos and William discover *Y Corff* (The Body) on the beach. Other commissions followed; among the more notable examples are drawings for *The Sailor's Song* by James Hanley in May 1954 and *Buchedd Garmon* by Saunders Lewis in January 1957. John Elwyn's contributions to the *Radio Times* were rendered in his incisive open line to withstand reduction for printing. Like his contemporaries Leonard Rosoman and Robert Micklewright he adopted some of the distinctive graphic devices of the day, such as multiple or dotted outlines and a short 'ticky' line feeling its way around the form.

In August 1953 Glyn Jones drew John Elwyn's work to the attention of Christopher Sandford, director of the renowned Golden Cockerel Press. Sandford was sent a portfolio of drawings and he suggested that he used wood engraving with stencilled colour to illustrate a fine limited edition when a text that was 'up his street' came along. 'I find your work most striking', he wrote, 'I think we must do a book together ... your colouring is particularly good compared with that of some otherwise good artists'.[92] Using colour line blocks John Elwyn designed dust-wrappers for Glyn Jones' *The Dream of Jake Hopkins* (Fortune Press 1954), *The Valley, The City, The Village* (J. M. Dent 1956) and *The Learning Lark* (J. M. Dent 1960).

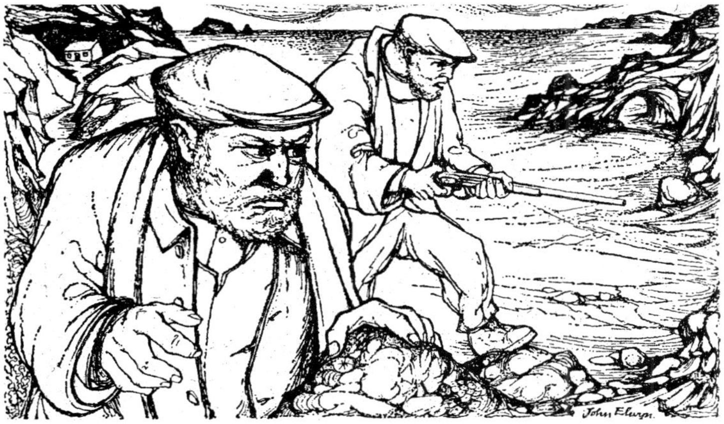

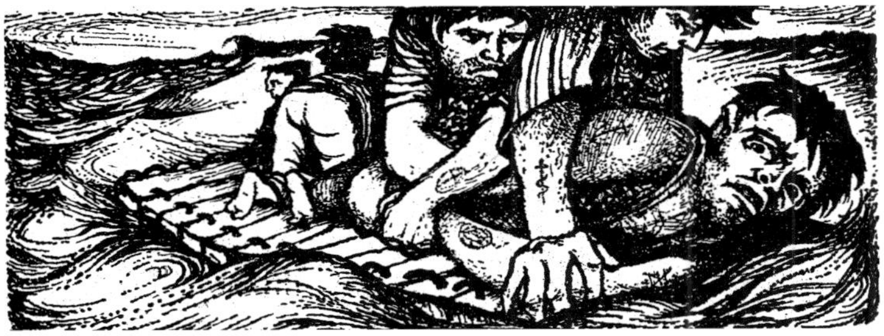

Y Corff (The Body)
February 1954
and
Sailor's Song May 1954,
ink on paper
[Radio Times]

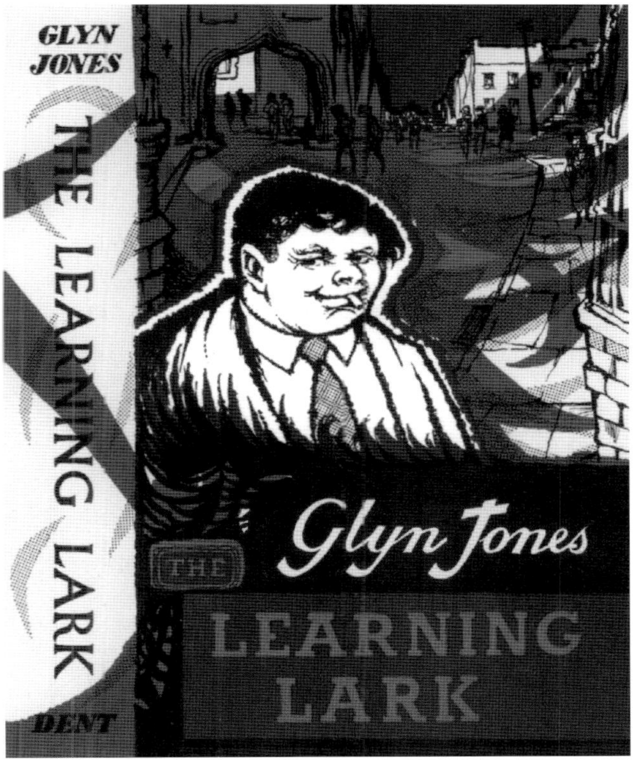

The Learning Lark
1960, line block in 4 colours on paper 8 x 6½
[J. M. Dent]

Winchester School of Arts and Crafts was then a small affair occupying the former St Swithun's School, a Victorian red-brick building on North Walls which it shared with the county lending library and other offices. It had occupied these so-called 'temporary' premises since the 1930s. The timetable was arranged to allow staff one day a week free from teaching and this gave John Elwyn time to investigate a new line of inquiry in painting. The social landscape of south Cardiganshire came under scrutiny once more, with its bustling farm yards, cattle pastures and the farmer with his wife working in apparent harmony with nature. Again he drew upon his fertile imagination, abundant repertoire of pictorial notes, and wide experience of the working life of the countryside. Those same people whom we saw dressed in Sunday best are now seen in their working clothes, undertaking the daily round of tasks that had been familiar to him as a child. *The Cat and the Cock* (1954), *The Broody Hens* (1955), *Feeding Time* (1955) and *The Inquisitive Geese* (1956) present an eirenical vision of rural life, and they characterise an attitude towards life in the country that was popularised by George Clausen and Jules Bastien-Lepage in the latter half of the nineteenth century. This halcyon view of life in the countryside, seen particularly in *The Pet Cockerel* (1953), also had its origins in Victorian narrative and Pre-Raphaelite landscape painting, recalling William Holman Hunt's *Strayed Sheep*, *Our English Coast* (1852) and John Everett Millais' *The Blind Girl* (1856). The intricate composition and the intensified realisation of the light conditions in Hunt's *The Hireling Shepherd* (1851–52) are echoed in *The Pet Cockerel* which he described as his 'small decorative mural'. (Plate XIX) The brilliant sunlit meadows around the central figures are rich in detail. Its Welsh title *Y Ceiliog Swci* is more indicative of the painting's intended significance, particularly in the relationship between the farmer's wife and her 'pet'. The orphaned cock has been hand reared and here its outstretched claws, straining neck and a vicious glint in its eye reveal a jealously protective side to its character.

The Adventurer (1954) is one of many smaller variations on the same themes as the S.E.A. and Eisteddfod exhibits that John Elwyn painted for the Leicester Galleries annual exhibitions of 'Artists of Fame and Promise' between 1950 and 1968. (Plate XXII) David Bell arranged his first introduction to Loftus Brown, a director at the Leicester Galleries in central London. In a letter to Mrs Coombe-Tennant, Oliver Brown observed a new confidence in the art market. From 1950 there had been a trend in the picture buying public away from the established names to art students and young artists. Walter Sickert and Matthew Smith had remained unsold yet in 1950 over sixty works by unknown artists had sold – and, he believed, it was not a matter of price.[93] In the healthy market that existed for contemporary art John Elwyn's paintings were frequently purchased by education authorities, private and public collections. This in itself was motivation to continue painting. Margaret Davies of Gregynog purchased *The Mothers* on behalf of the Contemporary Art Society for Wales and *The Milky Way* for her own collection which she bequeathed to the National Museum in Cardiff along with her internationally renowned French nineteenth-century paintings and sculptures. (Plate XVIII) From that same exhibition at the Leicester Galleries, Loftus Brown purchased *The Farmer's Wife*. (Plate XVII) In June 1954, J. T. Morgan, a wealthy collector and member of the Swansea Corporation Art Galleries Committee commissioned two oils to present to the Glynn Vivian Art Gallery: *Tree Architecture* and *Ydlan yn Sir Aberteifi*. (Plate XXI) David Bell travelled to Winchester and selected two works on behalf of the gallery. Morgan had known John Elwyn as a schoolboy and he still had dealings with his sisters at Emlyn Mill. Winifred Coombe-Tennant continued to follow John Elwyn's career and gained enormous satisfaction from the contribution she had made to his success.[94]

John Elwyn's landscapes of the meadows, dairy farms and barns of the Teifi and Ceri valleys and upland rural areas of Cardiganshire record different activities in the countryside at different times of the day and as they vary from season to season. These landscapes, in which farmers work the land, their wives look after the livestock and the farm-hands plaster a barn wall in *Pink and Grey Shapes* (1959), or wrestle with *The Broody Hens* and *White Leghorns*, occupied John Elwyn throughout much of the 1950s. David Bell observed that to John Elwyn the people:

> are an integral part of the landscape which *they* inhabit and *he* paints, just as much as that landscape is a part of him, and he paints them with the love and respect of familiarity ... because these are things he has known and this is where his heart is.[95]

War-time introspection continued well into the 1950s. Artists still turned to local and

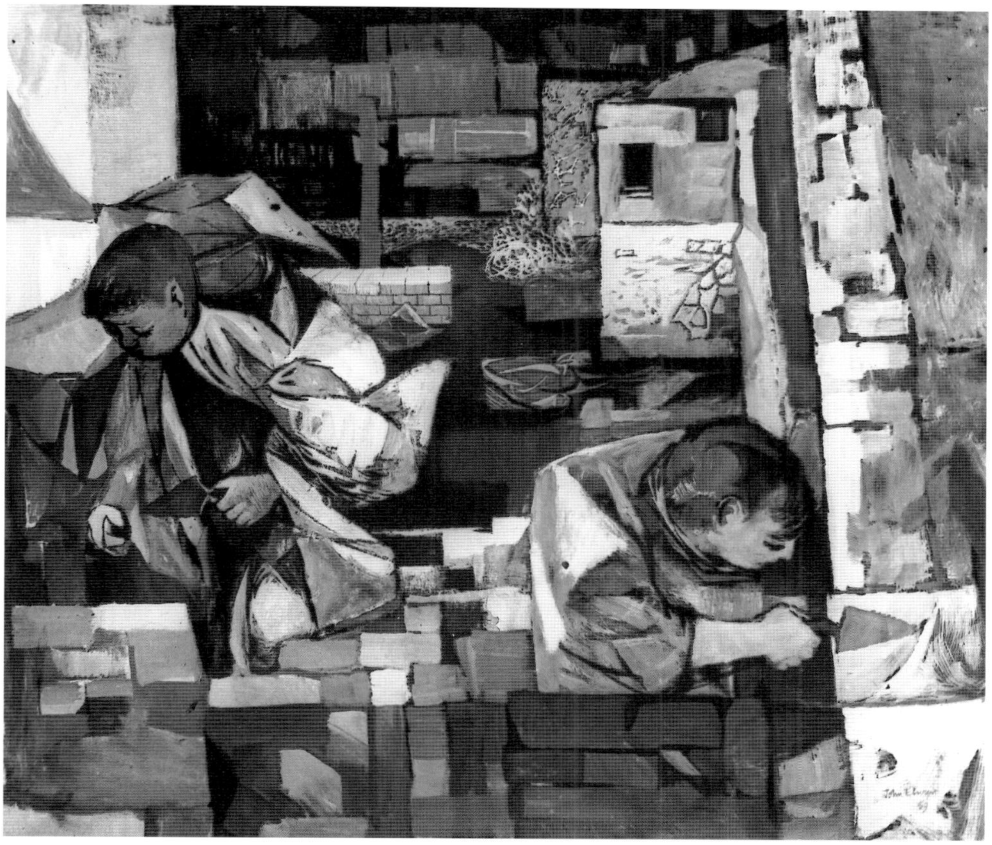

Pink and Grey Shapes
1959, gouache on paper 20 x 24
[Monmouthshire Education Authority]

provincial subjects for their paintings, albeit executed within the wider context of European realism – Joan Eardley amongst the Glasgow tenements, Lowry in the Lancashire mill towns, and the Kitchen Sink painters Derrick Greaves and Edward Middleditch working in Sheffield. In John Elwyn's farmyard paintings labour is seen as morally pure and dignified; the real hardship of working the land is overlooked. The commonly perceived view of the exposed, cold and wet Welsh countryside is rarely depicted. Whilst there is a slight brooding sadness about John Elwyn's mining subjects and farmyard paintings such as *The Sweeper*, his paintings never record the same ugliness and gritty urban realism as Greaves, Middleditch and John Bratby. (Plate XII) They all shared a common interest in workaday themes but John Elwyn's outlook was more cheerful and optimistic: his stylised figures set against decorative landscapes of formulised interlocking forms have more in common with John Minton's scenes along the River Thames and Prunella Clough's paintings of Lowestoft fishermen. *Windfalls*, purchased for the Contemporary Art Society for Wales by Evan Charlton from an exhibition of Contemporary Welsh Painting and Sculpture in 1956, presents a typical panegyric of country life, an attempt wrote John Elwyn:

> to paint the vivid and varied kinds of greens seen during a brilliant sunny spell following a heavy downpour, in August, in Cardiganshire. *Storom Awst* is occasionally accompanied by a whipping wind which is cruel to the heavily laden apple trees, causing them to shed tears of vivid emerald green. These tears are then gathered by the sometimes gossipy villagers as the first worthwhile windfalls of the year. It is a moment during such an episode that I have tried to paint. The figures are not portraits but types.[96] (Plate XXIV)

In September 1956 John Elwyn moved out of the Bannisters' lodgings in the centre of Winchester to The Vicarage, in the nearby village of Sparsholt, and here he continued his experiments with large decorative landscapes. The bright colours and almost Mediterranean light of *Shoni Winwns* (Johnny Onions) for example, painted in 1958, evoke a Continental landscape and in particular John Minton's paintings of Corsica in the late 1940s. (Plate XXVIII) *Shoni* depicts one of the many door-to-door onion sellers who travelled to Wales during the summer months from Roscoff on the coast of Finistère in Brittany. Their rented headquarters was a room at Sussex House in Newcastle Emlyn, just a few hundred yards from the family's mill. With a large bed in the centre of the room, tons of onions piled high in sacks all around, and reeds to string the onions stacked against the walls, they worked on commission, cycling miles to the outlying villages. *Shoni* is characteristically short and stocky, wears a black beret and carries his distinctive 'oignon rose de Roscoff', strung together with reeds, and hanging from a stick over his shoulder. *Shoni* was once a familiar sight around Wales; the Welsh had a particular affinity with them, and they found it easy to converse in Welsh because of its similarity to Breton.

Like an eighteenth-century artist in search of the picturesque, John Elwyn travelled around Cardiganshire to discover interesting and sensuous forms in a landscape of small enclosed valleys. The rhythmic, stylised forms suggest a sexualised landscape: the fertile valleys symbolise mysterious bud-like forms and analogies are made in paintings like *In the Hill's Elbow* (1959) between the contours of the landscape – mountain spurs, undulating hills, wooded valleys and writhing country lanes – and aspects of the human anatomy. The 'womb-like enclosures' of this fertile landscape are brimming with sexual symbolism. John Elwyn wrote:

> I am interested in how the inhabitants have dug themselves in – so to speak – to the sheltered corners and elbows of the hills and valleys. I am attracted by the way they have piled up stone upon stone and pink, blue or white washed them as evidence of life. The peeling coloured washes on barn walls and the activity within the farmyard during the ebb and flow of seed time and harvesting is my chosen field.[97]

In July 1959, John Elwyn adjudicated the Youth Section of the Arts and Crafts pavillion at the National Eisteddod in Caernarfon and there he met Kenneth Rowntree who was judging the Fine Art. In October he received a letter from Rowntree, then Head of the Fine Art Department at Durham University, asking him to consider producing advertisements for the *Shell County Guides*. The original idea for the guides had been taken up by Shell at Rowntree's suggestion. He was appointed art director for the *Shell Guides to the Countryside* which were dedicated to promoting the enjoyment of regional landscape and architecture. Illustrations appeared in various magazine features, the *Shell County Guides* (at 15/-), the *Shell & BP Guide to Britain* (at 30/-), and on covers of the popular *Shilling Guides* available from Shell-Mex and BP service stations. The correspondence between John Elwyn, Kenneth Rowntree and Edward Young of Rainbird & McLean Ltd, who were responsible for the book design and production on behalf of Shell, provides a remarkably detailed insight into commission procedures and is testimony to John Elwyn's patience and professionalism in his compliance with Geoffrey Grigson's meticulous attention to detail. Rowntree explained in his letter:

> My idea was that a composite painting be prepared; against a background of

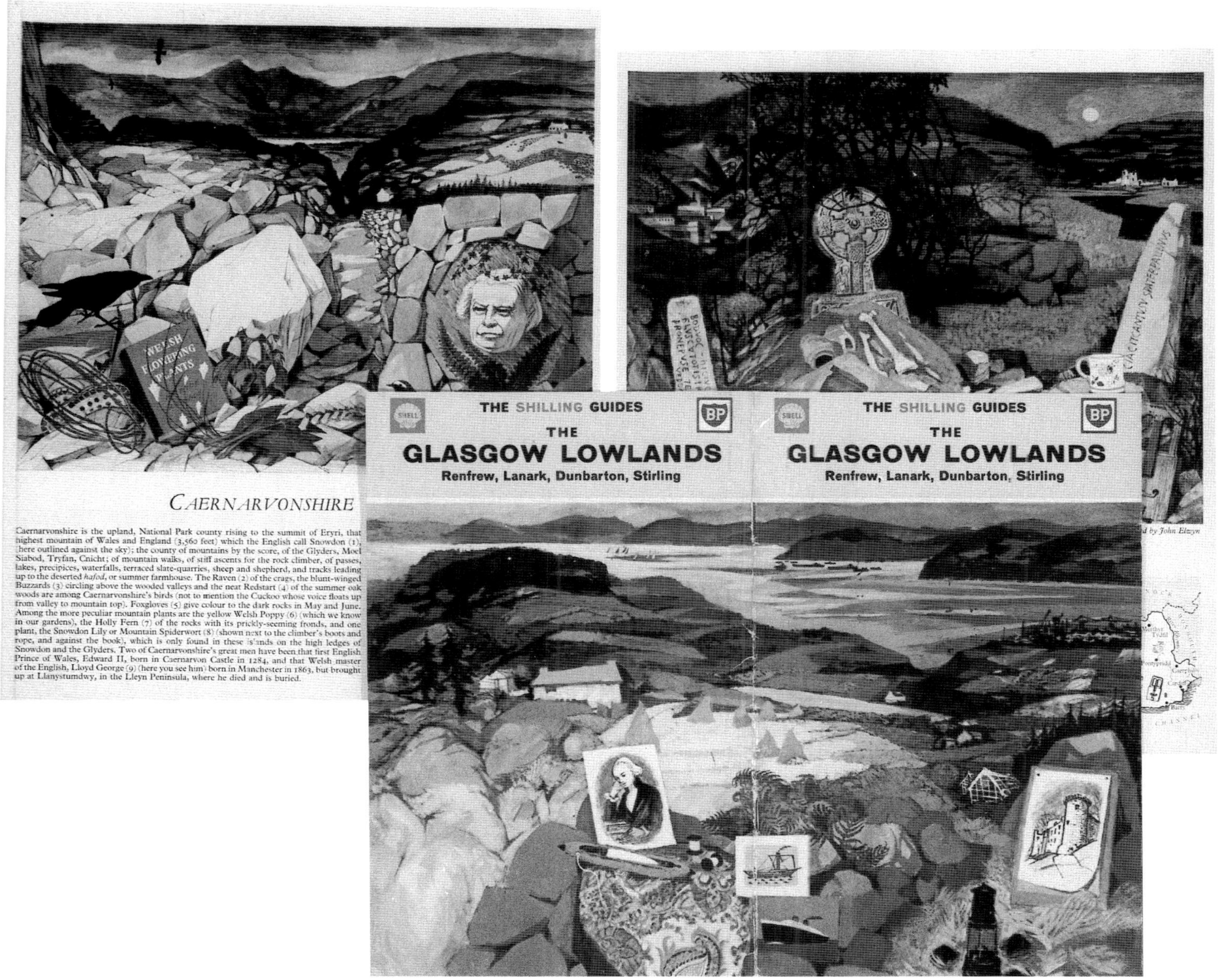

typical —shire, some buildings, earthworks, birds, flowers, portraits of famous people born in the county should be placed. The problem is really one of painting a still-life in a landscape, and the important thing is to incorporate and stress those characteristics which are absent in the other counties. The conditions are that you prepare a rough (a misnomer – Shell like it pretty polished), size 17 x 13 inches (landscape) and if passed, a finished painting, same size; the fee for completed painting is 150 guineas, plus £25 travel expenses ... after all this rigmarole would you like to do Caernarvonshire?[98]

Various formats in which the Shell commissions appeared, *Caernarfonshire* (top left), *Glamorganshire* (top right), *Glasgow Lowlands* (below)

Rowntree enclosed with his letter five pages of notes on Caernarfonshire prepared by the poet and critic Geoffrey Grigson in which he described the character of the landscape and details of the indigenous flora and fauna. After considering Grigson's *desiderate* John Elwyn incorporated into the landscape the following elements: the loneliness and wildness of Snowdonia, a terraced hill of slate quarries, scattered rocks, a lake, cloud, stone walls of mountain pasture, sheep being herded, foxgloves, a raven on a foreground rock, buzzards in the sky, a redstart, rock climbing gear, a portrait of David Lloyd George, and flora laid across a copy of Welsh Flowering Plants by Hyde and Wade – *Mecanopsis cambrica* (Welsh Poppy), *Polystichum aculeatum* (Holly Fern) and 'Mountain Spiderwort' (Snowdon Lily). The 'rough' was passed four weeks later subject to the panel's request to remove Lloyd George's initials, make more varied the pile of rocks on the left, and paint the sky less dark for the month of May. The finished painting was much admired and accepted by George Rainbird and the series editor Robin Golding. The art work was passed to Shell and three weeks later, just as the printing blocks were about to be made, Geoffrey Grigson caught sight of the painting and asked for further amendments. Robin Golding passed on Grigson's comments:

> the book, *Welsh Flowering Plants*, he says looks entirely different from the one he had in mind, i.e. the 1934 edition. The holly fern under Lloyd George is quite wrong, as the fronds are the wrong shape. He says he would never have recognised it and suggests that you might like to have a look on page 106 of Hyde and Wade's *Welsh Ferns*, 1940.[99]

John Elwyn agreed to correct the fern but when he looked up Hyde and Wade he discovered that Grigson's original instruction to consult 'plate 9, Polystichum aculeatum (Holly Fern)' was incorrect. *Polystichum aculeatum* is the Hard Shield Fern, plate 8 in Hyde and Wade. He queried which fern Grigson had actually meant and Grigson admitted through Golding that he had used the incorrect Latin name, but the important thing was that he was intent on the Holly Fern, adding that he still thinks 'that your drawing of Holly Fern is not as accurate or characteristic as it might be'.[100]

In spite of the problems of 'Polystichum Aculeatum', John Elwyn accepted Rowntree's invitation to undertake *Glamorganshire* in May 1960. (Plate XXIX) Grigson recommended that he paint a landscape based on Ogmore estuary with Ogmore castle in the distance. The foreground should indicate a rural and historical landscape, suggesting that the Vale of Glamorgan was 'well worth capturing, settling, and defending (Celts, Roman, English, Normans, in turn)'. Once more Grigson proposed elements he should like to see John Elwyn include, and among those included in the final painting were the red-stained bones of the 'Red Lady of Paviland' found in a cave in the Gower;[101] a Roman milestone re-inscribed in the Dark Ages to commemorate a Briton called Cantusus; the Budvoc Stone of about 550 in honour of the princely Briton Budvoc or Bodvocus; the eighth–twelfth century Great Cross of Conbeline; and specifically Welsh objects such as a *crwth* (fiddle), Swansea and Nantgarw porcelain, Bronze Age tomb pottery, *Anaphalia margaritacea* (Pearl Everlasting, a native of north America yet peculiar to Glamorgan), and laver bread, the Glamorgan delicacy – in its raw state, jellied at the fishmongers, and served on a plate with oatmeal. The 'rough' was presented on 2nd September and passed by the panel on the condition that he reduced the scale of the Great Cross of Conbeline and suggested the coal mining industry in some way. Mindful of the delight certain members of the public would take in finding fault, they also asked him to supply details of the Swansea and Nantgarw porcelain, and to give an assurance 'in writing' that these were after pieces that he had actually seen.

The final commission from Shell came on 25th August 1962 when Edward Young asked him to consider one of four Scottish localities for the *Shell Wayfarer Guides*. John Elwyn elected to paint 'The Glasgow Lowlands' (comprising the counties of Renfrew, Lanark, Dunbarton and Stirling). Shell gave very short notice: the picture was to be produced in four weeks. The rough was approved on 13th September subject to the panel's usual minor amendments. The scene is the Clyde, the sun breaking through cloud on to one of the world's great waterways with large merchant shipping and a small fleet of white sails. Ben Lomond, the highlands and Glasgow dockyards are in the distance, and the still-life elements comprise postcards of Bell's *Comet* launched in 1812 and the *Queen Elizabeth*, a portrait of James Watt who was a native of Greenock, and the thirteenth-century Bothwell Castle. A miner's lamp and a shuttle represent coal mining and cotton-thread manufacture respectively.

Other commissions followed. In June 1962, Richard Lloyd Jones of Glaxo Laboratories in Middlesex saw paintings by John Elwyn at the Leicester Galleries and immediately wrote to commission a painting 'that is, in essence, an impression of a characteristic Carmarthenshire rural scene'.[102] It was intended as a presentation to A. G. Beynon, distinguished President of the British Veterinary Association, himself a native of Carmarthenshire, to hang in the Council Chamber of the B.V.A. Headquarters. It was so well received that a second landscape was commissioned by Glaxo's chairman Dr F. J. Wilkins as a personal gift for Beynon. In September that year, David Jenkins, manager of Barclay's Bank, Carmarthen commissioned an oil painting of the Towy Valley for the Local Head Office in Swansea (Plate XXXIV), and in 1963 the General Post Office commissioned *Hambledon Village – the Cradle of Cricket* in Hampshire for the campaign 'Please use your correct address'.

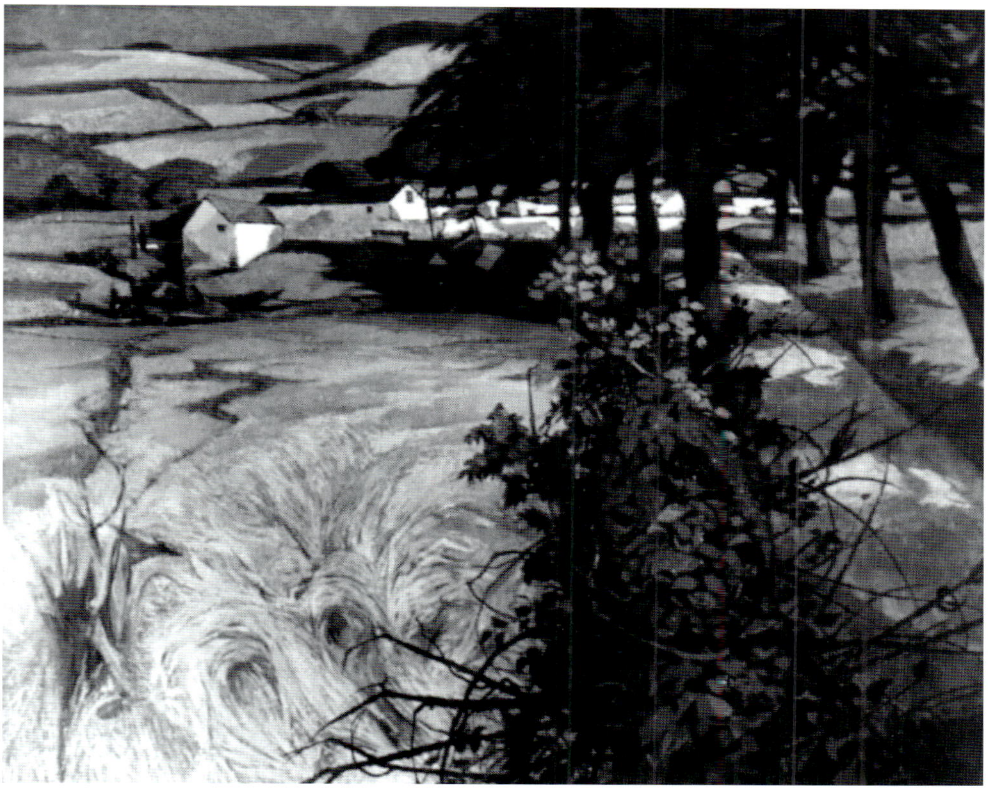

A Carmarthenshire Farm
1962, oil on canvas 28 x 36
[Glaxo Laboratories]

Chapter 5

once below a time I lordly had the trees and leaves:

nature remodelled

BY THE END OF THE 1950s John Elwyn's figurative subjects increasingly gave way to pure landscape. The strong geometrical aspects of the patterned landscape, organised and divided into fields with hedgerows and stone walls, especially appealed to his sense of design. (Plates XXIII & XXXI) *Off the Main Road* painted in 1959 is typical of the new formalised decorative surface created by the juxtaposition of interesting land forms and remote villages; the picture plane is fractured to lesser or greater degrees in his analysis of form. Sceptical of his gradual departure from traditional modes of representation, David Bell commented upon this new mannerism which he attributed to the characteristics of the Cardiganshire landscape itself:

> He seems to describe his forms by breaking them up into a pattern of facets of colour and tone, so that at times they appear to have a uniform appearance of paper which has been crushed and then flattened out not very successfully. In this way his surfaces tend to lose continuity and his forms their substance. I have always wondered whence this mannerism was derived until I stood one winter afternoon outside his home by the Teifi and looked across the river to the steep hillside opposite. Up it climbed the stone walls and the lime washed walls of house and farm and chapel, set amid the evergreen shrubs and the bare boughs in just such a mosaic of facets and with an appearance just as papery as John Elwyn uses with his brush.[103]

The titles he ascribed to paintings indicate the natural phenomena that inspired him: *Yellow Silence* (1957), *Carmarthenshire Green* (1957), *Cardiganshire Bay Blue* (1957), *Green Approaches* (1959) and *The Red Evening* (1960). (Plate XXX) Other paintings evoke seasonal variation or the quality of light at particular times of day: *Wet August Light* (1956), *September Evening Light* (1956), *June Morning Light* (1957) and *Late August Evening Light* (1959). Of *Carmarthenshire Green* John Elwyn explained:

> Here fields are surrounded by thick windswept hedges of blackthorn – where the dappled white-washed barn walls, dancing in and out of deep cast shadow, can be picked out on the hill slopes in the bright evening light – when the Dyfed greens are at their best and unique in their intensity – this quality of light lasts for a very short time when it does happen.[104] (Plate XXVI)

Ordinary subjects like tin sheds, paint-peeling gate posts, and crumbling barn walls with layers of white-washed surface falling away to recall generations of habitation, became of more interest and significance. He wrote:

> I did not look any more for a story, the bright sunlight falling on a peeling white-washed wall became an object of great excitement and filigree shadow producing a dappled pattern was itself a justification to paint it.[105] (Plate XXVII)

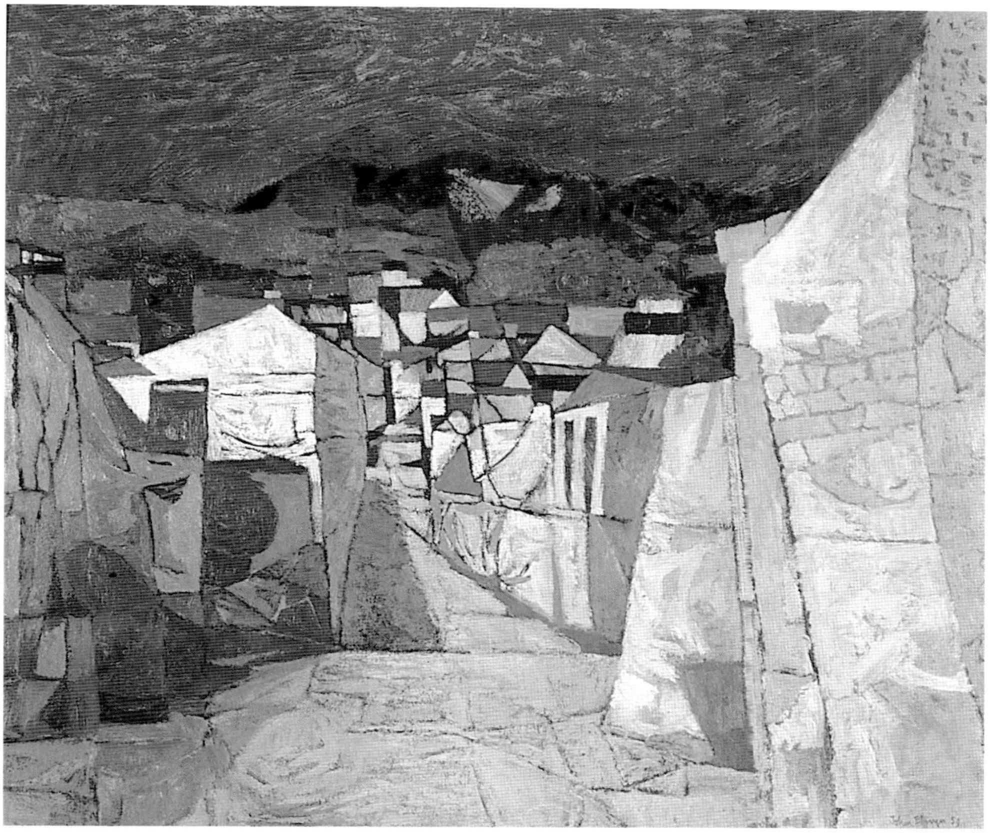

Off the Main Road II
1959, oil on board 20 x 24
[The University of Wales, Aberystwyth]

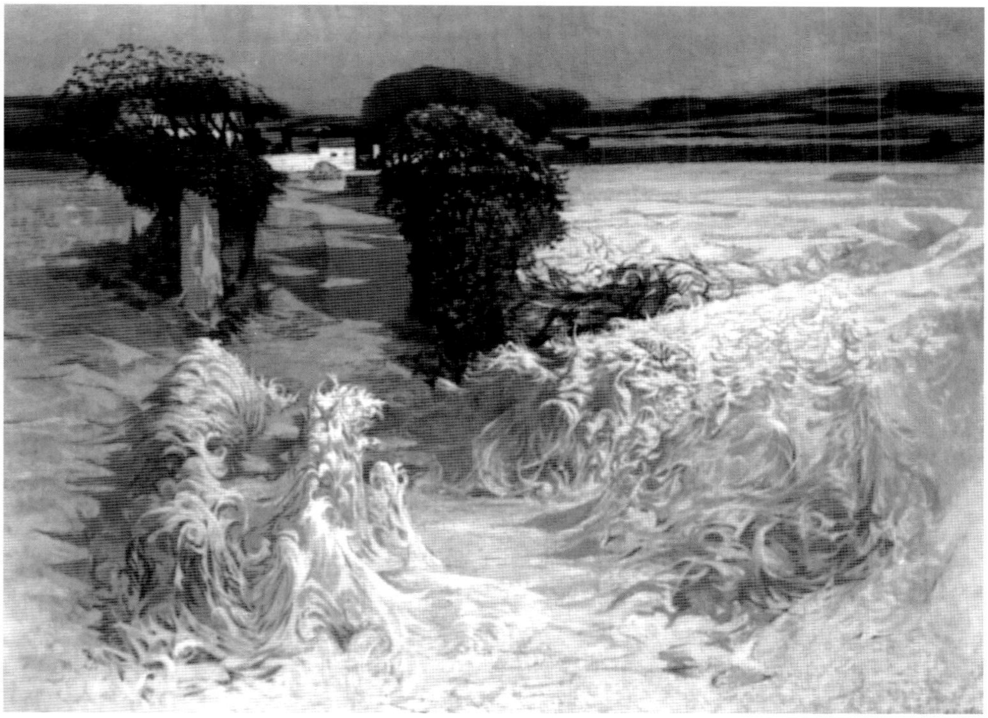

Yellow Silence
1957, oil on canvas 30 x 40
[Present whereabouts unknown]

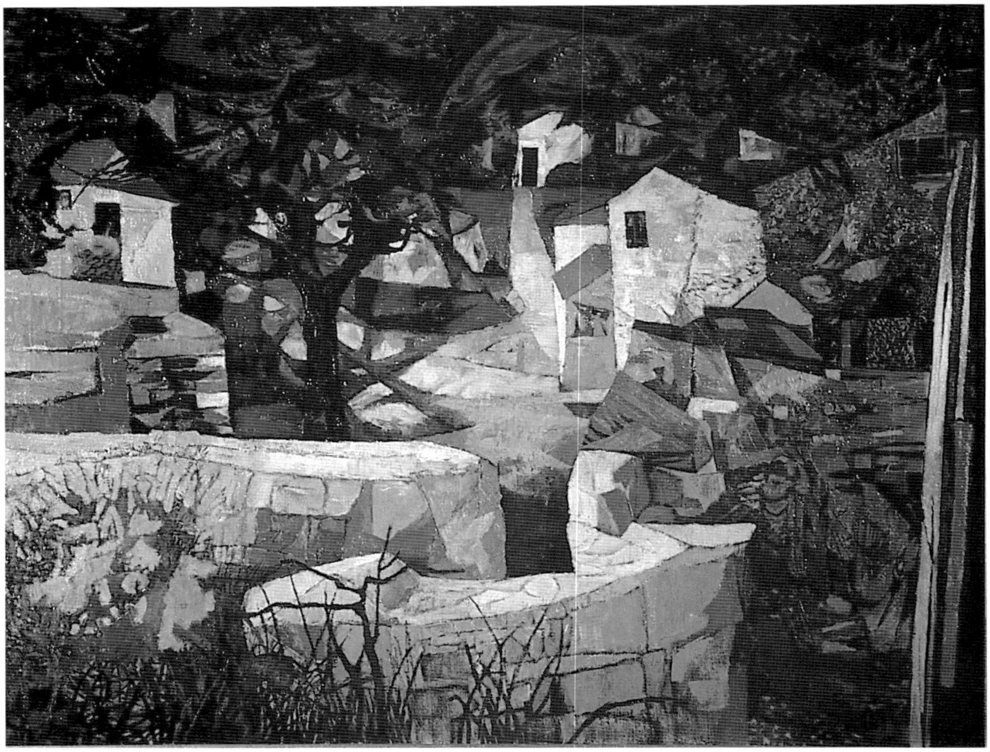

White Washed Walls
1958, oil on canvas 30 x 40
[Mr and Mrs Glyn Roberts]

In *Farm Shapes* (1961), for example, he sought out the more unusual forms in a landscape and enriched them with strong colour and the impression of bright sunlight. (Plate XXXII)

In 1961 John Elwyn spent the Easter vacation winding up the mill and family home at Adpar; his youngest sister Katie had died in October of the previous year following lengthy treatment and two operations in a fight against cancer. Mary, who was now alone at the mill, agreed to join her brother in Winchester, and in July 1961 they bought a semi-detached house on Greenhill Road.

In October 1960 the Coldstream Report was published on behalf of the National Advisory Council on Art Education. It led to the major re-organisation of British art schools which in turn brought a younger generation of abstract artists to the staff at Winchester. The Report recommended that art schools replace established training methods – learning the 'craft' of painting, the acquisition of technical skills, and the life class, etc. – with a modernist pedagogy that had originated in America and centred on the student's creativity. The Report came in the wake of the Tate Gallery's exhibition of 'Modern Art in the United States' which introduced the work of Franz Kline, Willem de Kooning, Robert Motherwell, Jackson Pollock and Mark Rothko to Britain in 1956. The exhibition fuelled the debate between the advocates of abstraction and those of more representational modes of painting, and created a dilemma for traditional painters. Mindful of his future, yet at the same time not wishing to compromise his convictions by taking on board fashionable avant-garde developments for the sake of it, John Elwyn's work was beginning to show signs of change.

As compositions became more economical and the formal passages more predominant he began to use nature more selectively. *Midnight Roses* and *Cockerels and Roses*, both painted in 1961, are from a series of imaginative nocturne landscapes worked from memory of his garden at night. (Plate XXXIII) These paintings were

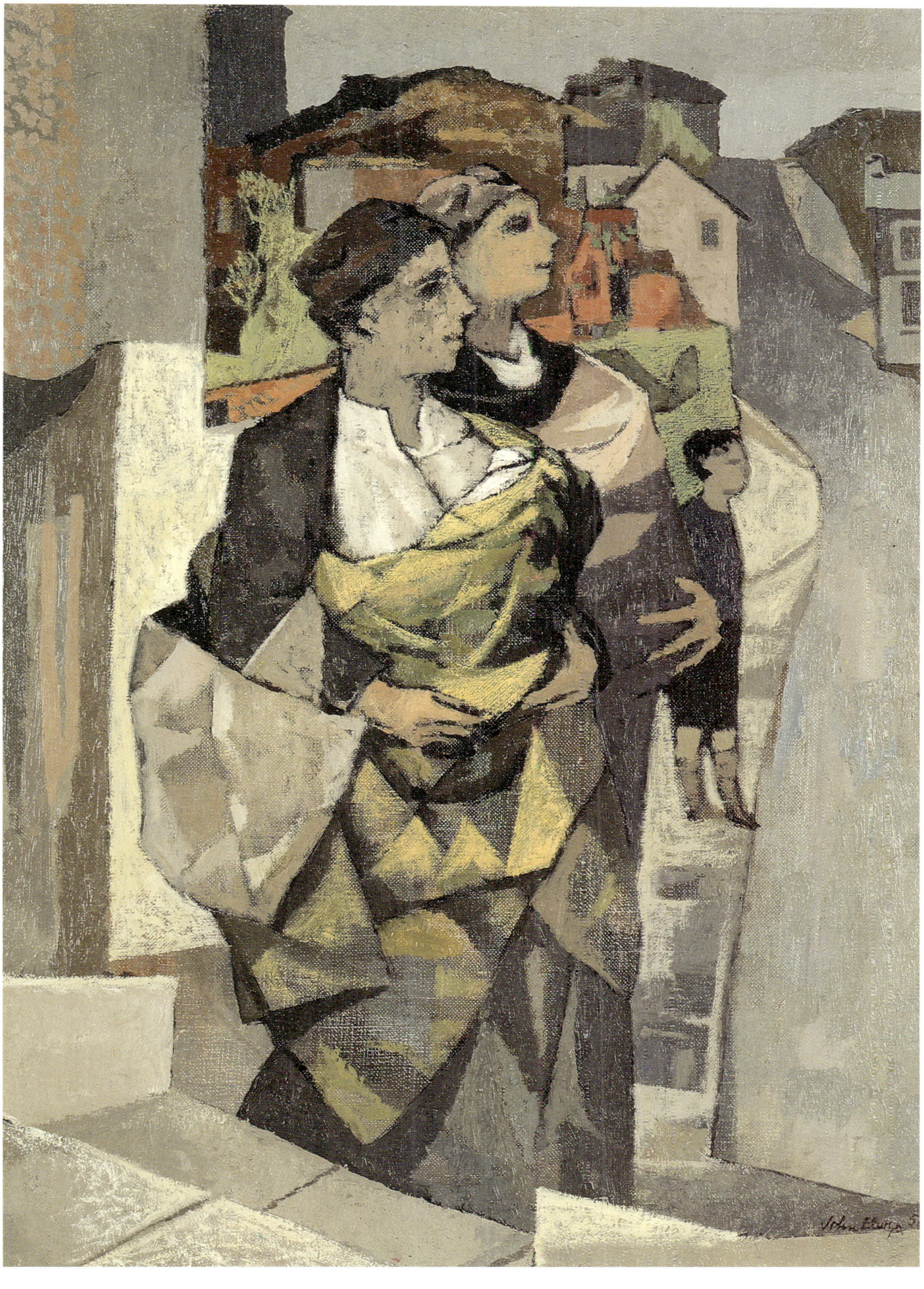

xx: *The Mothers I*
1954, oil on canvas, 20 x 16
[Contemporary Art Society for Wales / Newport Museum and Art Gallery]

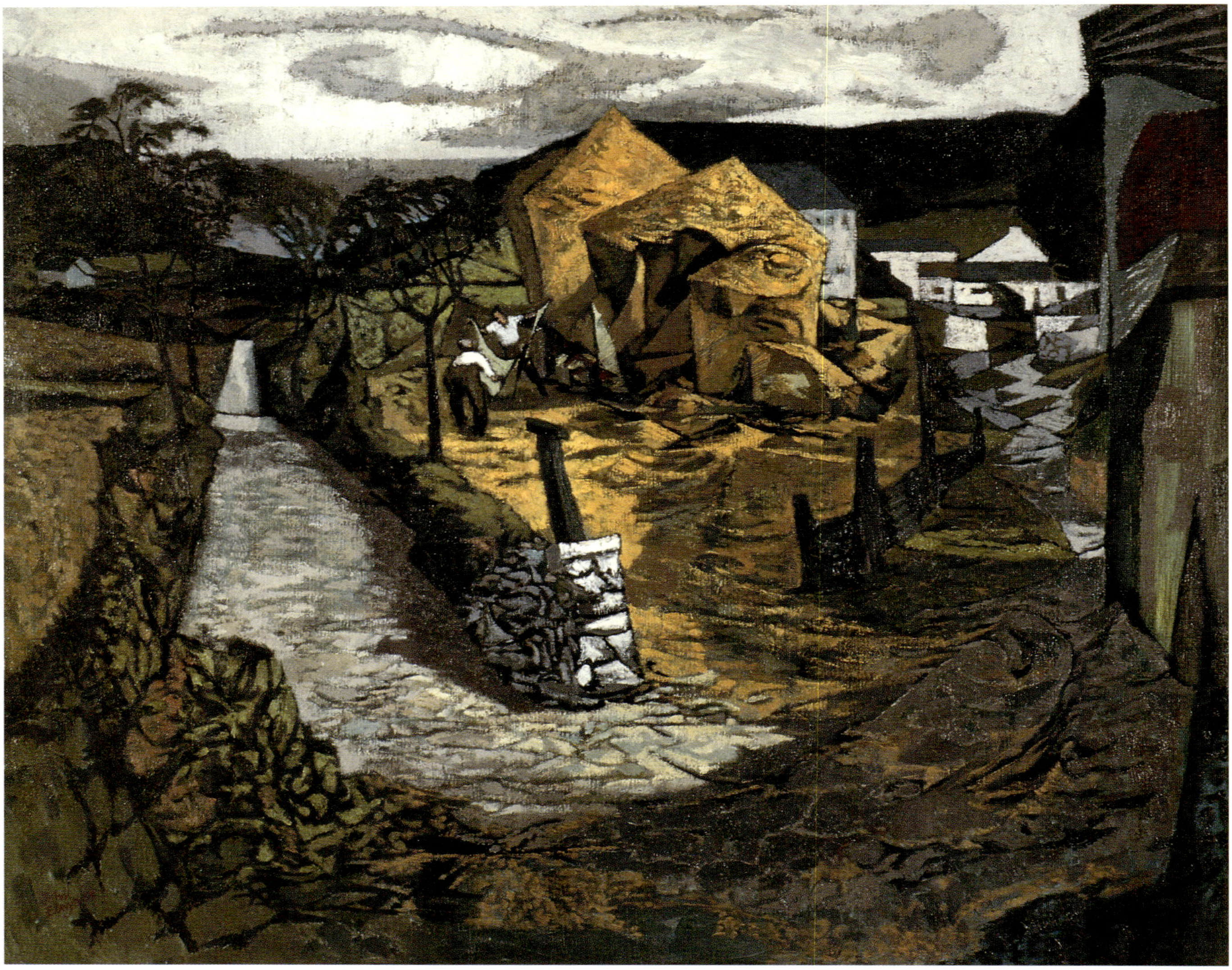

XXI: *Ydlan yn Sir Aberteifi* (The Rickyard)
1954, oil on canvas 20 x 24
[Glynn Vivian Art Gallery, Swansea]

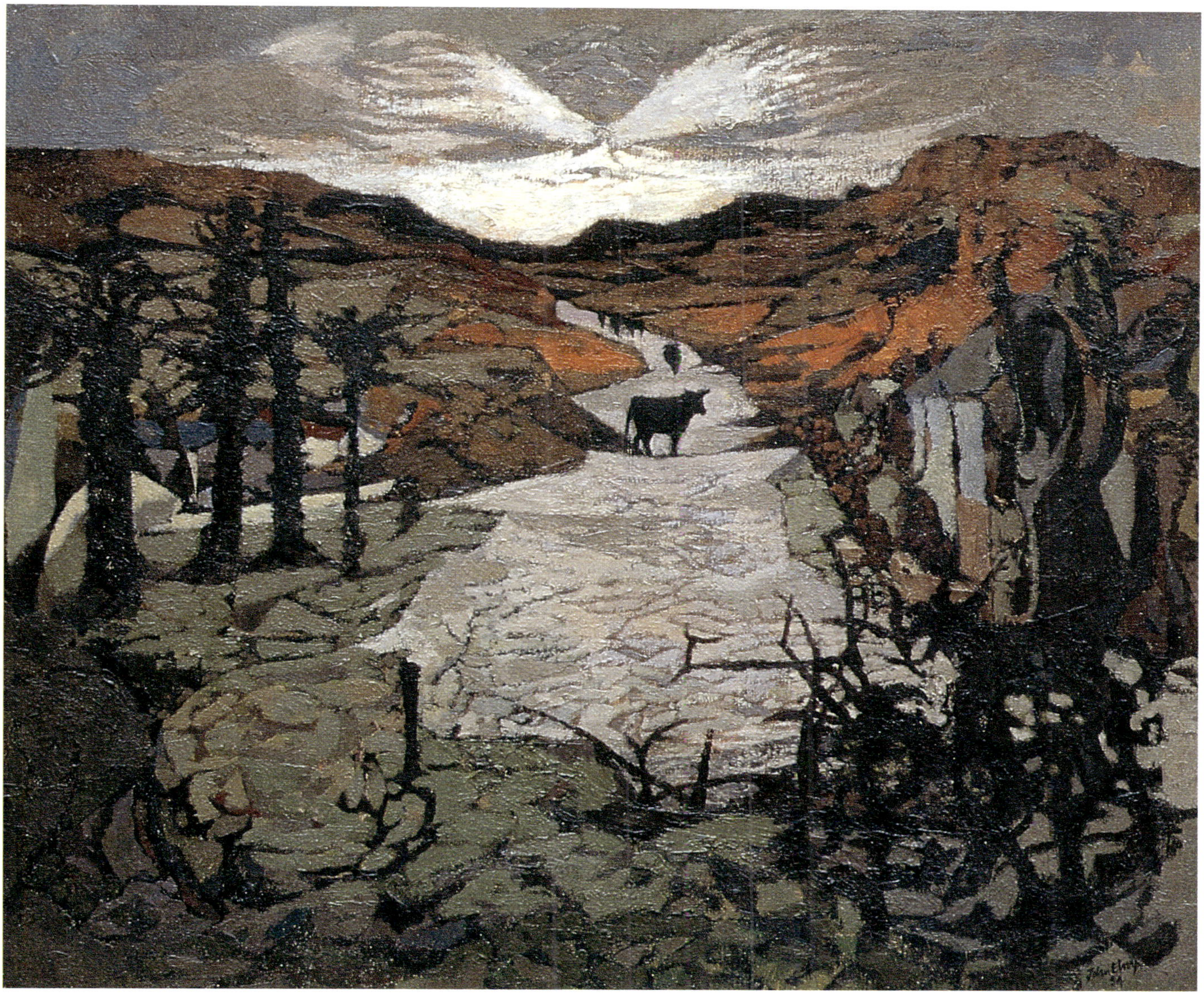

XXII: *The Adventurer*
1954, oil on canvas, 20 x 24
[Robert Meyrick]

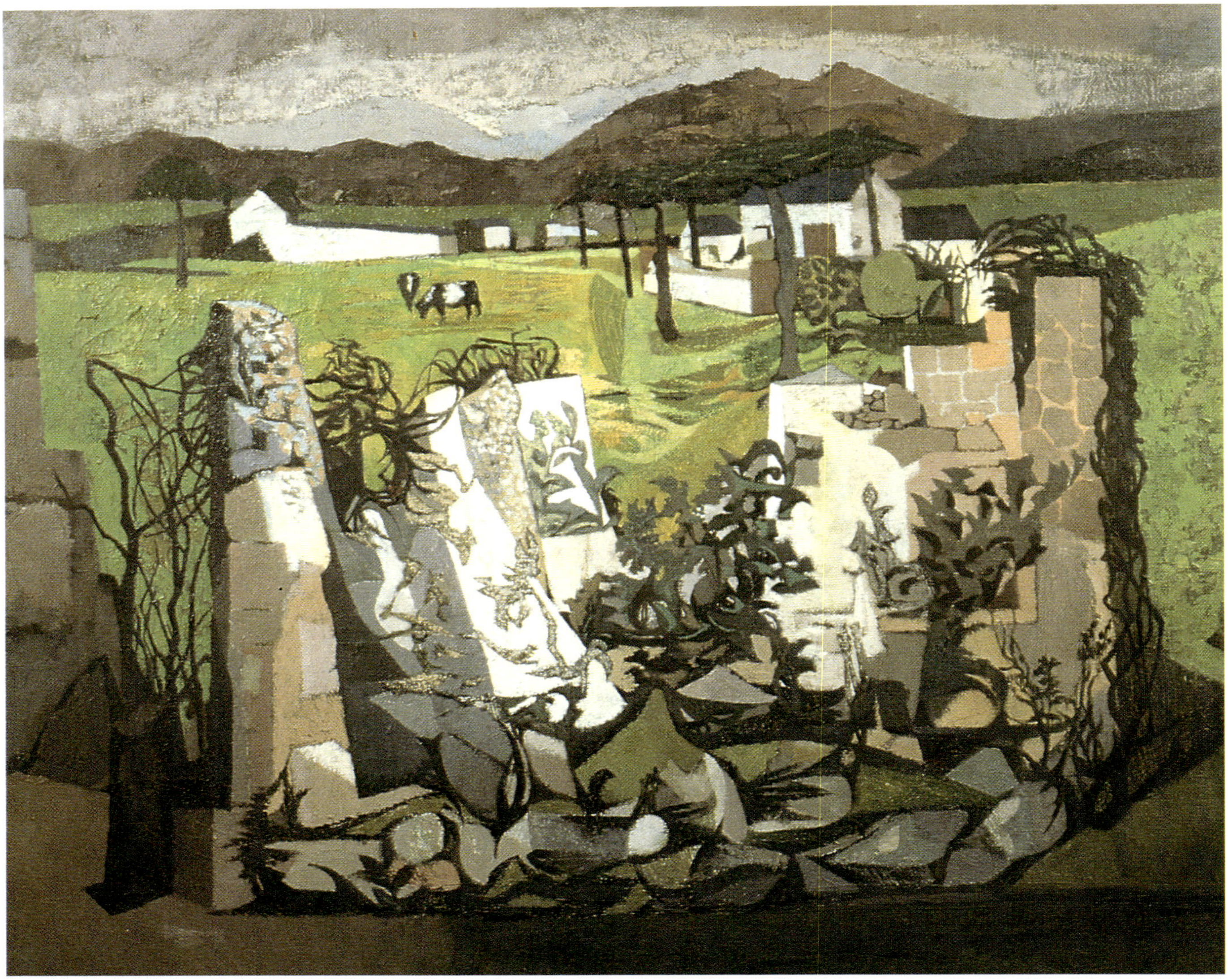

XXIII: *The Derelict Barn*
1955, oil on canvas, 24 x 30
[Martin Tinney Gallery]

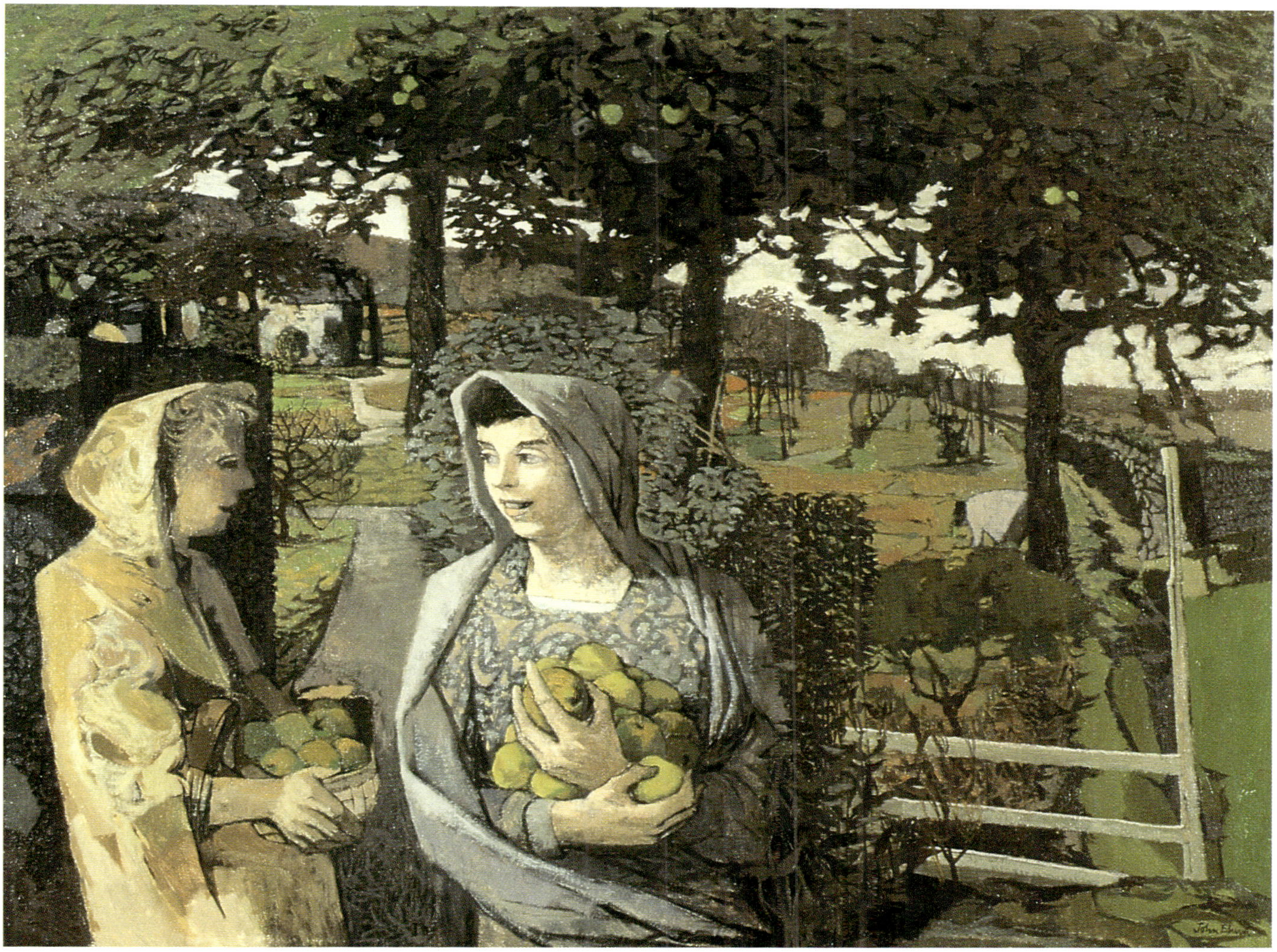

XXIV: *Windfalls*
1956, oil on canvas, 30 x 40
[Contemporary Art Society for Wales / National Library of Wales, Aberystwyth]

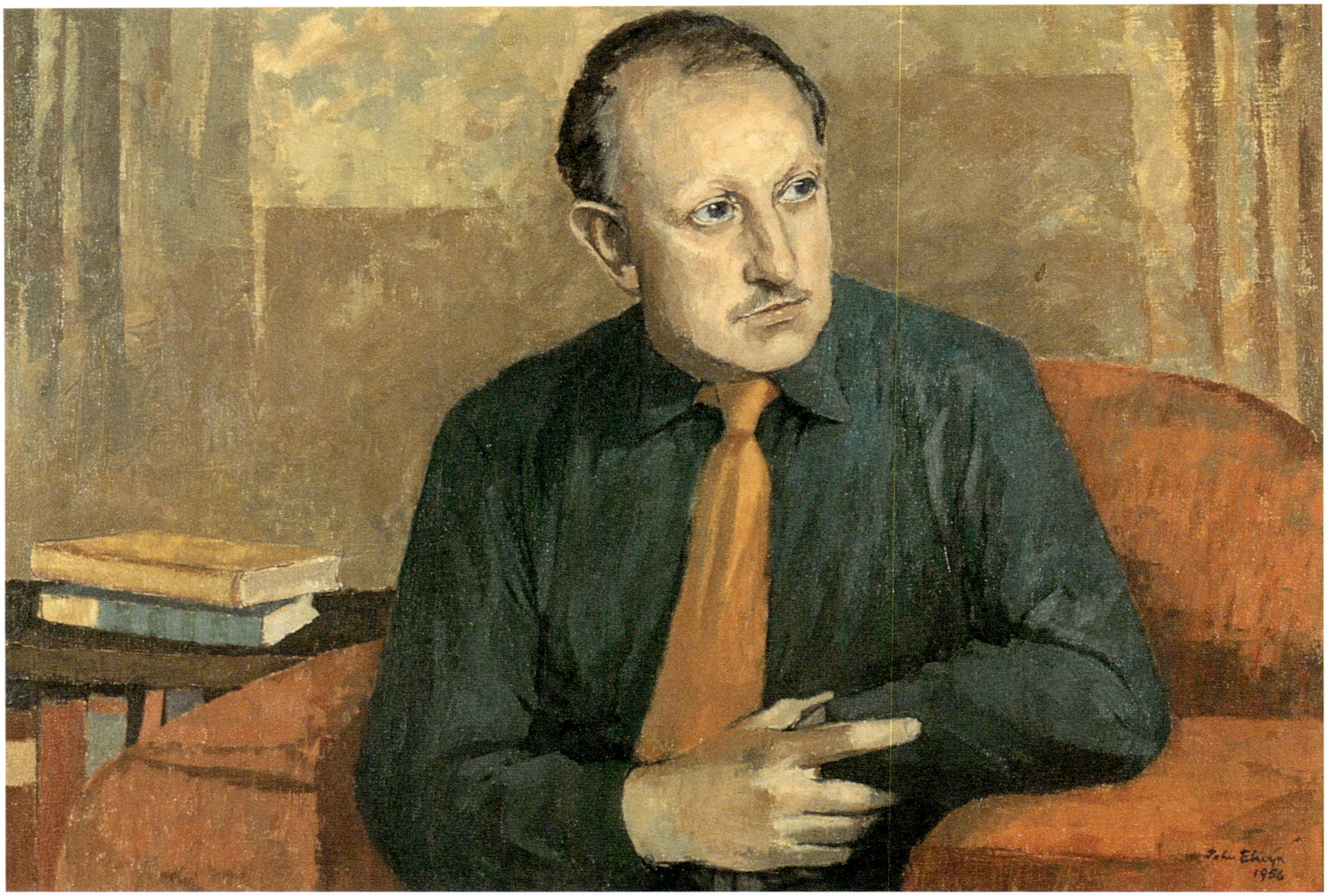

XXV: *Glyn Jones*
1956, oil on canvas, 20 x 30
[the late Doreen Jones]

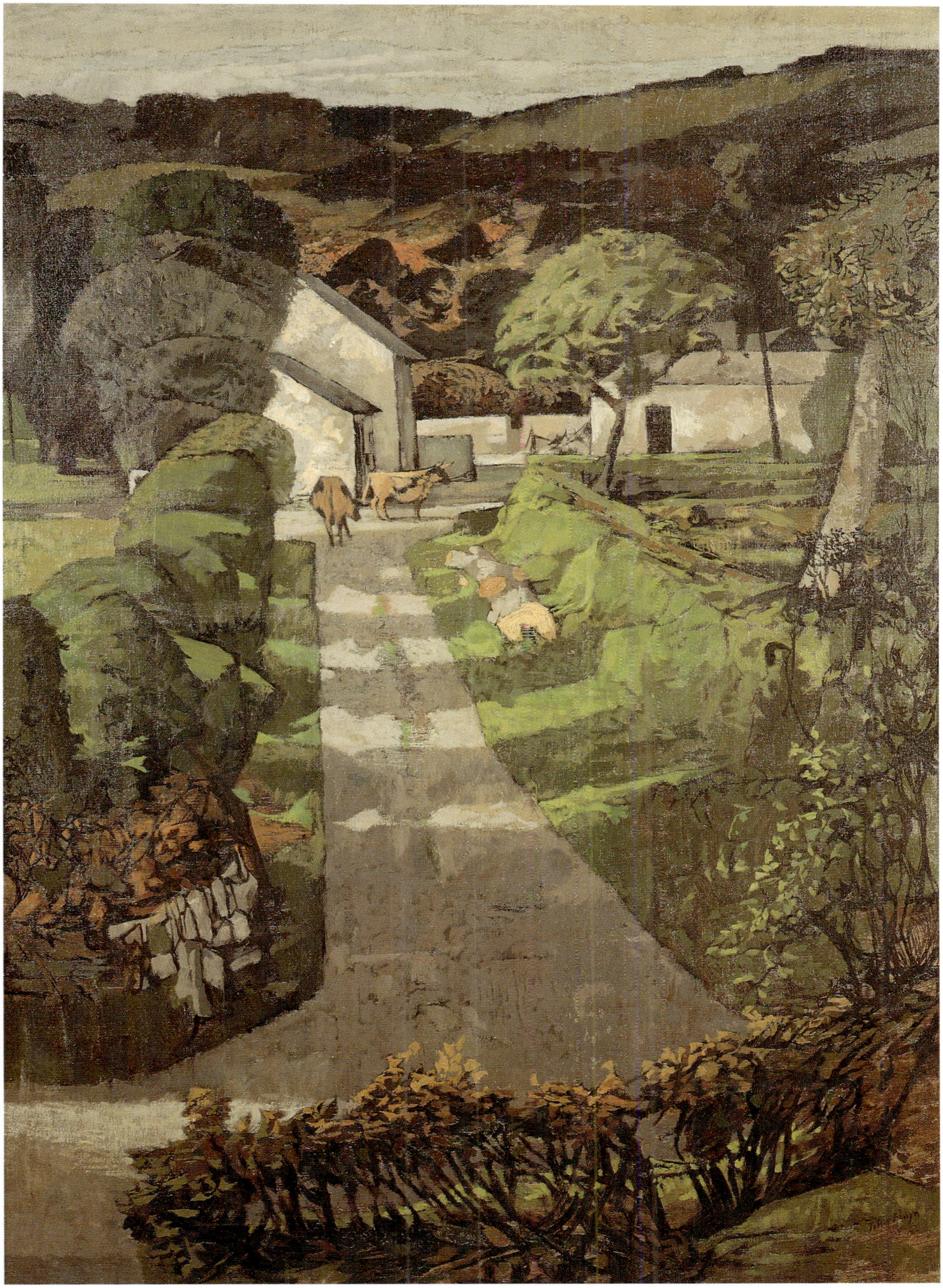

XXVI: *Carmarthenshire Green*
1957, oil on canvas, 40 x 30
[Newport Museum and Art Gallery]

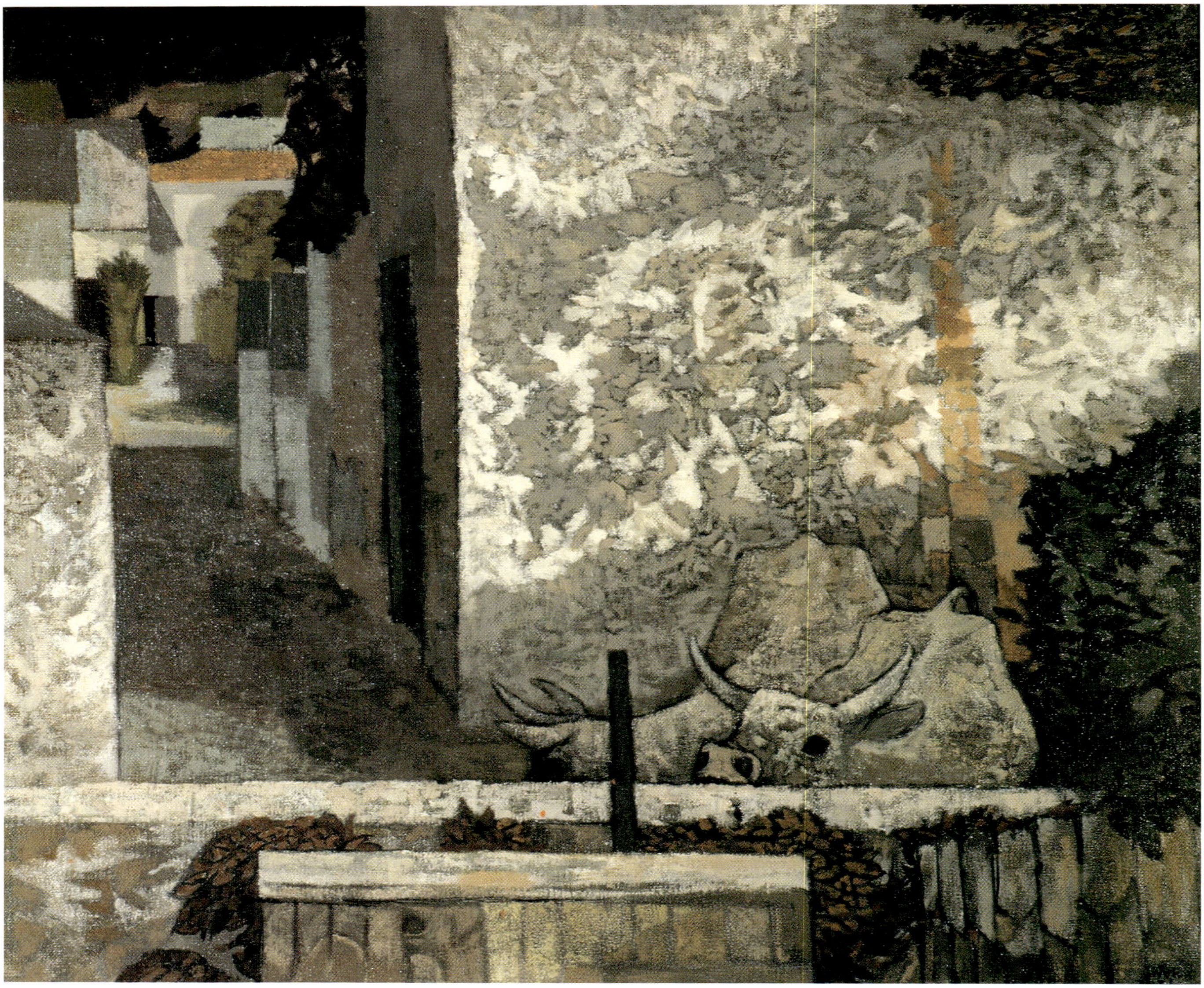

XXVII: *Barn Walls*
1956, oil on canvas, 20 x 24
[Dr and Mrs Huw Bevan Jones]

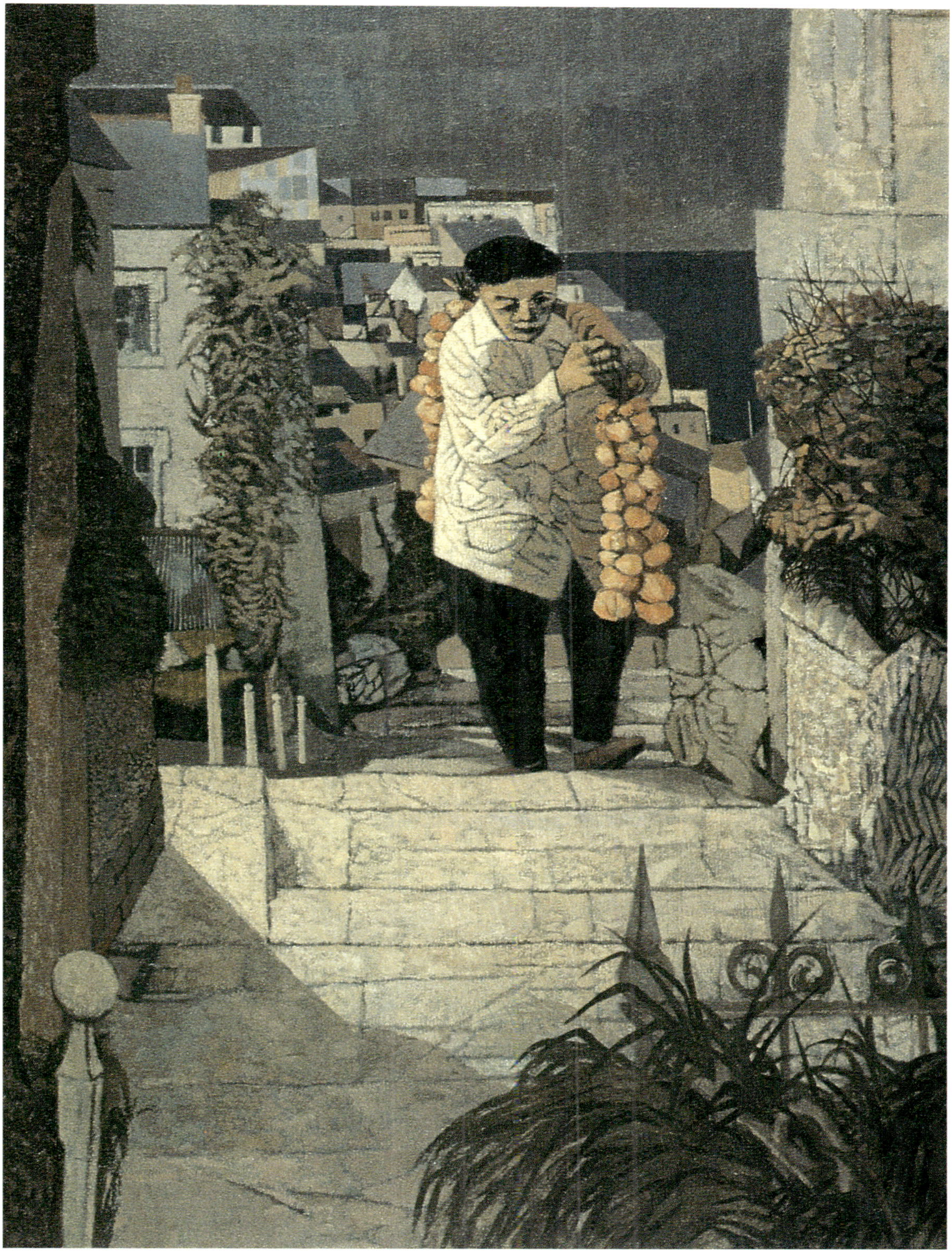

XXVIII: *Shoni Winwns*
1958, oil on canvas, 36 x 28
[Robert Meyrick]

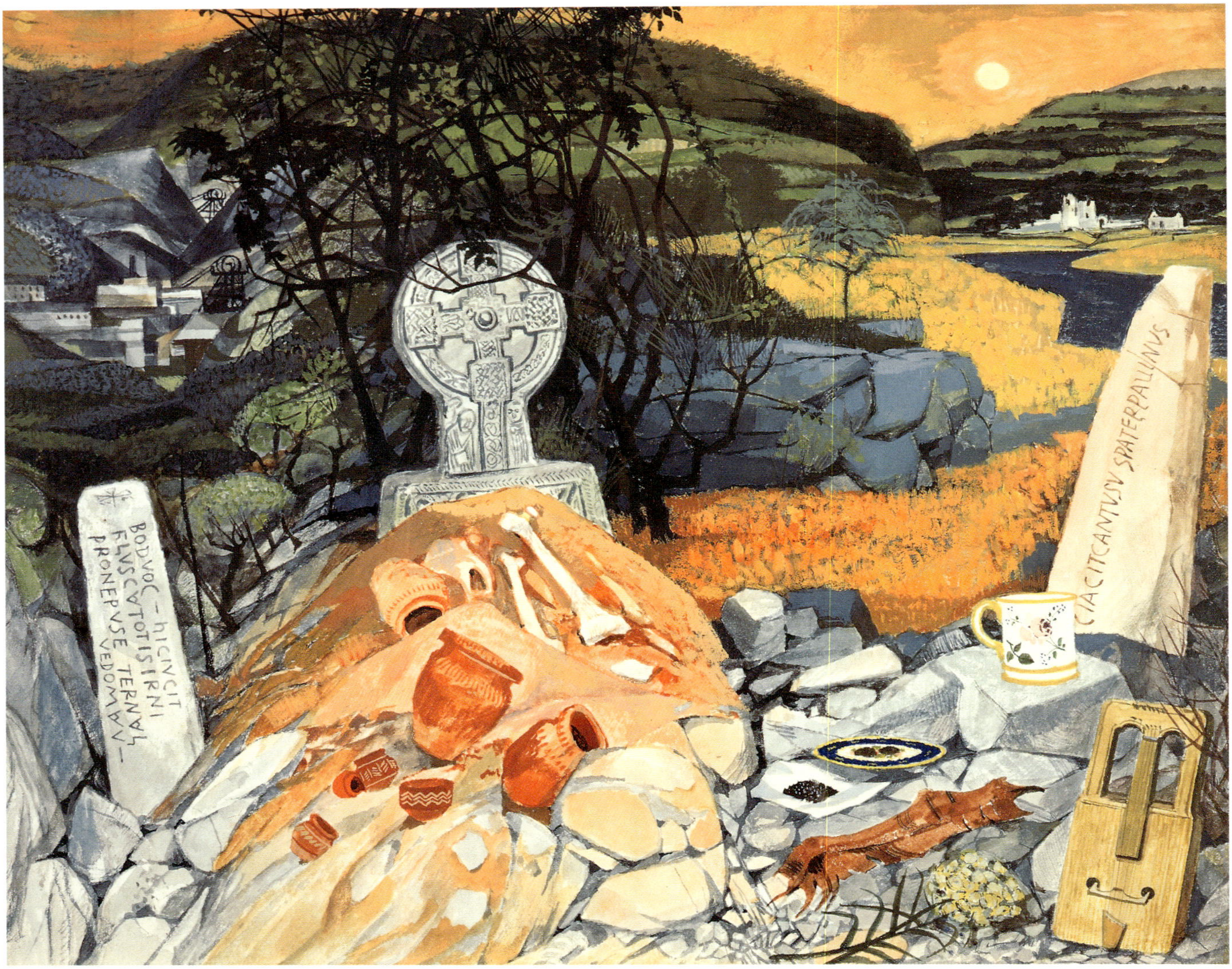

XXIX: *Glamorgan*
1960, gouache on paper, 13 x 17
[The Shell Art Collection at the National Motor Museum, Beaulieu]

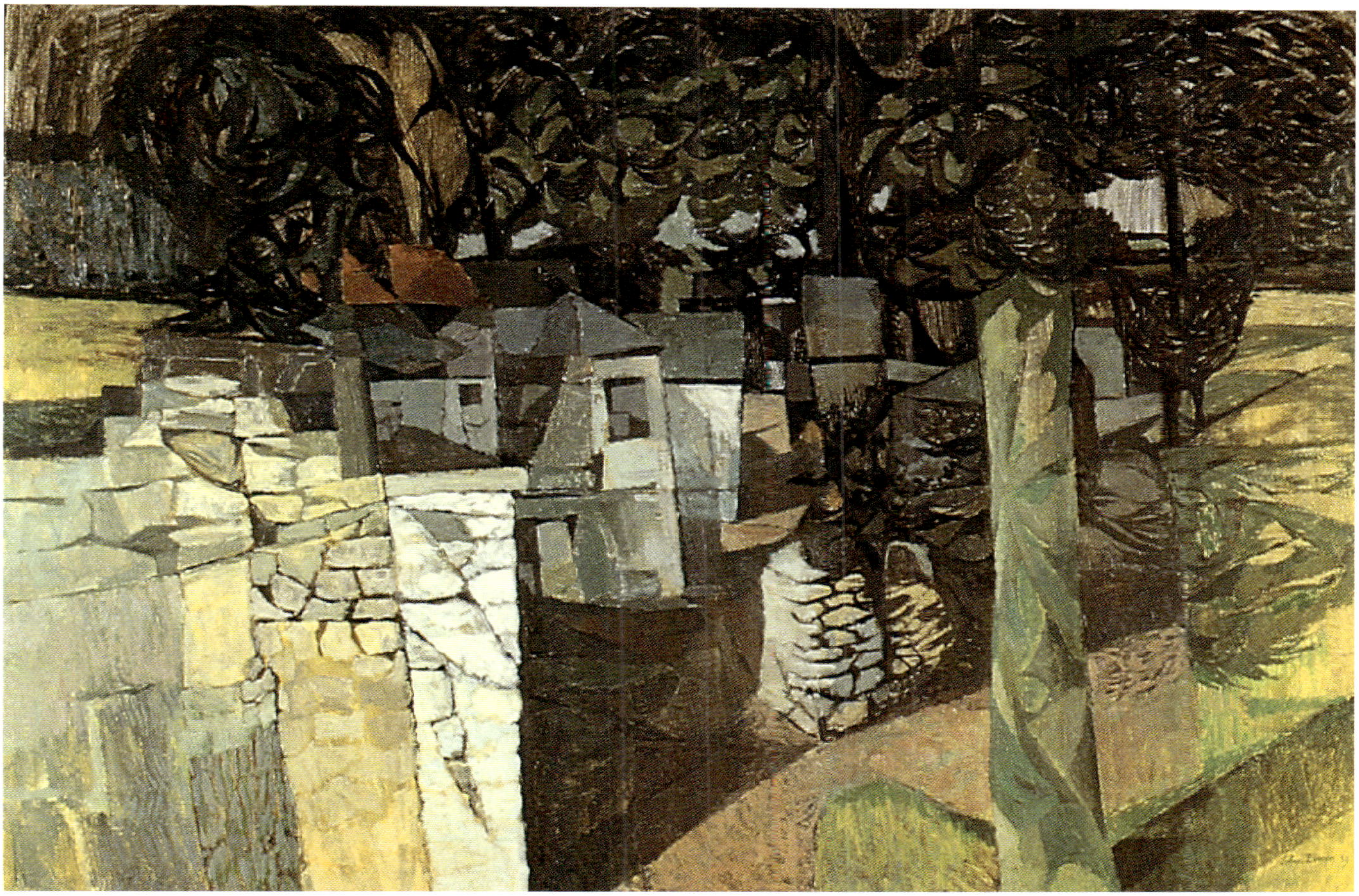

XXX: *Green Approaches*
1959, oil on board, 24 x 36
[Wil Aaron]

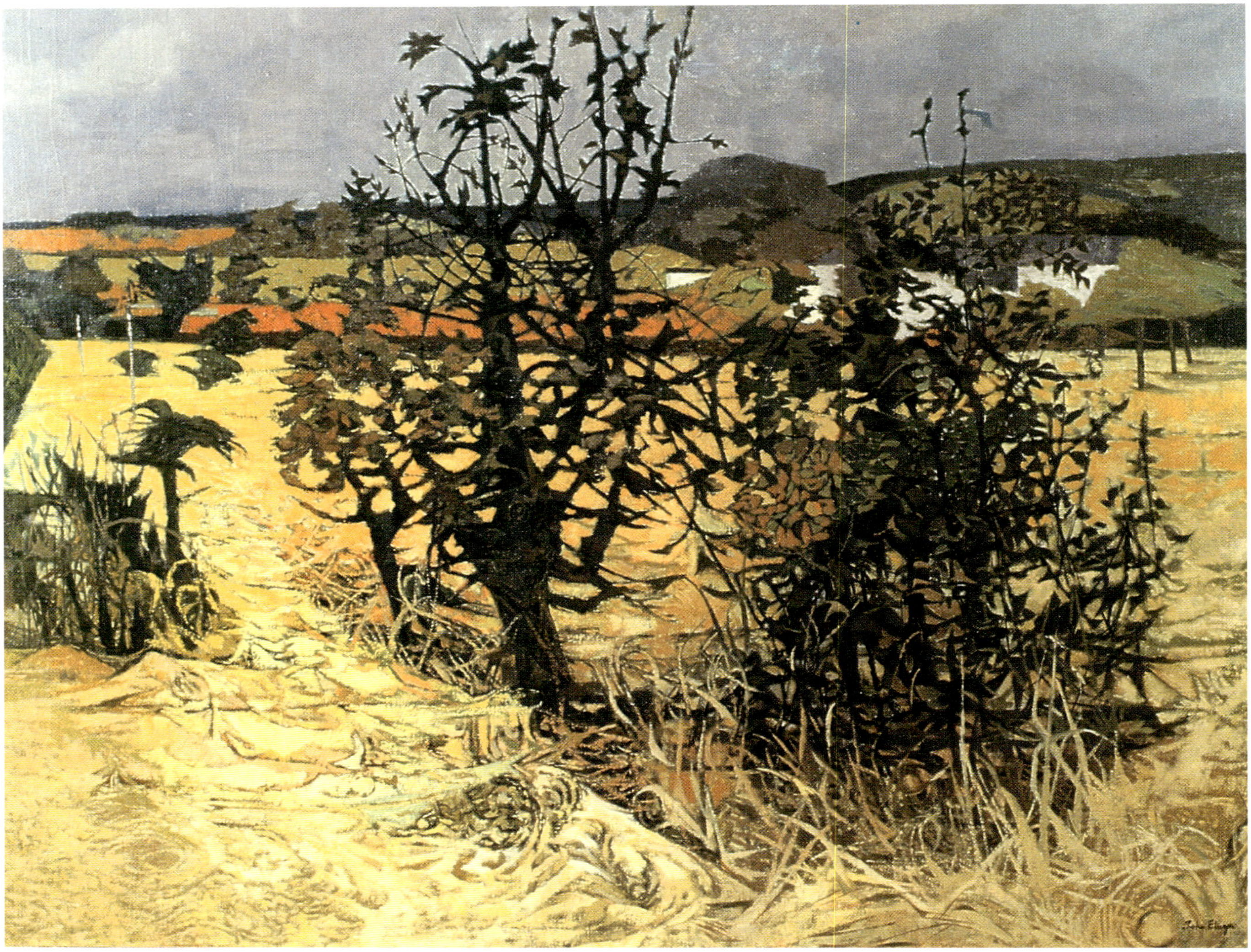

XXXI: *Cardiganshire Meadows*
1959, oil on canvas, 29 x 38½
[National Library of Wales, Aberystwyth]

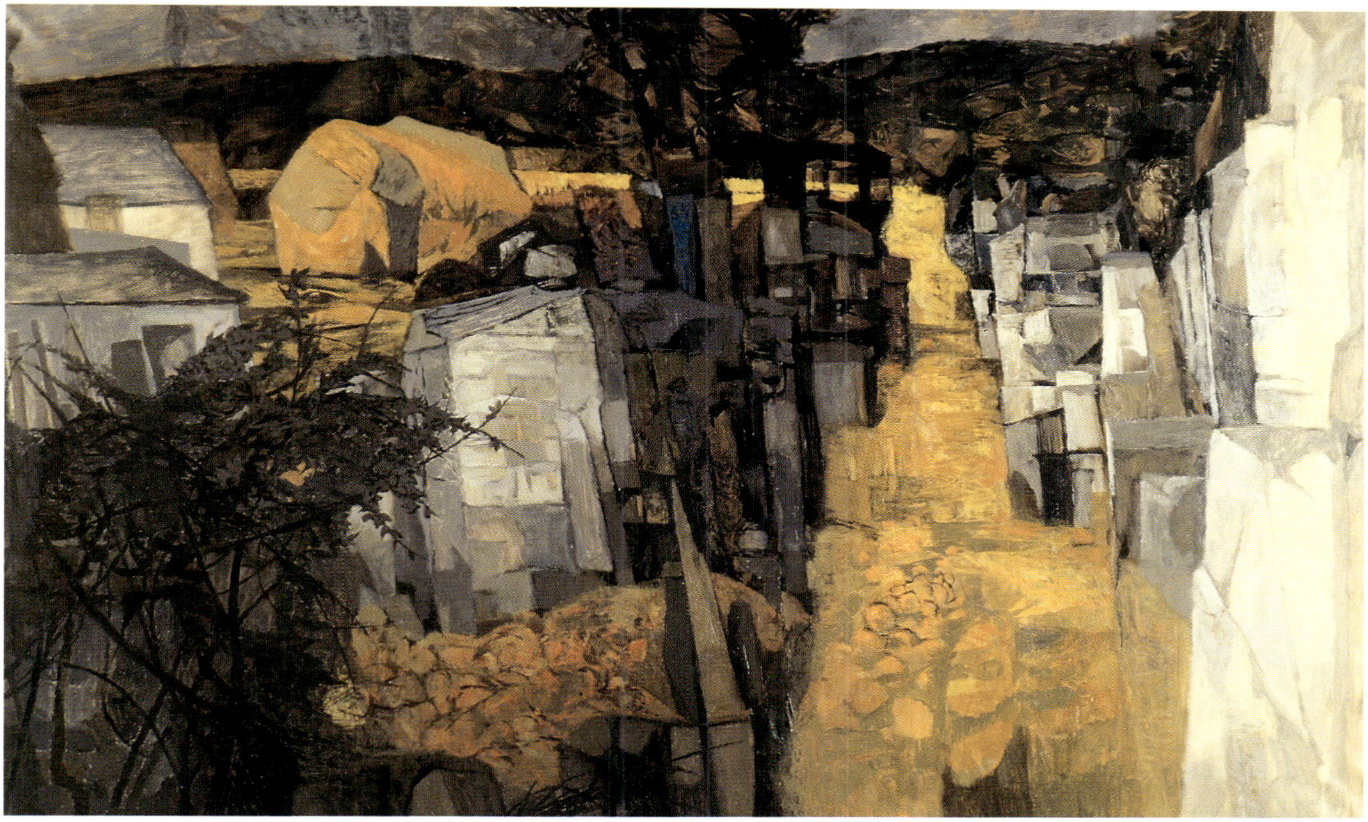

XXXII: *Farm Shapes*
1961, oil on canvas, 30 x 50
[Glenys Ormond Thomas]

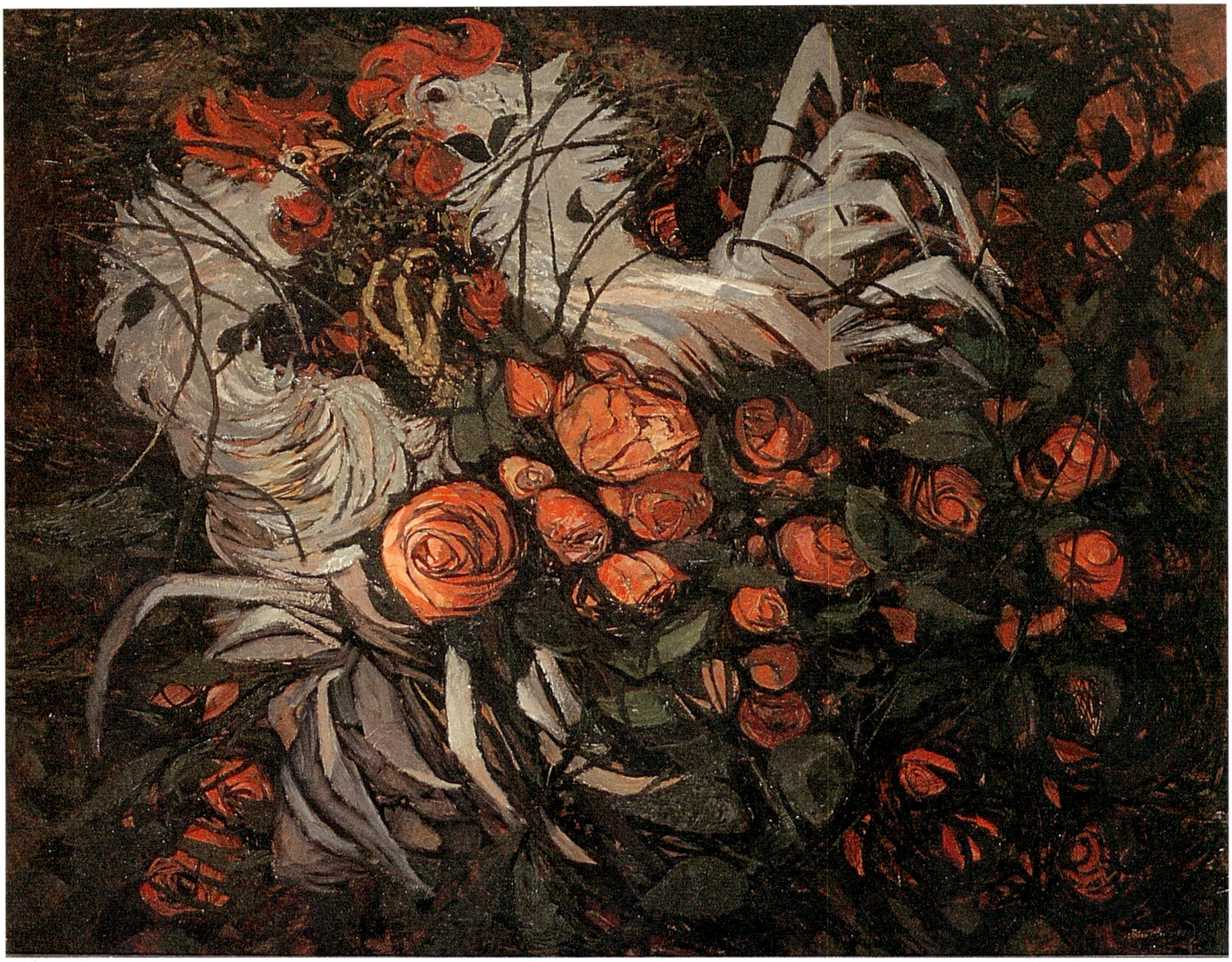

XXXIII: *Cockerels and Roses*
1961, oil on board, 28 x 36
[Dr and Mrs David Shedden]

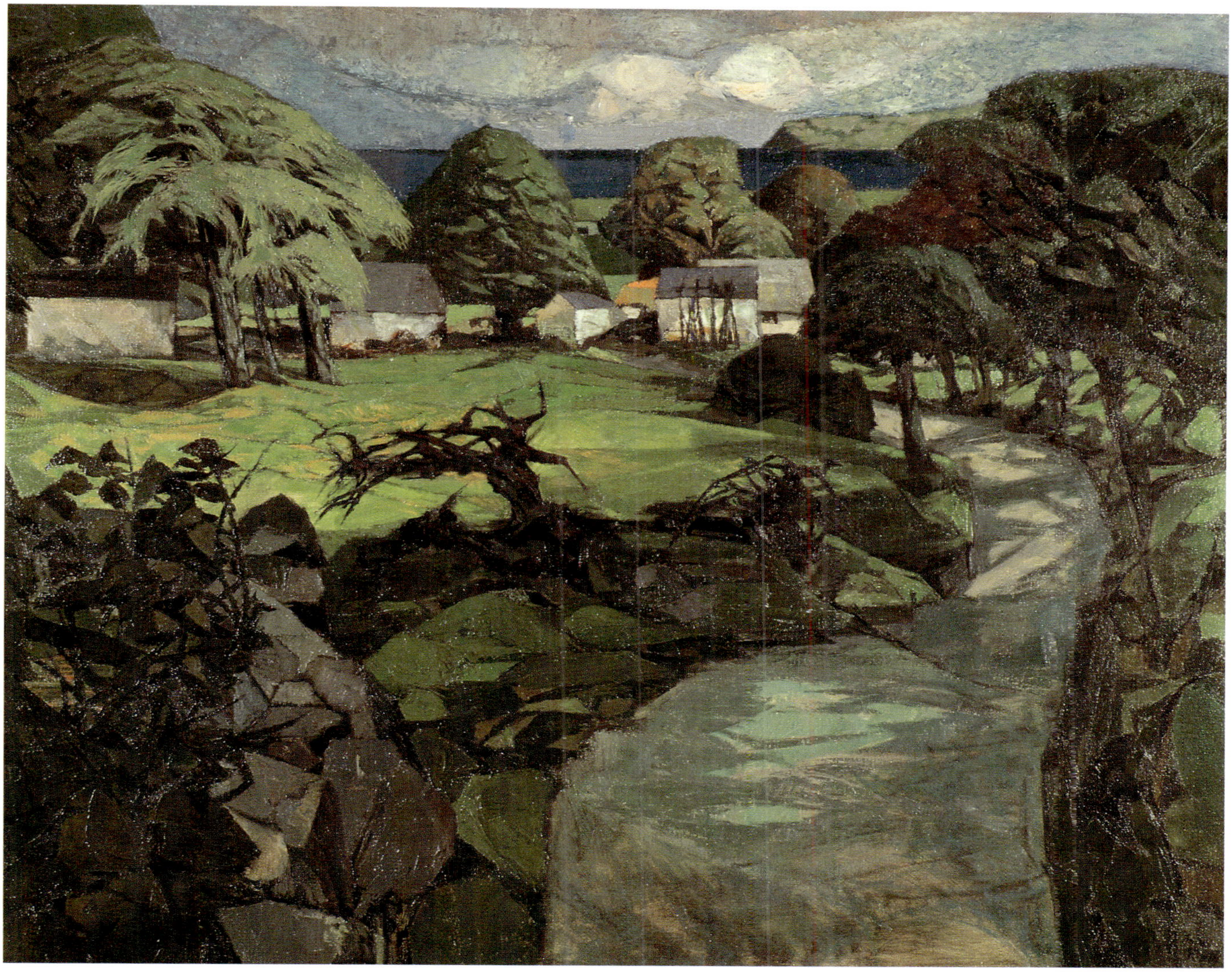

XXXIV: *The Road to Gower*
1963, oil on canvas, 28 x 36
[Huw Davies and Sian Vaughan]

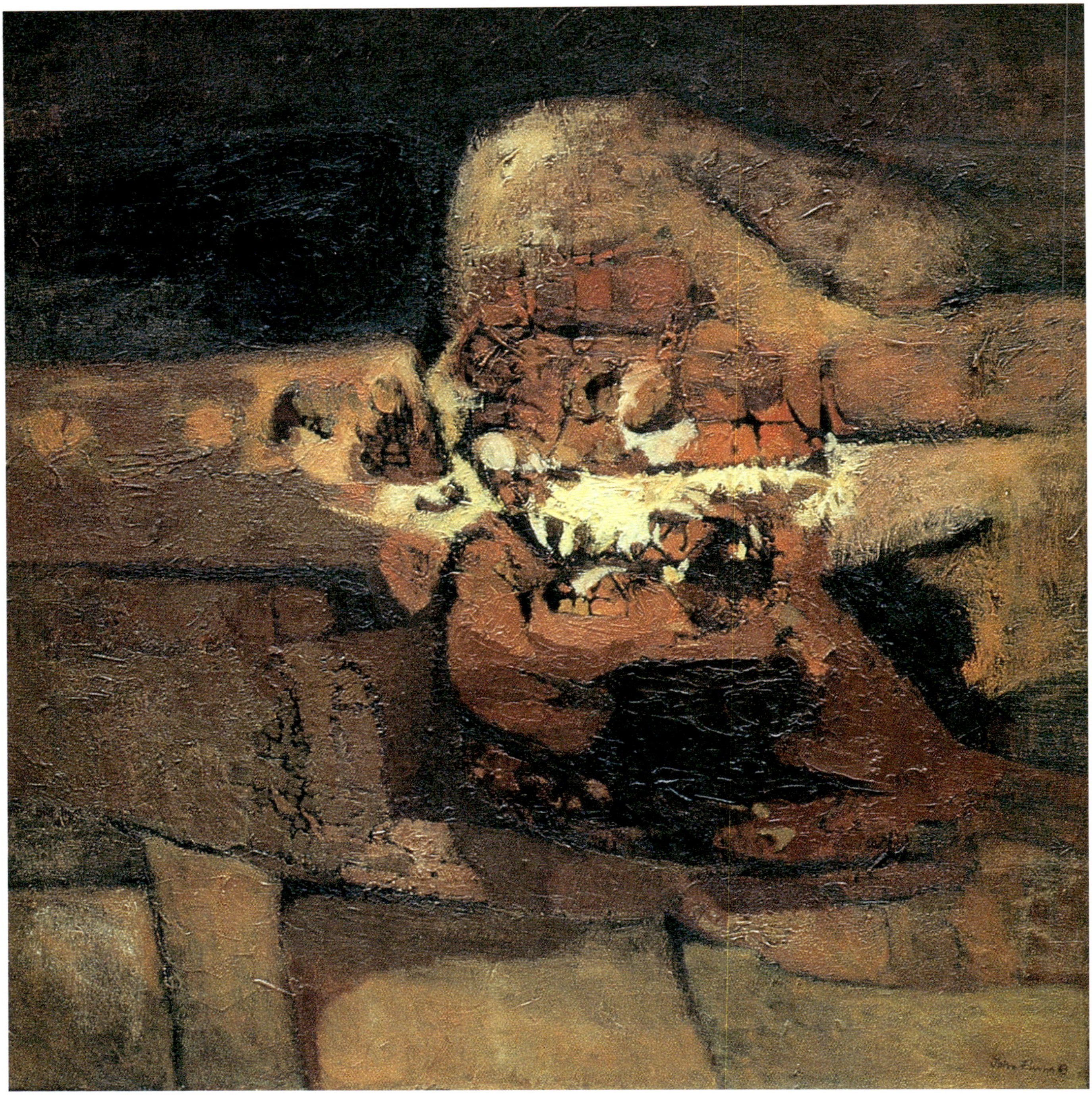

XXXV: *Landscar*
1964, oil on canvas, 30 x 30
[The Artist's Estate]

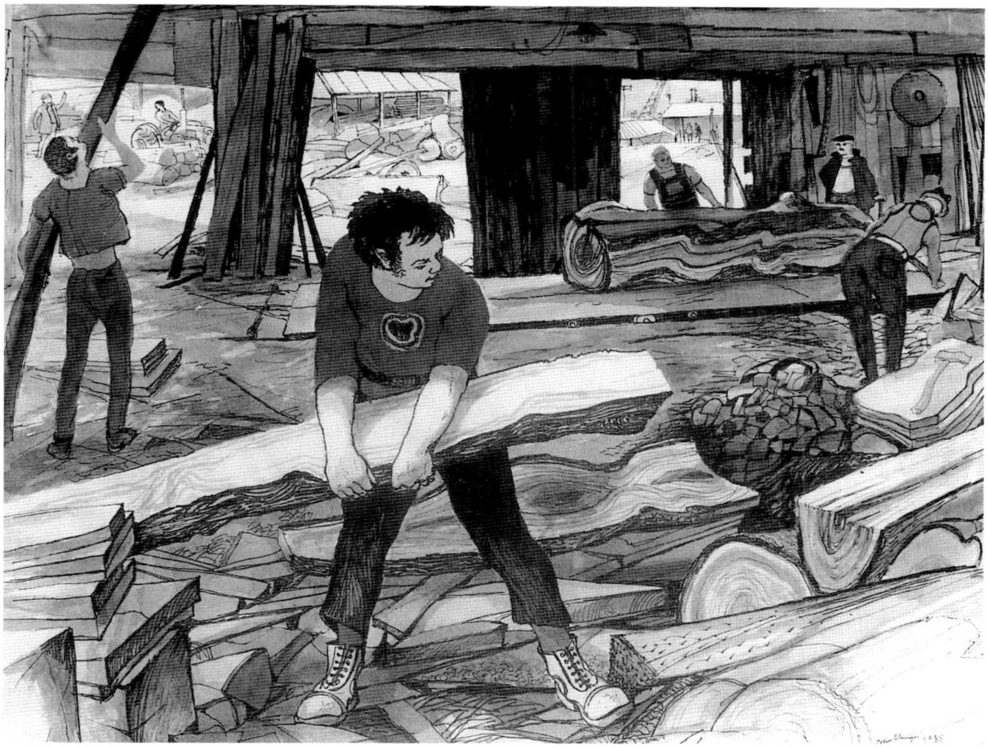

Ceri Mill
1985, ink and wash 20 x 27½
[The Artist's Estate]

among his first to move away from clearly recalled forms, and any subservience to direct observation to describe a perception of the experience. In 1962 he began to develop abstract compositions that were a synthesis of modernism and an imaginative transformation of natural elements. (Plate XXXV) Their origins, however, remained firmly within his experience and based on observation. Over the years he had made numerous drawings at Ceri Mill, the corn mill and saw mill in the Teifi Valley where his sister Sally lived, and had observed the large trees brought by farmers to be sliced up into large planks. He saw analogies between chunks of animal flesh and the freshly-sawn discs of beech; the deep ambers and hot reds when sliced were radiant for a few moments only before they quickly changed colour. On his way to Cardiganshire he also found that tree-felling in the Savernake Forest in Gloucestershire stirred the same emotions.

Sentiment and imagination replaced pure representation in the *Forest Ritual* series which represents the routine slaughter of the trees. The passion aroused in him by the destruction of large trees was channelled into the exploration of symbolic colour, applied to the canvas with a heavily loaded brush and knife to suggest the textural surface of the wood. The application of paint and the quality of the paint surface itself soon became as important to John Elwyn as the subject represented. Much was left to accident, he revised and significantly re-painted both naturalistic elements and abstract passages when motivated by forms suggested in the paint; he felt his way towards every mark as the act of painting became more intuitive. Details from sketch-book drawings were rationalised and ordered, cross sections of trees enlarged, forms broken down and reconstructed, and their identities made ambiguous to elicit a less conscious response from the viewer. Forms were manipulated until they took on a new identity and a new meaning, and were clearly intended to suggest foetal and skull-like forms. *Savernake* (1962), *Massacre Field* (1963), *Forest Enigma* (1963) and

Forest Ritual (1963) were among the large canvases that made up a solo exhibition in February 1965 at the new Mayfair premises of the Leicester Galleries. (Plate XXXVI) It was a critical and financial success, Frank Whitford commented in *Art News*:

> John Elwyn's pictorial language is solidly based on purely painterly effects, on the delicate negotiation between substance and texture, luminosity and opaqueness, and it is at once richly expressive and versatile. Occasionally his heavily impasted rectangular slabs of paint, whether knifed or brushed on, have something of the quality of De Staël's compositions from the early 'fifties ... although his abstraction is far more advanced, there is evidence that his compositions are more often than not inspired by landscape, and the sort of landscape that is heavy with romantic overtones.[106]

William Gaunt praised the exhibition in *The Times*. He thought the paintings were:

> abstract in the true sense of the word, that is in drawing out certain visual qualities from landscape which retain and convey something of its essential character ... Colour is more varied than the form which it holds in a subordinate and suggestive role ... John Elwyn does not lack a capacity for incisive pictorial structure.[107]

John Elwyn's interest in the symbolism of colour led him to Wassily Kandinsky's *Concerning the Spritual in Art: the Language of Form and Colour* (1912) which he read in April 1966. Kandinsky's observations on the mutual relationship between colour in the non-literal sense and form as an abstract entity were resonant in a new series of paintings for his second one-man exhibition at the Leicester Galleries in 1968. The book had drawn his attention to the importance of understanding the internal structure of form and encouraged John Elwyn to investigate more of the physical processes that occur in nature. He had an enduring passion for gardening and nurtured all manner of flowers and vegetables in his large garden in Winchester. He began to look at the structure of plants growing in his garden and made drawings that attempt to explain their underlying construction. He took cross-sections of various seed pods and studied the intricate forms of the inner structure. The paintings developed from drawings and paper collages of natural forms which he had made for the fabric design courses that he taught at the School of Art. These were integrated activities; designs prepared for textiles found their way into large-scale abstract canvases and vice versa. Carefully selected motifs are repeated and explored in search of harmony amidst the apparent chaos of nature. Tightly-balanced asymmetrical compositions combine expansive colour fields and small daubs of paint in central clusters. In an attempt to derive a more universal significance he made parallels between the creation of buds, leaves and flowers, and the natural processes of birth and death that control all living things. In their attention to the symbolic association between seed-pod and vagina, branches and limbs, etc., they recall Ceri Richard's series of abstract paintings of *The Cycle of Nature* 1952–1956.

Seedflight, *Arboreal* and *Germinal*, painted in 1968, are based on the ways in which pollination occurs. He also drew plants at different times of the day, recording their movement as they reacted to light and shade. Another aspect he studied was the seasonal variation of plant forms and the ways in which colour may be used to symbolise the seasons; from the sowing of seeds in spring, and the plants flowering in summer, to the seed-pods harvested in autumn, and the dormant period during winter when the sap returned to the roots. *Garden Episode*, *Equinoctial* and *Enigmatic Blossom* (Plate XXXVII) illustrate how a place, event or imaginative experience

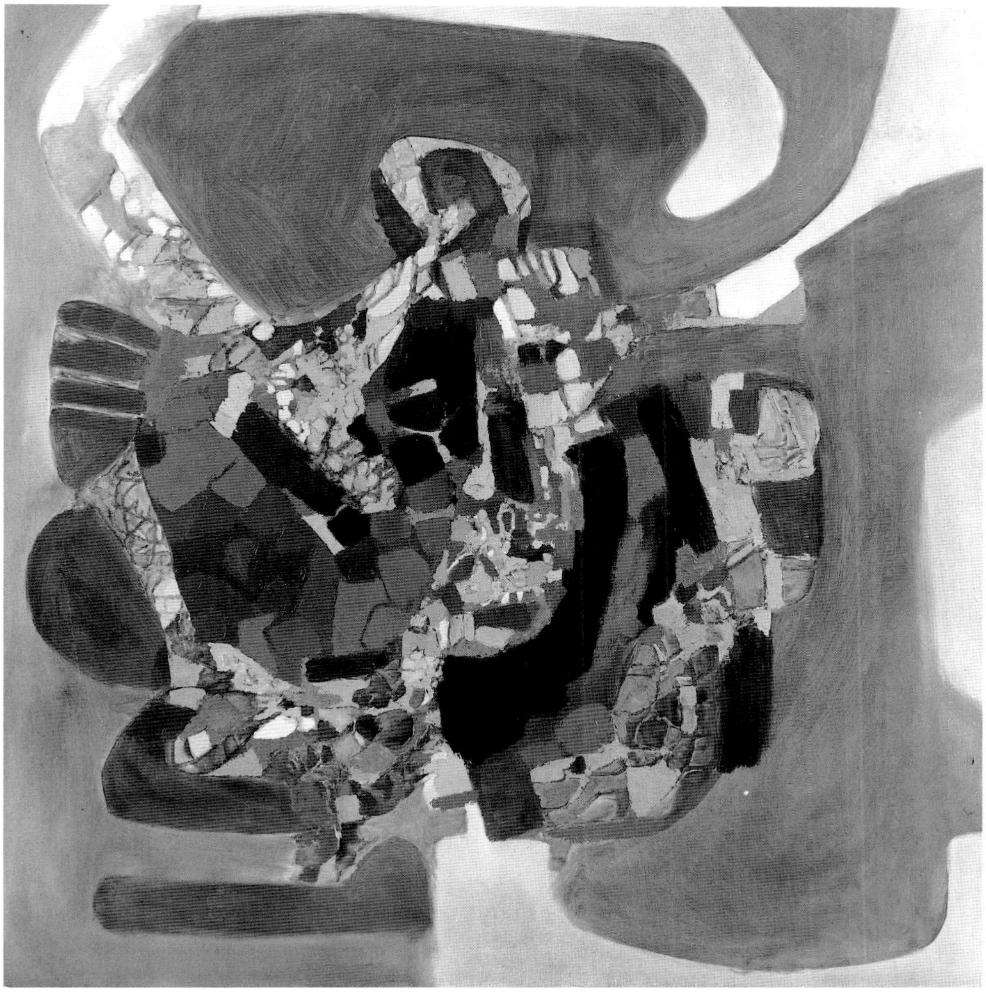

Equinoctial
1967, oil on canvas 48 x 48
[Present whereabouts unknown]

can make the familiar appear strange. The physical appearance of a seed-pod may have been the starting point for the drawings, but on canvas John Elwyn used colour to induce a particular response from the spectator. Liberated from pure representation, colour functioned independently of the object it described; it ceased to be secondary to narrative or a device to create spatial illusion. The paintings display a technical virtuosity and a facility for handling a broad range of exuberant colours. His understanding of the tonal values of colour, and his ability to observe and record them accurately, was always evident in the figurative paintings of the 1940s and 1950s. This facility was invaluable in his investigations of the expressive and emotional effects of vibrant colour.

In spite of a run of successful exhibitions of abstract paintings, John Elwyn had become marginalised by the more dominant younger generation of Systems, Minimalist and Conceptual artists on the staff at Winchester. Increasingly, fashionable London painters were invited to teach at Winchester for a few days each term. It was hoped that their association with the School would raise the profile of the institution. Their insensitive, and sometimes destructive criticisms undermined the students' self-confidence, leaving the full-time staff to pick up the pieces and rebuild their self-esteem. Generations of students have testified to John Elwyn's dedicated work as a teacher; he was sympathetic to both the needs of his students and the demands and

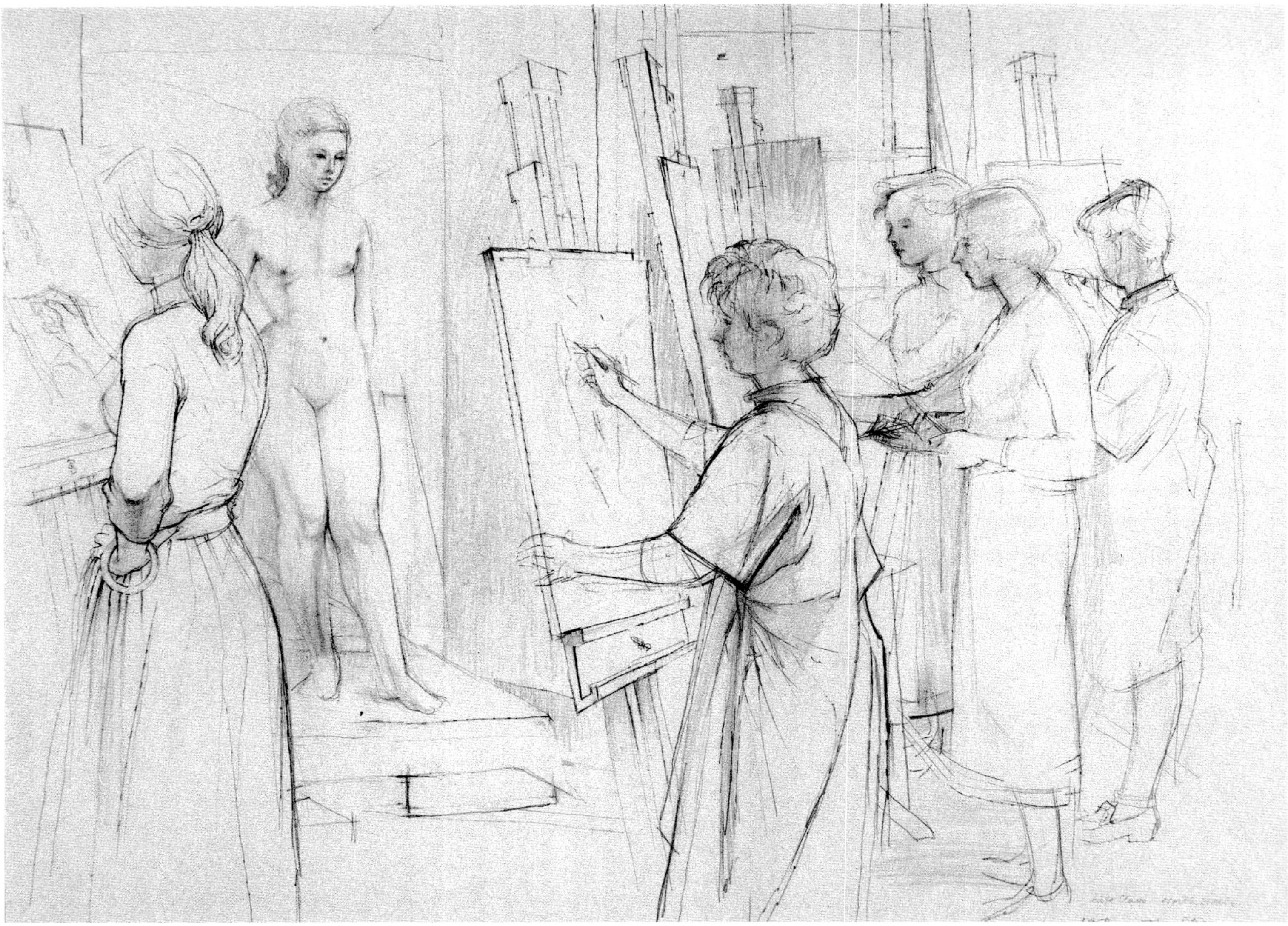

The Life Class at Winchester
1958, pencil on paper 20 x 26
[The Artist's Estate]

rigour of an art training. John Elwyn was always ready to praise the work of others and offer constructive advice. His role at Winchester, however, had become that of administrator, keeper of the materials store and 'father-confessor amongst the young people'.[108] Andrew Watchorn remembered being interviewed by John Elwyn in his narrow small office:

> He took as much interest in talking about my roots, being brought up on a farm, living and working in the country, as he did about the work in my portfolio. He was a man of integrity and sincerity and not someone trying to catch me out with obscure questions, [by this time he was being allocated very little teaching ...] which was such a waste! I so wish he had been more active in teaching as he had so much experience and knowledge to give. Not only did the staff not encourage him to actively teach, but I feel that many, if not most of the other students, certainly in my year, just did not recognise what John had to give.[109]

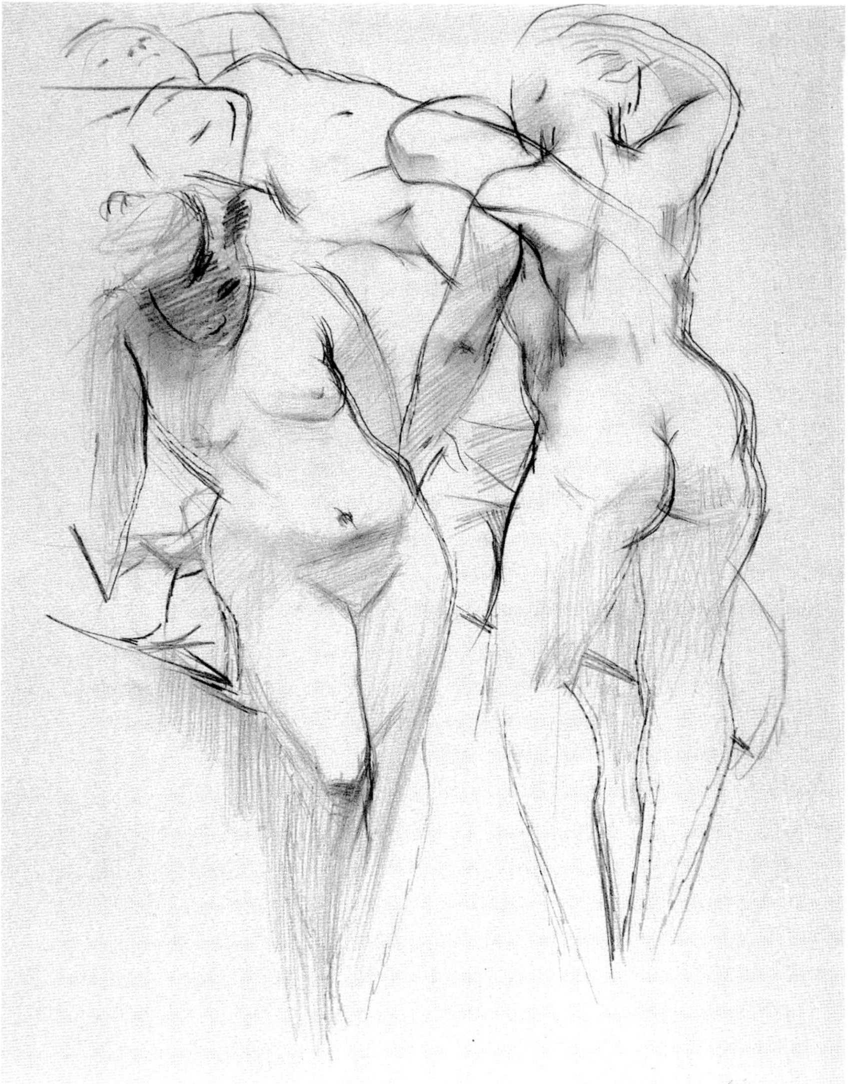

Figure Studies, Winchester
1960s, pencil on paper 22 x 15
[The University of Wales, Aberystwyth]

John Elwyn taught courses on methods and materials for artists, the techniques of past exponents, the 'craft' of handling paint and, not surprisingly, he especially gained satisfaction from teaching the science of how colours mix, the chemistry of pigments and colour theories. He realised that the knowledge acquired by students would not make them better painters, but 'perhaps may provide some stimulation and curiosity to think about colour in a more expressive way'.[110]

One area where John Elwyn made a significant contribution was in the life class and the drawings and paintings which date from his tenure at Winchester were all made as demonstration pieces for the instruction of students. He taught primarily by example, gathering students around him to demonstrate a particular approach or technical problem that they would be considering during the session. Some of the most interesting and unusual drawings are those he made of the model glimpsed between the backs of his students at work in the life class. He contrasts the rounded forms of the model with the geometric inter-locking forms of easels, chairs, drawing boards and studio furniture. These sensitive, carefully controlled line drawings were an antidote to the spontaneous studies in pencil which convey movement, and the quick chalk studies with broken texture on rough paper. These 'summary drawings' use *chiaroscuro* to define the essential body masses, drawing with an equal distribution of black and white chalk. Working on toned paper provided a convenient middle tone for quick studies. The practice of evaluating and describing the principal tones, rather than defining outline, was an effective solution to short poses.

In command of his own life class, he favoured not the heroic poses set by Percy Horton at the R.C.A., but quiet and introspective poses. He delighted in the sensuality of the gently undulating female form: its subtle twists and turns, the body's musculature, the distribution of weight in attaining balance, the harmony created by the angle of a hip raised on a weight-bearing leg, and a shoulder relaxed to counter-balance the posture. In contrast to his abstract paintings of plant forms at that time, John Elwyn never distorted, exaggerated or departed from the naturalistic representation of the human form as a means to other ends. He was an artist fascinated by human nature and he responded to it in his work. John Elwyn was a consummate draughtsman working in the 'classical' sense as understood by the greatest exponents of the European figurative tradition.[111]

Chapter 6

golden in the heydays of his eyes:

the Cardiganshire landscape revisited

IN 1966, after thirty years in 'temporary' accommodation, Winchester School of Art moved to purpose-built premises, and there John Elwyn met Gillian Butterworth who had joined the staff as lecturer on the newly established Foundation Course in Music. Gillian, who was born in Newport, Monmouthshire and trained at the University of Manchester and the Royal Manchester College of Music, is a professional pianist and has accompanied many well-known soloists and musicians. In her teens she made her first broadcast for the BBC. Gillian is a tutor with the Open University and until recently examiner for The Associated Board of

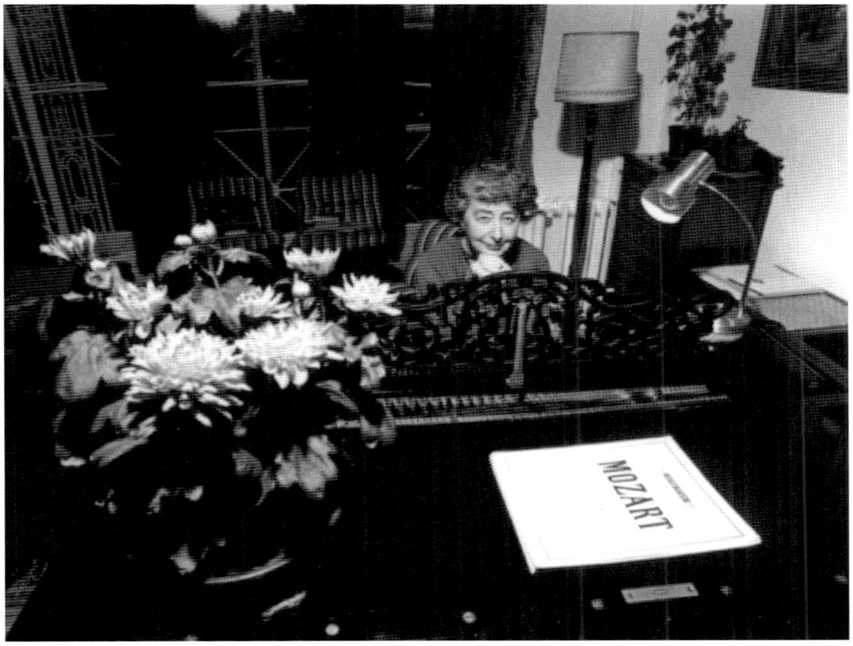

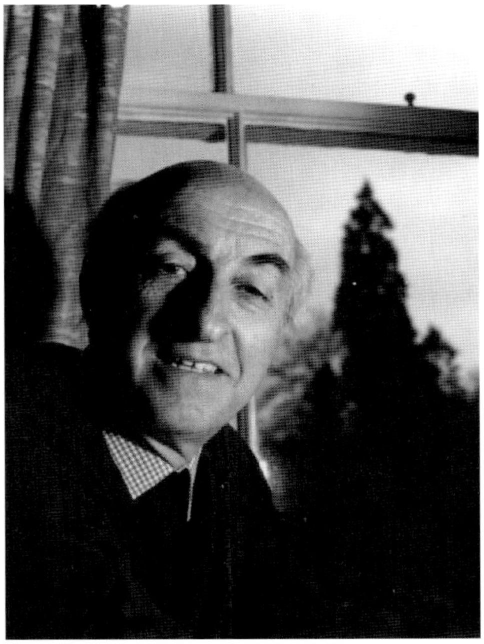

John Elwyn
1983
[Photograph by Joe Low]

Gillian Butterworth
1983
[Photograph by Joe Low]

the Royal Schools of Music. Their courtship was initially tentative, it was John Elwyn's first relationship with a woman; his family and friends had assumed he would remain a 'confirmed bachelor'. In addition, he was concerned about his sister Mary's predicament; she had become dependent upon him since she had given up the Mill to live with him in Winchester. Many Saturday evenings had passed in Gillian's sitting room watching *The Forsyte Saga* on the television before the couple eventually became engaged in December 1969. They married three months later on 3rd March 1970, when John Elwyn was fifty-three, and moved into a large Victorian house in Winchester with Gillian's young children by her first marriage, Robin and Louise. On the ground floor they created an apartment for Mary.[112]

John Elwyn's life style changed enormously from the start of his courtship with

Gillian; he made a much wider circle of friends, they visited the theatre and concerts regularly, entertained guests, and travelled extensively on the Continent and to Egypt. (Appendix 3) Consequently, these new enthusiasms encroached upon the time he had available to paint – and at a time when he was being invited to exhibit with more commercial art galleries than he was able to supply with new work. (Appendix 1) So, when David Pare retired as Principal of the art school in 1976, John Elwyn

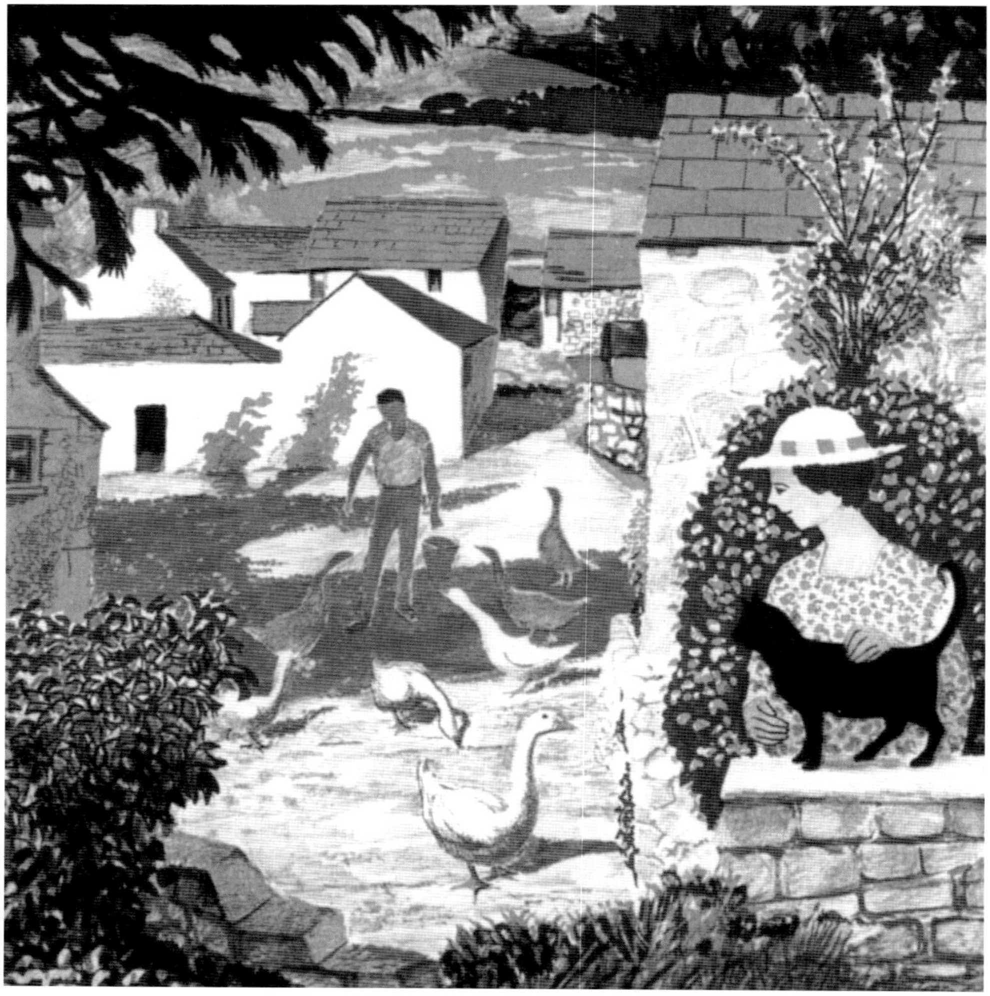

The Farmer's Wife
1967, lithograph on paper 17 x 17
[The Artist's Estate]

also decided to leave and concentrate on painting full time, returning to the more direct representations of the Cardiganshire landscape that were popular with the galleries. He lived and worked in relative isolation in Winchester and reflected:

> If you hang on long enough, it's interesting how things come together. The statement "John Elwyn's *In the Hill's Elbow*, extends the Neo-Romantic vein of Graham Sutherland's landscape" – pleased me very much. If I had known about it twenty years ago things might have been different, because I never thought myself as belonging to any group or style at all. I wish I had, it would have been a help and have brought about a certain confidence that was necessary to sustain some quality that I was attempting to achieve. This was elusive and in a way I pursued the commercial element in many galleries at that time.[113]

In his studio in Winchester he worked from memory and from sketch-book annotations. All his life he had drawn from nature as an *aide-memoire* for paintings, although the drawings invariably never correspond exactly to completed paintings. He felt that they never contained enough information to suggest how a painting might progress. The sketch books contained only details – the forms of a valley, a configuration of farm buildings and groups of people. He worked out his problems

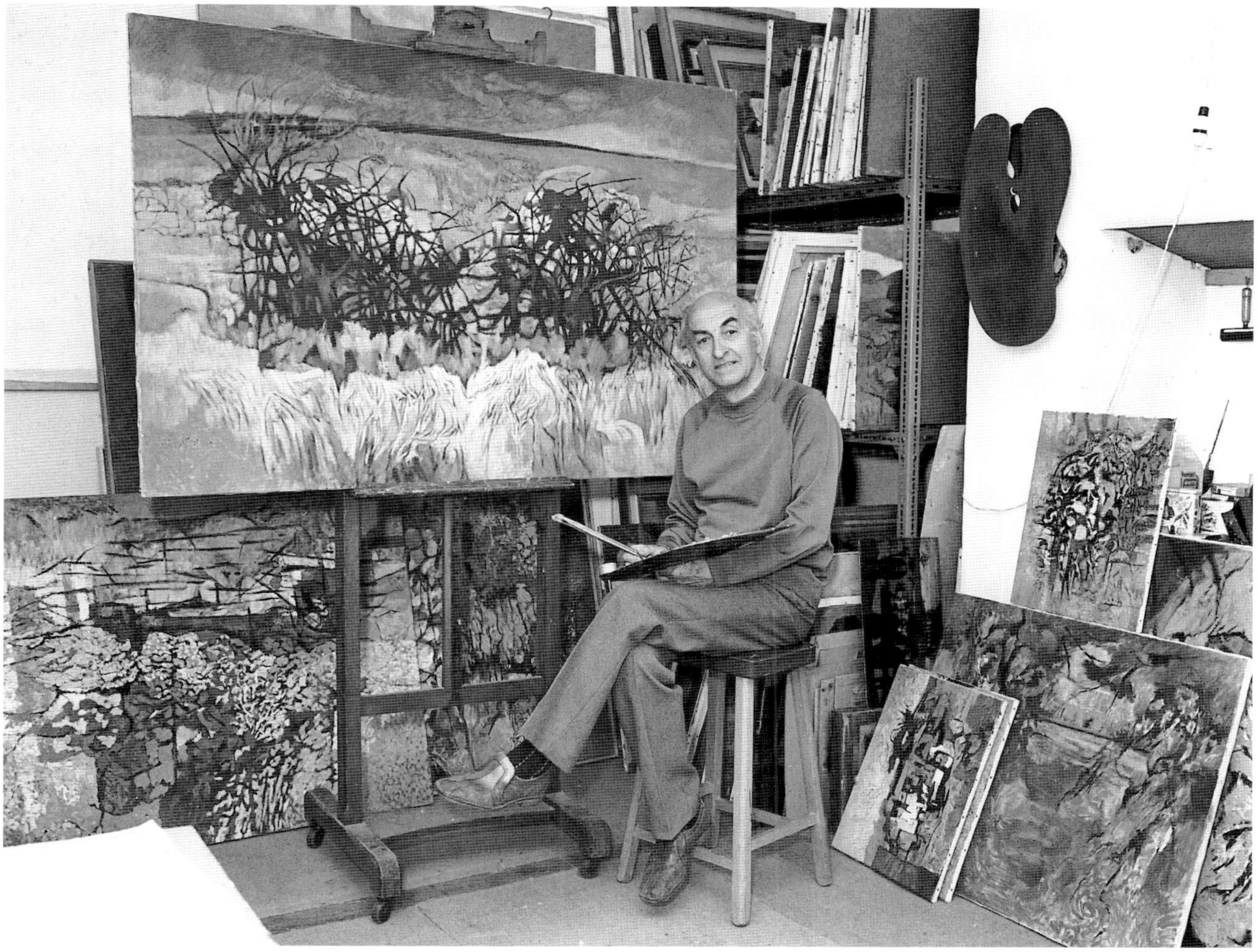

John Elwyn, Winchester, April 1982 (*Dyfed Moors* is on the easel)

on the canvas – if he did not know what the subject was going to look like he painted vertical marks, continuing until something suggested itself. Paintings developed from a germ of an idea which might first have emerged years before and may already have existed in his mind's eye. He wrote:

> I am old fashioned and a romantic at heart and before I start working on a painting I must have some inspiration from outside such as a shower of rain in April or perhaps a line of poetry. Something to make the imagination move and start creating a mirror of thoughts and reflection of feelings. Then it is better not to know exactly what will follow – leave the painting to take over in a way. There is always hope that something interesting will happen if this takes place.[114]

Paintings such as *Between the Barns* (1974) steer a path between the pastoral and modernist tendencies in art; they are half-remembered landscapes that fall between naturalistic representation and abstraction. (Plate XXXVIII) The meandering arabesques of a Cardiganshire lane are central to many of his paintings, rising then disappearing from sight over a hill or behind a hedgerow, only to re-appear horizontally displaced and continuing its journey to the horizon. Fields of corn undulating in

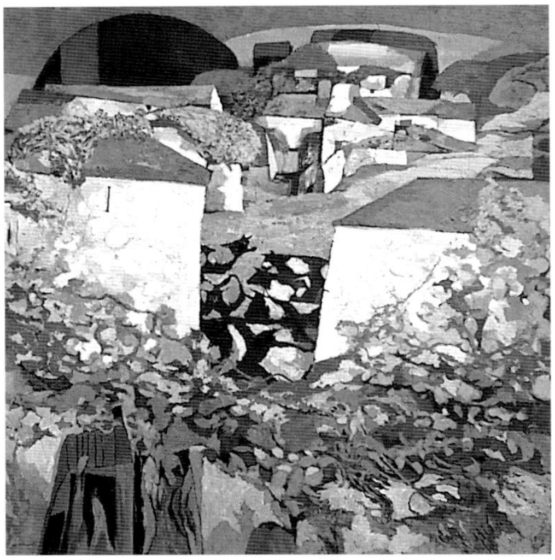

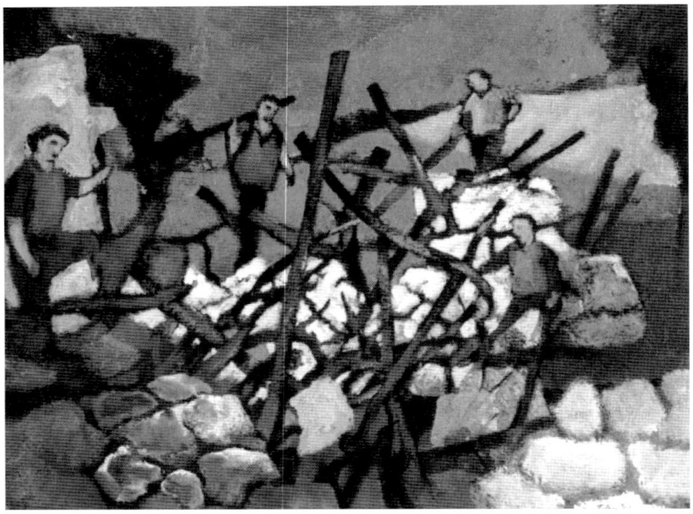

Cattle Between the Barns
1977, oil on canvas
[Dimensions and present whereabouts unknown]

The Collapsed Barn
1994, acrylic on paper
11 x 14½
[Robert Meyrick]

the August gales create unexpected waving forms, whilst inquisitive farm animals peer through a hedge, a felled tree, or between barn walls. The sky is seldom given prominence, low viewpoints place the horizon high on the picture plane. He remembered as a child at infant school being given a small card at the end of the week for good attendance. Each card was usually of a different a scene in Canada, but ultimately they all looked the same; a road leading through rich vegetation or a thorn bush with objects fragmented behind its tangled branches. In the landscape of Cardiganshire he recognised too that a gnarled hawthorn bush, or the jagged skeleton of a collapsed barn silhouetted against golden pastures shortly after the hay harvest, had potential for dynamic compositions. Vivid green, yellow and orange sunlit fields, storm-threatening skies, shimmering white-washed barns, and a winding country lane, describe the geometrical shapes of a domesticated landscape compartmentalised by fences, hedgerows and stone walls. These were the recurrent motifs in John Elwyn's late works and he painted many variations on the same theme. Titles such as *Off the Main Road*, *Welsh Hill Farm*, *Entrance to a Farm*, *White Washed Walls*, *Dyfed Landscape* or *Upland Farm* (Plate XLIII) frequently occurred amongst the many paintings he made of the:

> luscious meadows and banks of the river Teifi and Ceri where the cottages are tucked away behind the apple trees in the elbows of the hill, and dappled white-washed walls can be picked out in the morning sun from the patchwork quilt of hedge and fields.[115]

John Elwyn visited Wales and regularly corresponded with family and friends, many of whom were involved in the arts and kept him abreast of new developments – the painter and stained-glass artist John Petts, the poet and film-maker John Ormond, but none more so than Glyn Jones. Most of these letters were written in

English, but John Elwyn possessed solid linguistic roots and loved the language of his homeland, and he used every opportunity to speak or write in Welsh to his family and friends in the Teifi Valley. Welsh and Anglo-Welsh poetry continued to spark off John Elwyn's imagination, inspiring him to interpret landscape in a more personal and expressive way. Glyn Jones' evocative descriptions of a peaceful Carmarthen-

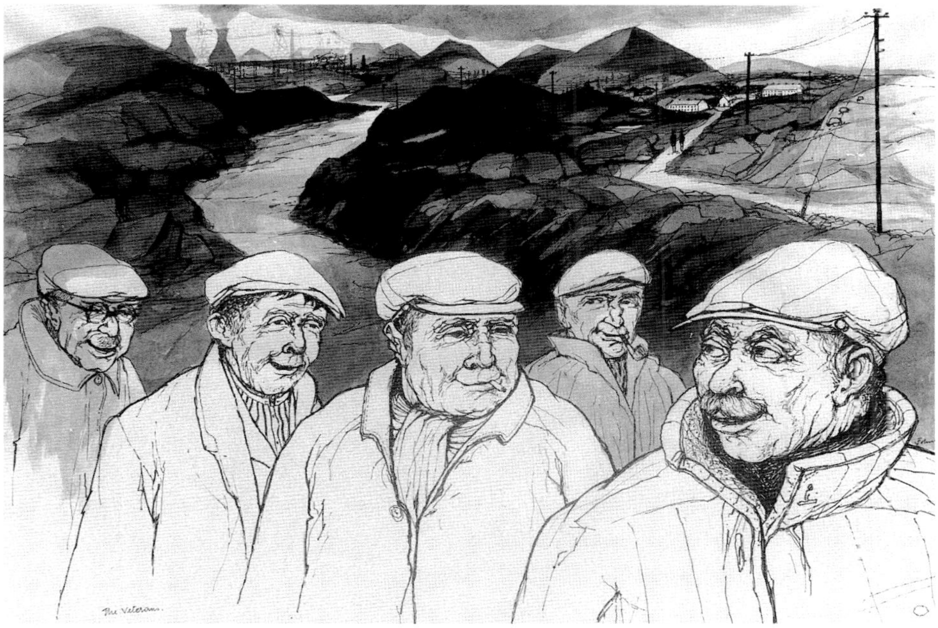

The Veterans
1985, ink and wash on paper
18½ x 27
[The Artist's Estate]

shire countryside naturally struck a chord with John Elwyn. *Cwmcelyn* for example, and the poem *Easter*, in which Jones described the soft 'plush-pile of the grass-like wheat, the green velvety nap of springing corn burst forth', inspired several paintings. Another influence was the Welsh poetry of Waldo Williams, his friend and fellow Quaker, which dealt with many of the principles of brotherly love held dearly by John Elwyn. It was many years before John Elwyn had been able to shed completely the order and dogma observed by the Nonconformist church and participate fully in the silent worship of Quaker Meetings. After years as attender, he became a full member of the Friends in 1984 with his wife Gillian. Towards the end of his life John Elwyn's faith became increasingly important to him. He took seriously the roles of Overseer and Elder in the Winchester Meeting, each of which had a tenure of three years.

His fascination with the cycle of the seasons, and their bearing on the community, led him once again to the poetry of Dylan Thomas. Like John Elwyn, Thomas had also discovered his passion for nature, in all its diversity, during his childhood in Wales. The poem *Fernhill* (1946), which famously begins 'And as I was young and easy under the apple boughs, about the lilting house and happy as the grass was green', has become an archetypal romantic poem about landscape and childhood experience. In 1977 John Elwyn made a series of formal and lyrical interpretations of *Fernhill* which are, like the poem itself, concerned with imagination, harmony, rhythm and form. (Plate XXXIX) He also painted a series of watercolours of the sandy beaches and limestone headlands of the Towy estuary from Dylan Thomas' small boat house at Laugharne near Carmarthen.

In his seventies John Elwyn returned to illustration with large drawings such as *The*

Veterans (1985) and book projects for the private presses. In 1988 he illustrated *Norris's Ark* for the Tidal Press in Maine, USA and in 1993 Nicolas McDowall invited John Elwyn to illustrate a selection of works by the medieval Welsh poet Dafydd ap Gwilym – on the themes of love, nature and the seasons – for the Old Stile Press in Monmouthshire. It seemed appropriate that John Elwyn should be paired with Dafydd ap Gwilym, for the poet had spent time in Newcastle Emlyn when his uncle Llywelyn ap Gwilym was a constable of the castle in the fourteenth century. As a child he too had wandered the banks of the Teifi and discovered his muse. McDowall's long-standing interest in British romantic painting of the 1940s and 1950s, led him to suggest that John Elwyn produce:

> a series of shamelessly and wonderfully nostalgic and romantic pictures on the theme of love and nature in Wales ... I would hope that you would dive back into the period that excites me so much, and perhaps relive the pain and joy of those years in and after the war when you were on the land and clearly living and thinking so richly.[116]

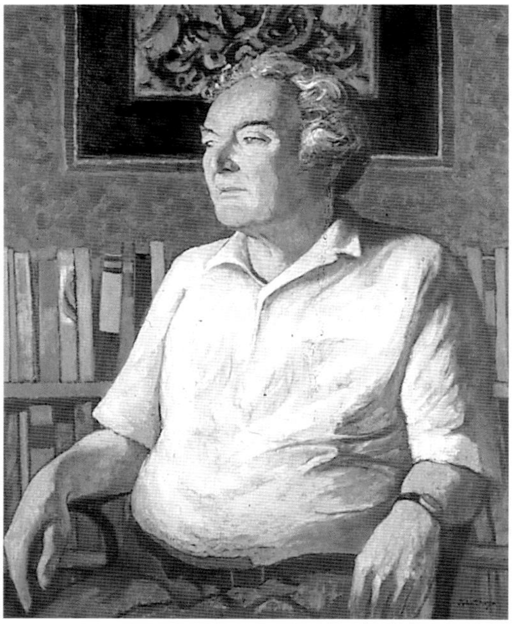

John Ormond
1980, oil on canvas 24 x 20
[Glenys Ormond Thomas]

Periodic returns to portrait painting sharpened John Elwyn's powers of observation and expression. He painted several portraits of his literary friends such as Glyn Jones, Leslie Norris, Jack Jones, and commissioned portraits of Sir Alun Talfan Davies and Dr Raymond Edwards. He began a portrait of the Swansea-born poet, broadcaster and film maker John Ormond in August 1980 when he was staying with him in Winchester on the occasion of his poetry reading at the cathedral. Ormond established his reputation as a writer for *Picture Post* and was founder, producer and director of the BBC Wales Documentary Film Unit and made over 70 films in America and Europe. He was one of the foremost Anglo-Welsh poets of his generation; his poetic vision and powers of observation appealed to the painter who valued their friendship greatly. Ormond had been a very close friend of Graham Sutherland and provided a tangible association with an artist whose painting, and especially his writing on art, John Elwyn had long admired. Ormond wrote:

> Who was it said (something like) "No portrait is liked by those who know its subject"? Well, he was wrong. ... your portrait of me has brought gasps of recognition and admiration of your work from those who have seen it; and certainly it has got me, and further, it is a fine piece of painting in its own right ... Graham Sutherland once told me that when a subject and family came face to face with the portrait for the first time so often, without a word being said, such a silence would descend as he (GS) could only liken to the silence after a deep snowfall. I can assure you that that's not been the case here.[117]

John Elwyn's subject matter was far more diverse than is commonly recognised. Even during the 1960s he was not so totally absorbed in abstraction that he abandoned figuration totally. He painted lively studies of women enveloped in brightly coloured pac-a-macs braving the wind and rain, and spirited paintings in oil or gouache like *Plastic People by the Sea* (Oil, 1964) and *Plastic People* (Gouache, 1965). In the 1970s he returned to still-life painting incorporating vases of flowers and potted plants on the windowsill or on Gillian's Steinway piano with its elaborate fret-work music stand. He also painted interiors of the sitting room, the conserva-

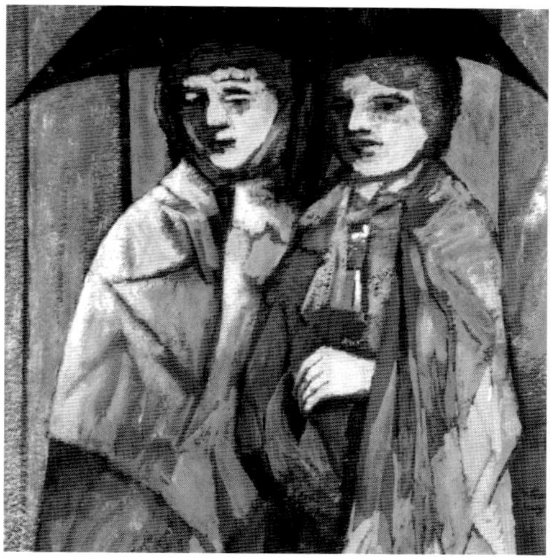

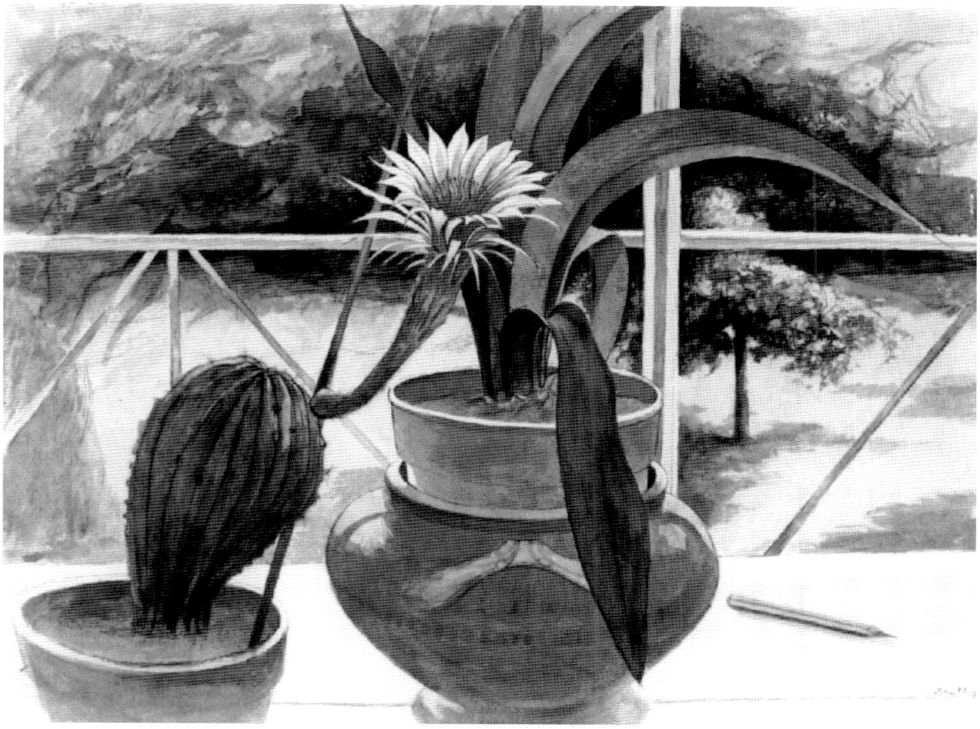

Plastic People
1965, gouache on paper 11 x 11
[Robert Meyrick]

Flowering Cactus
1975, watercolour and pencil on paper $15\frac{1}{2}$ x 22
[Robert Meyrick]

tory, and views from the studio looking down on to the walled garden, its trees laden with blossom. (Plate XL) Until the end of his life John Elwyn remained a keen gardener and nurtured a well-stocked kitchen garden and flower beds. He also invented garden situations such as *The Topiarist* and *Paddock Bird*, both painted in 1985. (Plate XLI) Conversely, in the 1970s when his work was principally concerned with the Cardiganshire landscape, he began to investigate the relationship between painting and music, especially the correlation between the seven colours of the rainbow and the seven notes within an octave, between colour and the sound and rhythms of music. Each chosen passage of music led him to a create visual metaphor for the image it suggested. He wanted each painting to stand as an end in itself, as an expression of feelings like a poem or piece of music, and not be bound to representation.

John Elwyn also kept sketch-book journals of Spain, Italy and Greece whilst on holiday with Gillian. Alongside watercolour drawings he wrote day-to-day accounts of his activities, observations on the architecture, and peculiarities of the landscape, climate, farm animals, vineyards and olive groves. As one might expect there are frequent references to the comings and goings of the locals as he watched them about their routine; he recalled his encounters with them and meal-time conversations. He took a genuine interest in everyone he met and could strike up a conversation immediately. The days were occupied with long walks into the countryside and visits to

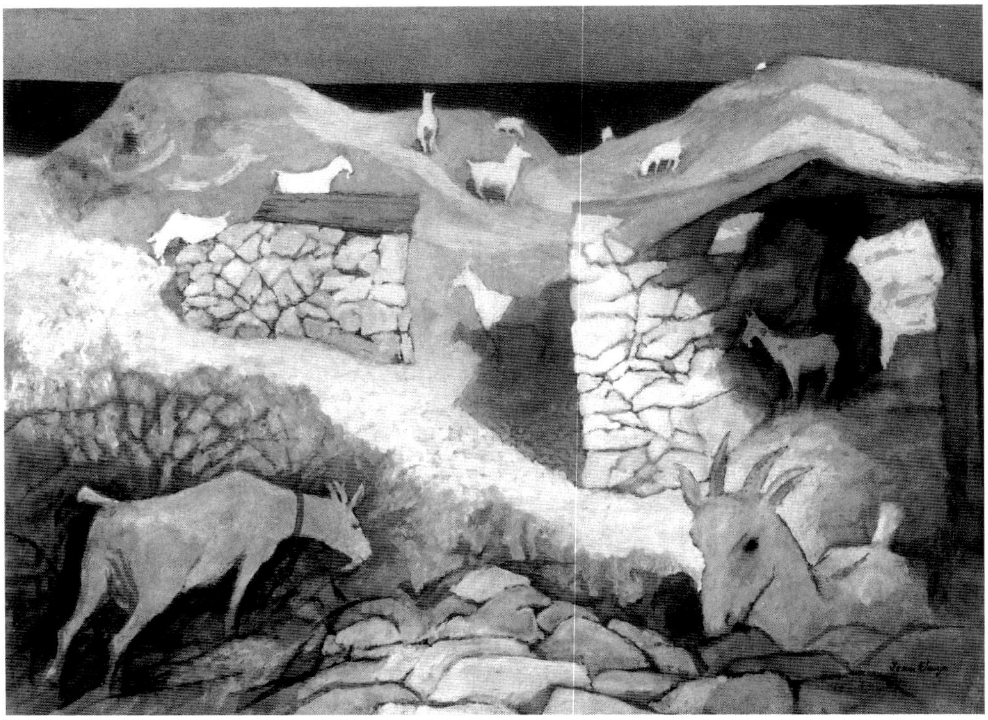

The White Goats, Cos
1985, gouache on paper 15 x 20¼
[The Artist's Estate]

places of interest. A particular interest was visiting the homes of artists and musicians. Back in Winchester he used his sketch books as a source for paintings in acrylic and oil, and for smaller works on paper. In a letter to Glyn Jones he described an oil painting that he was in the process of working up from a small holiday drawing:

> the subject is the market at Compostela, Spain – it really could be anywhere – but it's a starting point. We saw a lot of chickens and cockerels there being sold on the pavement – with their feet tied together or individuals holding one cockerel up at a time – quite decorative, not for the bird though.[118]

John Elwyn took his last trip abroad in 1991; by then he felt physically weakened after major surgery in the previous year when it was discovered he had cancer. He was content to remain at home, taking short breaks to Wales and accompanying Gillian who regularly travelled around Britain in her role as Associated Board examiner. However, he was happiest when left alone to spend all day in his studio and retreat into the solitary landscape of paintings such as *On the Dyfed Coast.* (Plate

XLII) These increasingly became a vehicle on which to project his own emotions. As early as 1959 he was describing this personal approach to landscape:

> however important the appearances of things may be it is the reaction to these appearances in oneself that is to me of value in painting. If one responds to the mood of the surrounding countryside, if one can become aware of the pulsating earth around one, one can get nearer to the essence, the *genius loci* of the place. To arrive at that point and to be able to express the experience of environment and convey it on to a canvas is what I would like to achieve. It should be a personal and individual synthesis of the chosen subject.[119]

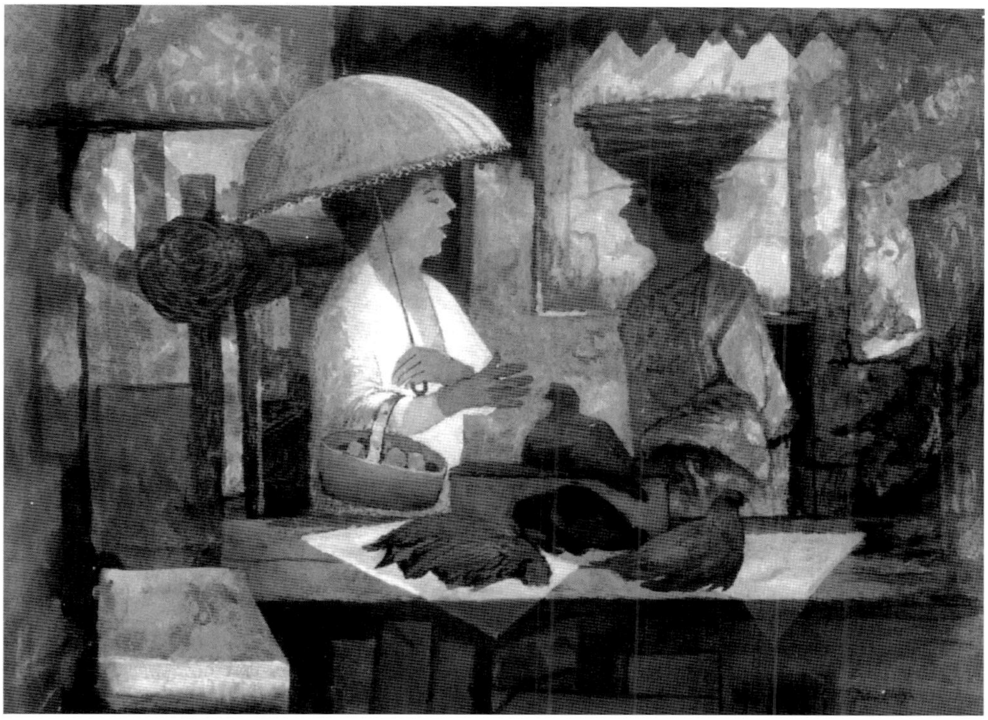

The Market, Santiago da Compostela
1989, gouache on paper 14 x 18
[The Artist's Estate]

In his later career John Elwyn gained enormous pleasure from the many accolades that were bestowed upon him. He was invited to become full Honorary Member of the Royal Cambrian Academy in May 1965 by the power invested in the Council to invite artists of exceptional merit to become Academicians. He was elected a Member of the Royal Institute in 1979 and Honorary Member of the Gorsedd of Bards in 1982. In 1996 he was awarded an Honorary D.Litt. by the University of Wales in recognition of his contribution to art in Wales, and the National Library of Wales paid tribute to a distinguished career with a major retrospective exhibition surveying sixty years' work. He staged his last one-man show at the Martin Tinney Gallery in Cardiff in 1997. John Elwyn died at 4.30a.m. on 13th November 1997, the result of a head injury sustained when he fell in his garden on 22nd October. He was cremated on his 81st birthday at Southampton. A Quaker Memorial Service to celebrate the life of John Elwyn took place in the Friends' Meeting House in Winchester on 14th December; a large number of his paintings were displayed on the walls. His ashes were interred on 6th April 1998 in a plot alongside his parents and sisters in a remote and peaceful cemetery outside Newcastle Emlyn, overlooking the meadows and gently undulating pastures of Cardiganshire that had meant so much to him, and sustained him throughout a long and active career as an artist. (Appendix 5)

John Elwyn consistently found inspiration in a familiar environment. His extensive knowledge and love of the south Cardiganshire landscape recalls Samuel Palmer's 'Valley of Vision' at Shoreham, John Constable's affection for Suffolk, and Stanley Spencer's devotion to Cookham-on-Thames. He shared with these artists the ability to go beyond 'likeness' and capture the essence of his secluded country villages, lonely farms, cottages and barns. His paintings of rural west Wales, however, are anything but provincial or local. As John Piper once remarked:

> Romantic art deals with the particular. The particularisation of Bewick about a bird's wing, of Turner about a waterfall or a hill town, or of Rossetti about Elizabeth Siddall, is the result of a vision that can see in these things something significant beyond ordinary significance: something that for a moment seems to contain the whole world; and, when the moment is past, carries over some comment on life or experience besides the comment on appearances.[120]

John Elwyn's work represents the quieter strain of Neo-Romanticism in British landscape painting, not its wild excesses. The paintings are Romantic for his interest in the particular, his spontaneous paint application, and in his use of intensified colour for the portrayal of peculiar and inspiring episodes of nature. In the literary sense, many ideas developed from reading romantic Anglo-Welsh poetry and prose. They are Romantic too in their statement of emotion; in his depiction of rural ceremonies and rituals he represented a breadth of poignant visual experiences with considerable drama.

Inversely proportional to his diminishing visits to Newcastle Emlyn, paintings such as *September* (1996) became increasingly Arcadian. (Plate XLIV) These intimate and consoling landscapes possess a real feeling for 'place' that has characterised so much British landscape painting and literature. They draw upon the same rich seam of childhood experience, the 'land of lost content' and 'blue remembered hills', that fuelled A. E. Housman's *A Shropshire Lad* in 1896. The solitary world into which he retreated is perhaps nowhere more poignant than in his last completed work, *The Lonely Servant* (1980–1997), a moving portrayal of an isolated and vulnerable farm worker. (Plate XLV) His starting point might well have been the Welsh landscape but the paintings tell us equally about the artist himself. He was modest and unassuming. His gentle temperament was not instrumental in drawing attention to his work, nor did he court the media like many artists in the post-war period. His career was dependent in part on the assistance of those in a position to help, such as Winifred Coombe-Tennant who made his name known to patrons, curators and dealers, and David Bell who arranged contacts with the Leicester Galleries in London and organisations in Wales. John Elwyn's paintings were not dependent upon any indigenous Welsh tradition: they developed within the British landscape tradition. However, the way in which his career developed was clearly indebted to the widespread interest in the visual arts in post-war Wales, and to the individuals who fought to establish and nurture some sort of Welsh National School.

John Elwyn was a 'popular' painter in the true meaning of the word. The appeal of his paintings has been widespread, they have been purchased consistently by public and private collectors, and have sold equally well outside Wales. His work is represented in numerous private collections all over the world – many have been acquired

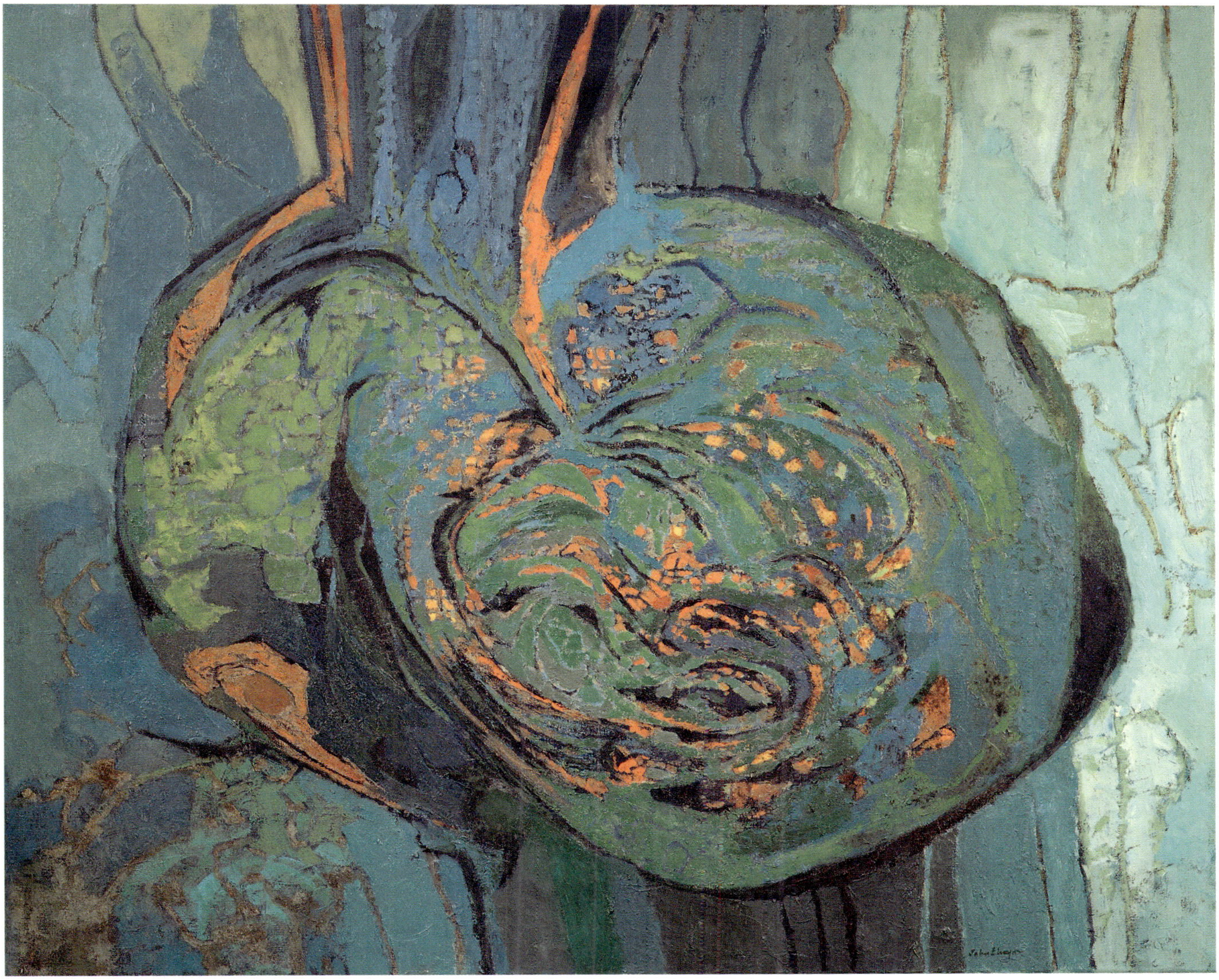

XXXVI: *Forest Enigma*
1964, oil on canvas, 40 x 50
[The Artist's Estate]

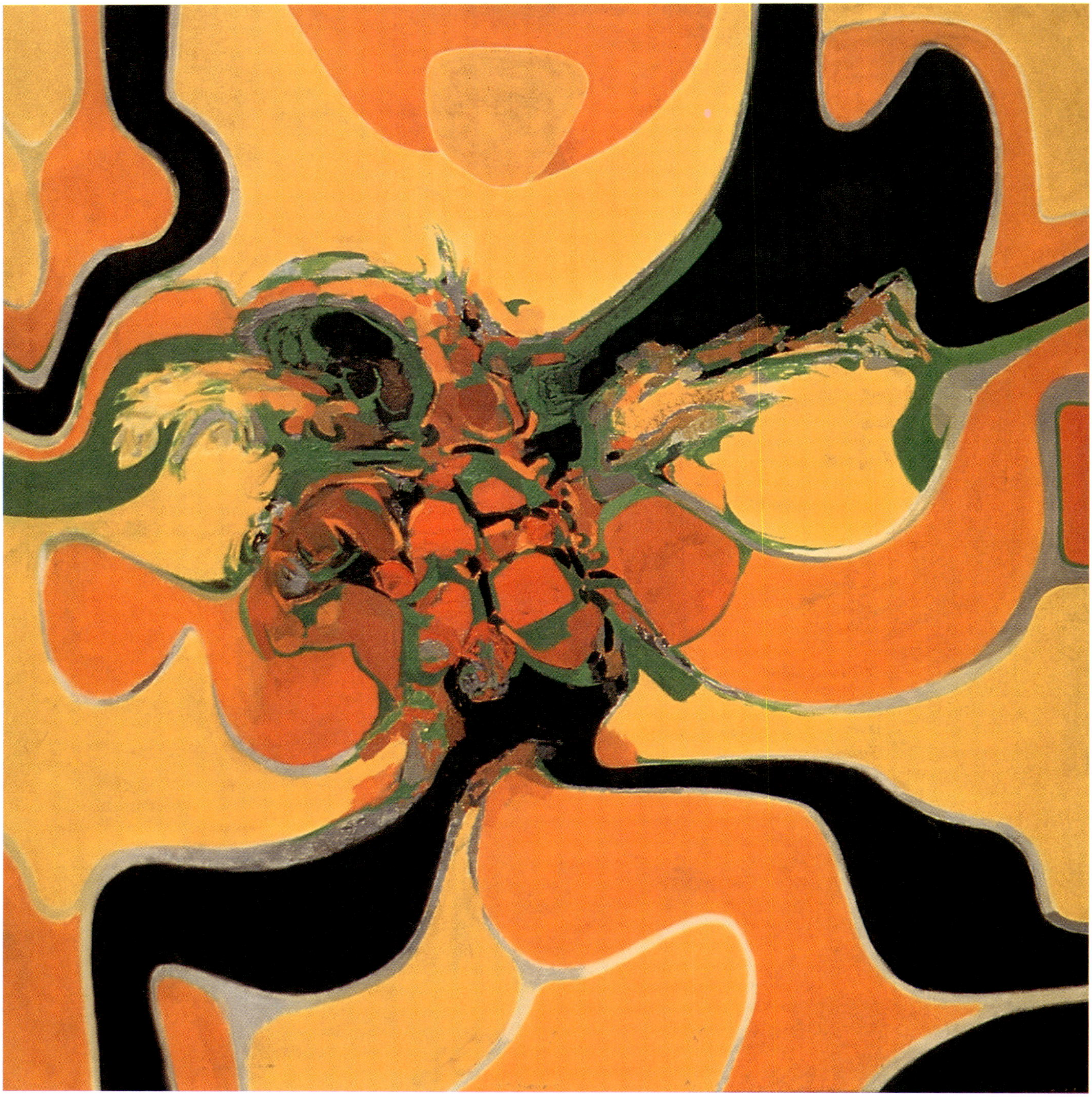

XXXVII: *Enigmatic Blossom*
1967, oil on canvas, 60 x 60
[The Artist's Estate]

XXXVIII: *Entrance to a Barn*
1967, oil on canvas, 28 x 36
[Percy Thomas Partnership]

XXXIX: *Fernhill III: And the sun grew round that very day*
1977, oil on canvas, 36 x 48
[University of Wales, Cardiff]

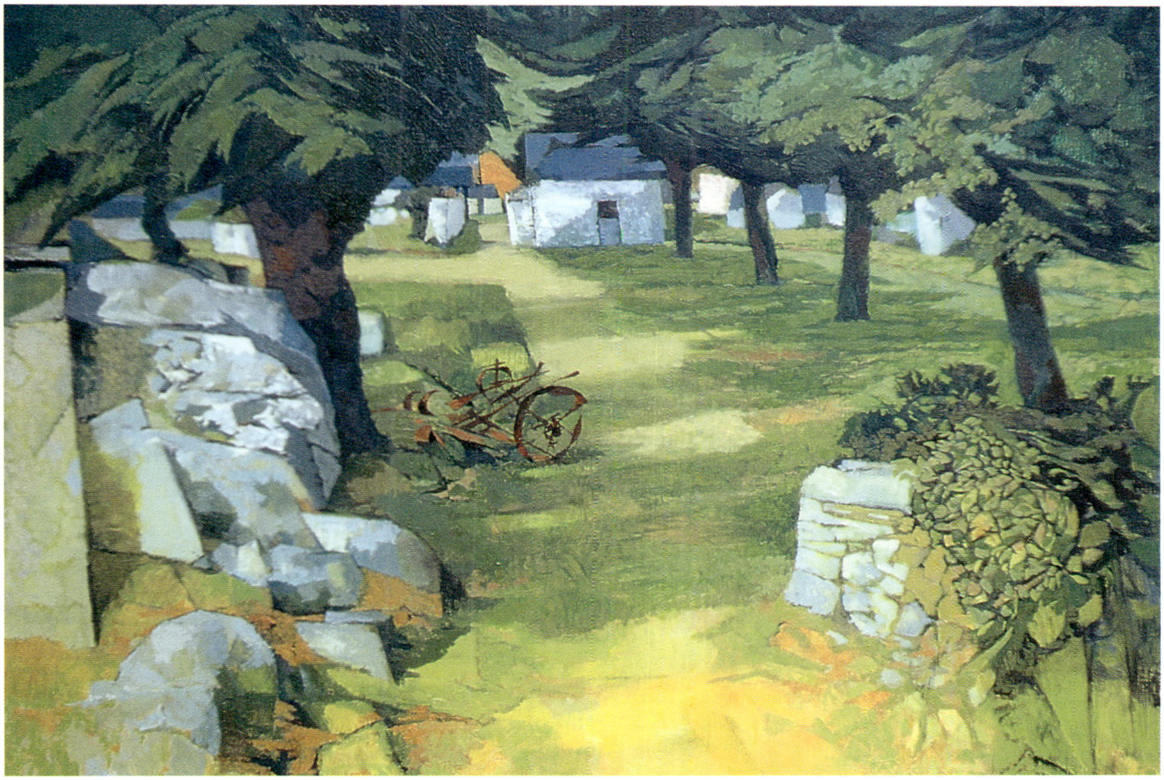

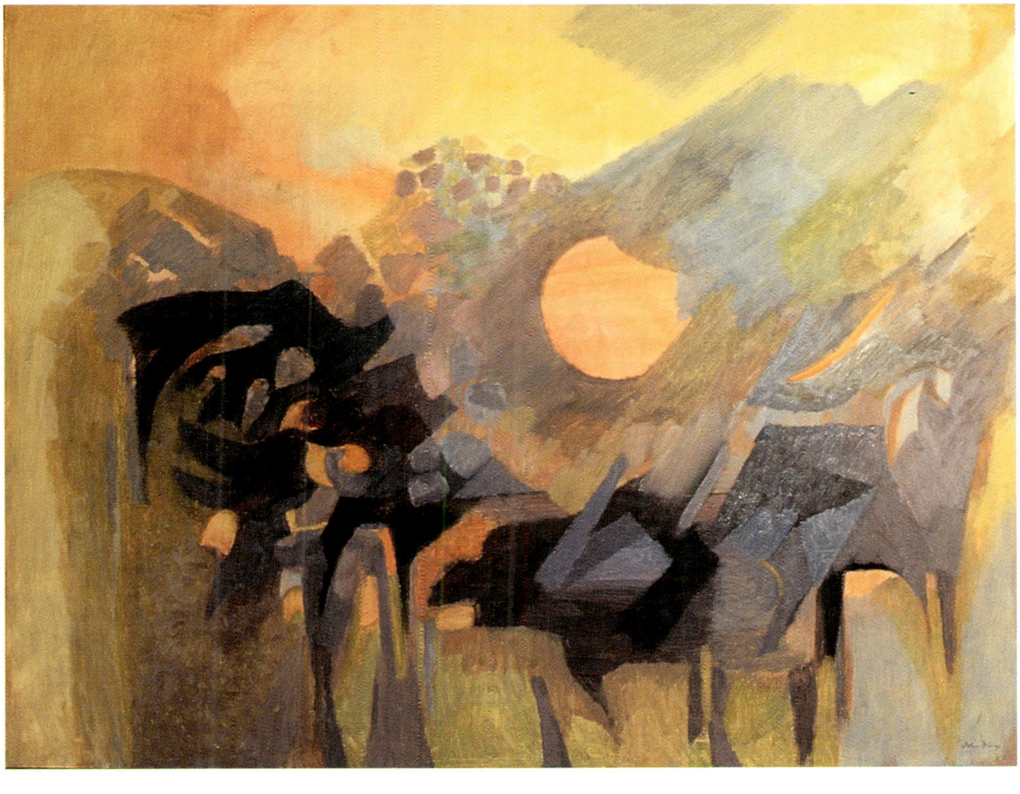

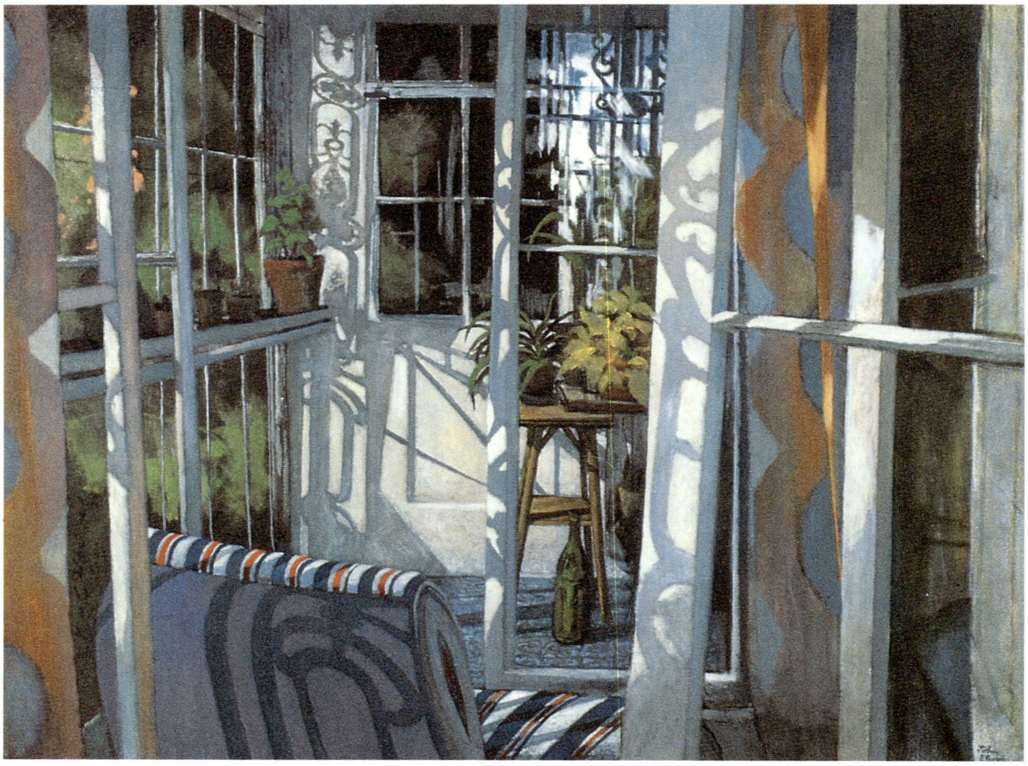

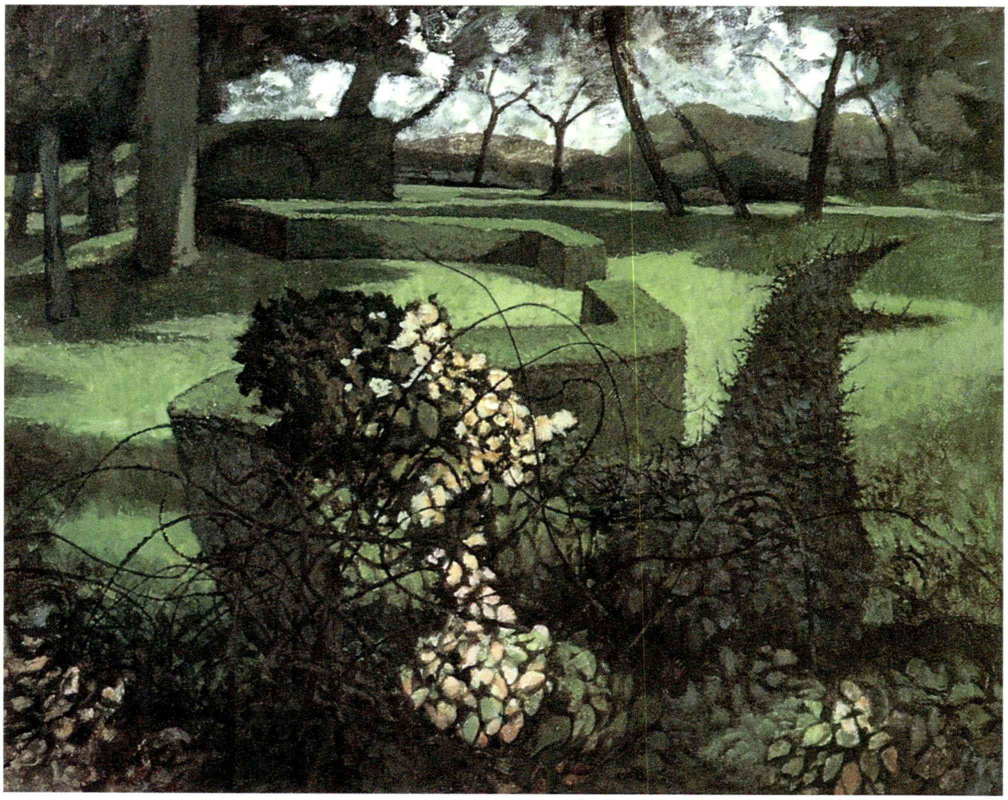

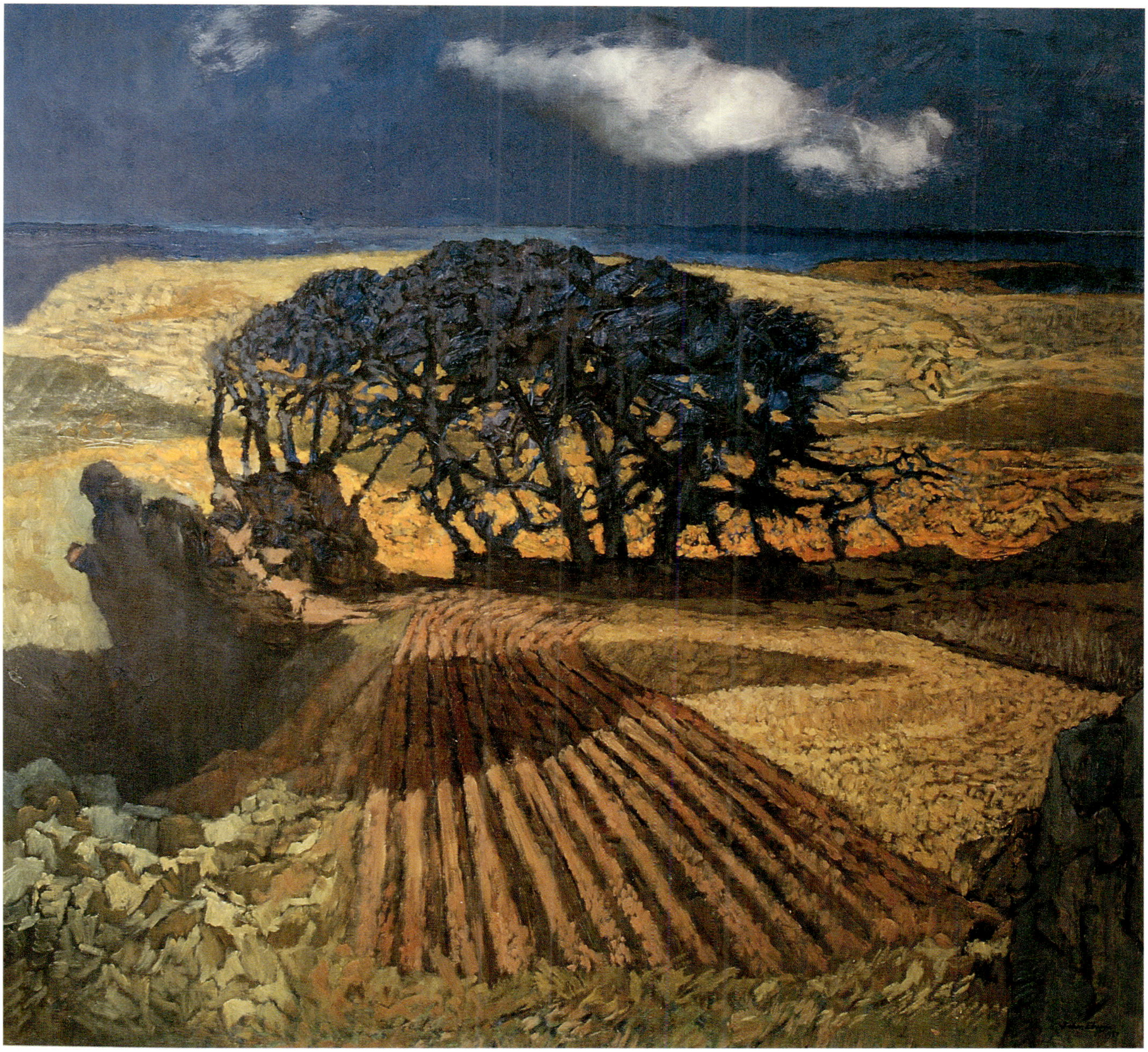

XLII: *On the Dyfed Coast*
1987, oil on canvas, 36 x 40
[Dr and Mrs David Shedden]

XL: *The Enclosed Balcony*
1980, oil on canvas, 28 x 36
[Miss G. Cemlyn Jones]

XLI: *Paddock Bird*
1985, acrylic on paper, 21 x 29
[Donald Moore]

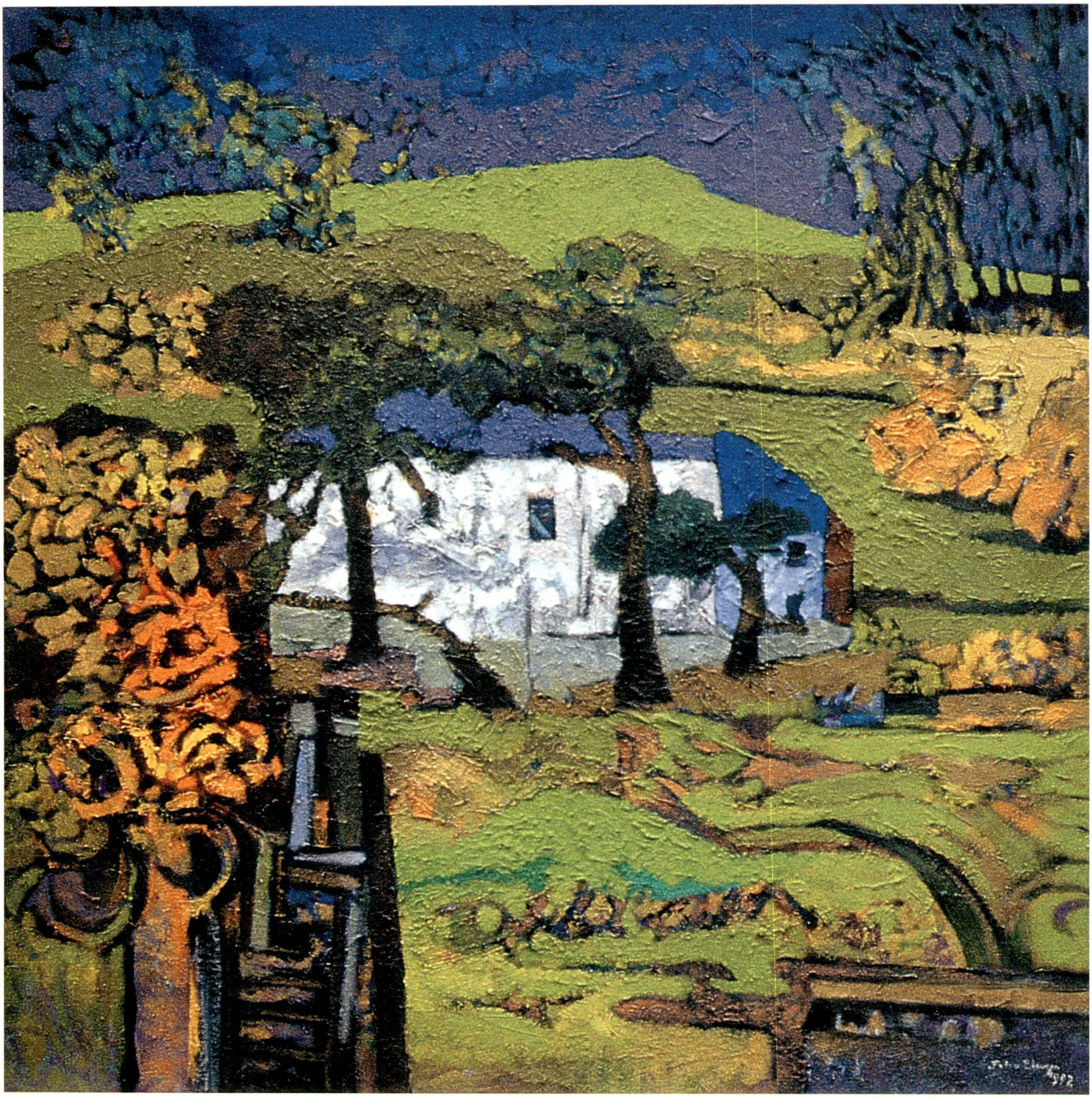

XLIII: *Upland Farm*
1992, oil on canvas, 30 x 30
[The Artist's Estate]

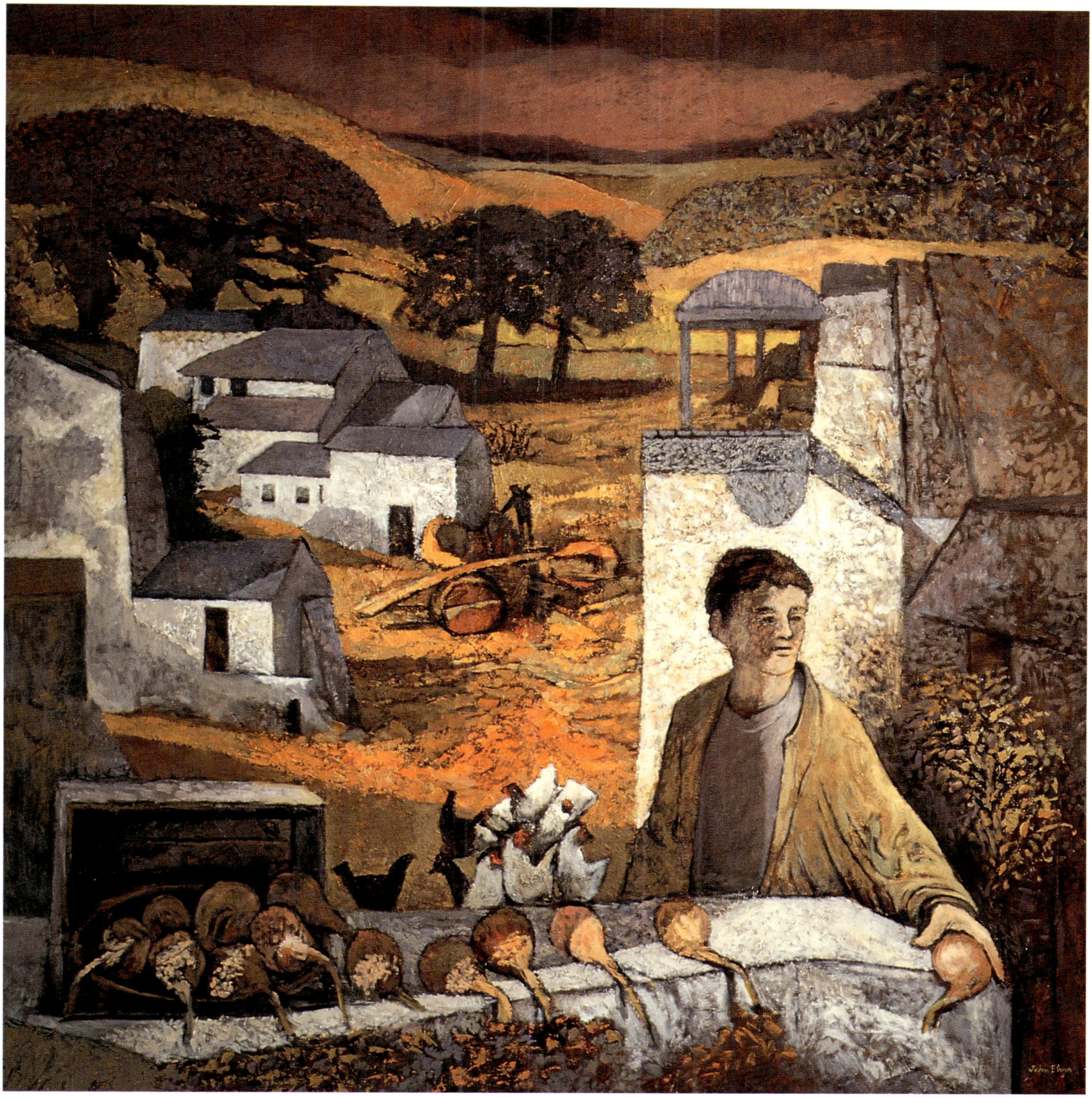

XLIV: *September*
1996, oil on canvas, 48 x 48
[Dr and Mrs Huw Bevan Jones]

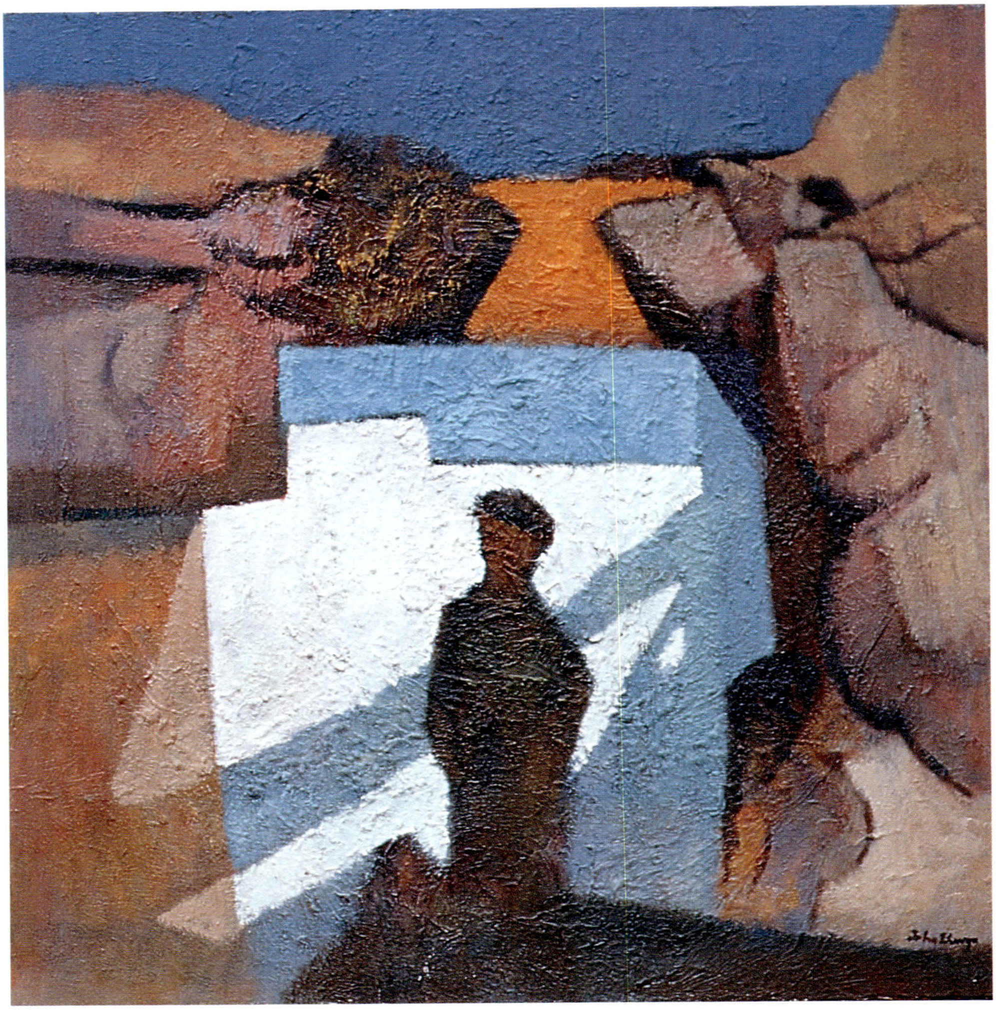

XLV: *The Lonely Servant*
1980–97, oil on canvas, 20 x 20
[The Artist's Estate]

by ex-patriots who have bought them for their perceived Welshness. (Appendix 2) John Elwyn was intensely proud of his origins in west Wales and the paintings are a tribute to his undiminished enthusiasm and nostalgia for his home land. He invariably drew upon his memories of a happy childhood and it is doubtful that he could have sustained the intensity of his conviction had he remained in Wales. The paintings are unashamedly nostalgic, escapist, insular and anti-progressive – that has been their appeal. They have been described as 'illustrative' in the pejorative sense, but such a term also serves to ally his work to the greater part of the European tradition in art. John Elwyn was the first to admit that it was not in his nature to be an innovator. He held great store by the writings of other artists; he quoted Matisse, Delacroix and Kandinsky, and would often site their observations, especially when these artists so eloquently reinforced his own beliefs. He would quote the philosophy of Renoir, that one should be buoyant and adaptable like a cork on the ocean. Rouault's attitude towards creativity was especially pertinent, as is evident in the following extract which John Elwyn read aloud whilst opening an exhibition in Petersfield:

> I am a believer and a conformist. Anyone can revolt, it is more difficult to obey our interior promptings and to spend our lives finding sincere and fitting means of expression for our temperaments and our gifts – is it not better to be a Chardin or even much less, than a pale unhappy reflection of the Great Florentines.[121]

It is fortunate that John Elwyn had faith in his convictions and remained true to these ideals. He may have painted landscapes of the mind, but they have a place in reality – based as they are on real places and real situations. The paintings are about his own experiences and as such they are imprinted with his personality and reverence. He wrote:

> recollections of this kind would enable me to keep working away because that is what the artistic bug makes you feel. You can't stop even if you are not painting. One is always dwelling in that area of visualising everything on canvas or paper. This is not inspiration as I understand the term, but is on the way towards it because it is very rare that it can happen as an isolated occurrence, but only by sustained effort and attention to hard work ... It is impossible to predict the result. It has to be experienced or lived through and projected before it manifests itself, whether in sound, colour or words.[122]

Notes

Chapter 1

1 John Elwyn: unpublished autobiographical notes. 'Shilgot' is a tiny fish commonly known as a minnow. John Elwyn could not swim, but never fell in the river. Other parents in the village thought he was a very 'sensible' companion for their children.

2 David Davies (born Pencarniced, Llandysul 7th June 1871, died Adpar 21st April 1947, aged 75), the oldest of six children of Thomas Davies, a cooper known locally as 'Tomos Top', and his wife Sarah (née Davies). Anne Lewis (born Newcastle Emlyn 6th November 1872, died 26th September 1942, aged 70) youngest of six children to David Lewis and his wife Hannah Bowen of Craigyrhuad in the Ceri Valley.

3 David Thomas Davies (born 28th May 1904, died 1st June 1904, aged 3 days). Sally Anne Davies, known as 'Sis' (born 27th April 1905, died July 1991, aged 86), married 8th April 1939 at Ebenezer Chapel, Newcastle Emlyn to David John Jones (born 17th July 1898, died 13th October 1972, aged 74), a farmer and manager of Ceri Mill, Cwmcoi. Hannah Mary Davies (born 27th May 1908, died 25th April 1982, aged 72). Katie Tegwen Davies (born 13th May 1911, died October 1960, aged 49). Sally was always addressed 'chi' (thee/thou, formal) and not 'ti' (thee/thou, familiar) by the younger children.

4 Joyce Eaborn: letter to the author, 6 September 1998. As a child, Joyce Thomas lived in the nearby Cilgwyn Lodge. She was told the circumstances surrounding John Elwyn's birth by her twin uncles Cecil and Cyril Thomas. They had accompanied their mother when called to the mill to act as midwife to Anne Davies, since the doctor was out on his rounds in the remote farmsteads. She was untrained but had borne several healthy children herself.

5 John Elwyn: letter to the author, 7th October 1997.

6 In the National Library of Wales, Aberystwyth. The single volume that is the *Emlyn Factory Account Book* spans nearly the first four decades of the twentieth century. It records transactions of merchandise such as wool, stocking yarn, blankets, grey flannel, shirts, drovers' shirting; all local clients and those as far afield as Dowlais, Pontypridd, Ebbw Vale and Treorchy; merchantile customers in Kidderminster and Rochdale; dates on which the bull had the cows each year; drills of potatoes put aside in exchange for merchandise; wages for workers at the mill; and recipes for rhubarb wine and marmalade, as well as home-made tinctures for neuralgia, cough and codle pick-up.

7 These have now been deposited at the National Library of Wales, Aberystwyth. I am extremely indebted to Ainsleigh Davies who translated the original manuscripts (all undated) into English.

8 John Elwyn: letter to the author, 7th October 1997.

9 John Elwyn: letter to the author, 7th October 1997.

10 As the new barrel of lubricating oil was rolled into the mill the old one was recycled. In an open space by the mill his father put 'saithlan' (seven wools) into the barrel and set it alight, rolling the wooden barrel on its side, to burn away remnants of the oil. The cleaned barrel was used for animal grain, over-wintering the potatoes, or cut in half to make tubs in which the wools could be dyed.

11 J. Geraint Jenkins *Dre-fach Velindre and the Woollen Industry* Gomer Press, Llandysul 1976.

12 As a school boy he had lodged in Carmarthen for a time due to the poor transport in the area.

13 J. O. Francis: R.N.E.W. Exhibition Catalogue, Tenby 1936.

14 Cyril Cox: catalogue for 'Exhibition of Contemporary Welsh Art', 1935.

15 In 1938 the fees per session (3 terms) was £32 and it was estimated that students required a minimum subsistence of £80 per annum to cover board and lodgings.

16 Sidney Morse-Brown: letter to John Elwyn, 18th July 1938. [NLW]

17 Anne Davies: telegram to John Elwyn, 5th July 1938. [NLW]

18 Denis William Reed (1917–1979) joined the West of England College of Art in 1934 on a four year course in Drawing & Pictorial Design. The career of this Bristol-born painter of still-life and local landscape was hampered by recurrent ill health. He exhibited rarely, at the R.A., R.B.A., N.E.A.C., and the Royal West of England Academy of which he was a full member. He died suddenly on 23rd February 1979. Richard MacDonald (1919–1993) was born in Yeovil, Somerset. He taught at Camberwell School of Art 1951–55 and from 1954 worked in films. Eventually, he moved to Los Angeles where he was an Art Director and Production Designer in Hollywood. His last film was *The Firm* starring Tom Cruise.

19 Denis Reed: letter to John Elwyn, 4th September 1938. Fifteen letters from Denis Reed to John Elwyn, written between 4th September 1938 and 15th June 1957, are preserved at the National Library of Wales, Aberystwyth.

20 Denis Reed: letter to John Elwyn, 13th September 1938. [NLW]

Chapter 2

21 Denis Reed: letter to John Elwyn, 13th September 1938. [NLW] Once a month a public criticism of students' work was held at the College.

22 John Elwyn: April 1939. Catalogue number 20 was *Dans le Parc du Chateau Noir* (1900).

23 Joyce Eaborn (née Thomas): letter to the author, 6th September 1998.

24 John Elwyn: lecture notes, undated, Cardiff circa 1944.

25 John Elwyn: lecture notes, undated, Cardiff circa 1944.

26 David Davies: undated manuscript. [NLW]

27 Richard MacDonald: undated letter to John Elwyn, 1940. [NLW]

28 Reed went on to do general farm work in Wiltshire, was head porter at the Royal Hotel in Weston-Super-Mare, did a two week stint as fire-watcher, and was a farm hand at Stratford-upon-Avon before he eventually signed up.
29 John Elwyn: interview with Rhian Evans, 'Artist still inspired by hiraeth 50 years on', *Western Mail* July 1996.
30 Denis Reed: letter to John Elwyn, 24th November 1940. [NLW]
31 E. M. Bush moved from Cardiff in November 1943 to the Stone Bower Fellowship, Burton-in-Lonsdale near Carnforth in Lancashire where she died on 4th January 1945, aged 72 years.
32 Denis Reed: letter to John Elwyn, 4th November 1941. [NLW]
33 Denis Reed: letter to John Elwyn, 4th November 1941. [NLW]
34 Denis Reed: letter to John Elwyn, 29th November 1941. [NLW]
35 In addition to books of poetry Glyn Jones wrote several volumes of short stories and novels, notably *The Blue Bed* (Jonathan Cape, 1937), *The Water Music* (Routledge, 1944), *The Valley, The City, The Village* (J. M. Dent, 1956), *The Learning Lark* (J. M. Dent, 1960) and *The Dragon Has Two Tongues* (J. M. Dent, 1968).
36 Very early works are signed 'Elwyn Davies', some dating from the 1940s are initialled 'J.E.D.', but all works after about 1950 were signed 'John Elwyn' or initialled 'J.E.'.
37 John Elwyn: letter to Winifred Coombe-Tennant, 8th March 1948.
38 John Elwyn: notes towards an exhibition in a letter to the author, 1994.
39 John Elwyn: undated autobiographical notes.
40 John Elwyn: letter the author, 7th October 1997.
41 John Elwyn: interview with the author, 15th March 1997.
42 John Elwyn: letter to the author, 24th January 1997.
43 John Elwyn: interview with the author, 15th March 1997.
44 Vera Adie: letter to the author, 15th August 1998.
45 John Ward: letter to the author, 9th August 1998.
46 Rodney J. Burns, a part-time member of staff in the Painting School, awarded John Elwyn a prize of two guineas for a landscape painting of Adpar.
47 Gilbert Spencer, Professor of Painting, Royal College of Art (1930–1948), testimonial for John Elwyn, 21st July 1947. [NLW]
48 Percy Hague Jowett, Principal, Royal College of Art (1935–1947), testimonial for John Elwyn, 7th July 1947. [NLW]
49 Charles Cyril Mahoney RA, Tutor, Painting School, Royal College of Art (1928–1953), 17th July 1947. [NLW]
50 Percy Horton, Senior Assistant, Painting School, Royal College of Art (1930–1949), 14th July 1947. [NLW]

Chapter3

51 Ceri Richards: letter to John Elwyn, 24th July 1947. [NLW]
52 Ceri Richards had written to him suggesting he exhibit and that he knew the Director, Arthur Howell, and would mention him. On 6th September 1947 Richards wrote a second letter urging John Elwyn to contact Arthur Howell who had asked him to see some work for the exhibition of Welsh painters.
53 Morland Lewis: postcard to John Elwyn, 16th October 1939. [NLW]
54 As well as her contribution to the visual arts in Wales, Winifred Coombe-Tennant was also known as a 'communicator' of messages to this world from the dead. George Routledge Ltd published her book under the assumed name Mrs Willett, transmitted by Geraldine Cummins and edited by Signe Toksvig, *Swan on a Black Sea: A Study in Automatic Writing: The Cummins-Willett Scripts.*
55 Winifred Coombe-Tennant: letter to John Elwyn, 25th February 1948. [NLW]
56 Winifred Coombe-Tennant: letter to John Elwyn, 19th February 1948. [NLW] Evan Walters had received an almost identical letter – and subsequent friendship, encouragement and introductions – following her purchase of a small oil painting from his one-man exhibition at the Glynn Vivian Art Gallery in Swansea in 1920.
58 Winifred Coombe-Tennant: letter to John Elwyn, 25th February 1948. [NLW]
59 Anthony Eyton RA (b. 1923), studied at Camberwell, taught at Portsmouth from 1951. From 1955 he taught at Camberwell.
60 Anthony Eyton: letter to the author, 22nd June 1998.
61 Vivian Pare: letter to the author, 29th January 1999.
62 John Elwyn: Imprisoned Splendour: *A Study of Creative Inspiration* compiled by Jack H.Wallis, privately printed, Winchester, January 1994 p.36.
63 John Elwyn: notes towards an exhibition in a letter to the author, 1994.
64 John Elwyn: unpublished autobiographical notes, undated.
64 Glyn Jones 'An Afternoon at Uncle Shad's' first published in *The Welsh Review*, Vol.1, No.1 February 1939 pp.8–15. Later re-issued as 'An Afternoon at Ewa Shad's' in *The Water Music* (Routledge, 1944). This extract, and a little more from 'An Afternoon at Uncle Shad's' was read by John Elwyn's widow at his funeral service.
65 John Elwyn: *Imprisoned Splendour: A Study of Creative Inspiration* compiled by Jack H.Wallis, privately printed, Winchester, January 1994 p.36.
66 John Elwyn: *Imprisoned Splendour: A Study of Creative Inspiration* compiled by Jack H.Wallis, privately printed, Winchester, January 1994 p.35.
67 John Elwyn: notes towards an exhibition in a letter to the author, 1994.
68 Winifred Coombe-Tennant: letter to John Elwyn, 11th August 1948. [NLW]
69 Winifred Coombe-Tennant: letter to John Elwyn, 1st July 1948. [NLW]
70 J. T. Morgan: undated letter to Winifred Coombe-Tennant, summer 1949.
71 John Elwyn: letter to Winifred Coombe-Tennant, 27th August 1950.
72 John Ormond: letter to John Elwyn, 4th March 1987. [NLW]
73 John Elwyn: letter to Winifred Coombe-Tennant, 4th April 1950.
74 John Elwyn: notes towards an exhibition in a letter to the author, 1994.
75 John Elwyn: letter to Winifred Coombe-Tennant, 9th July 1951.

Chapter 4

76 The Arts Council was set up by the Labour government in 1945 to develop and encourage state patronage for the arts. It replaced C.E.M.A., the Council for the Encouragement of Music and the Arts, which had been established in Britain in 1940 by the Pilgrim Trust, an American foundation.
77 See Peter Lord *Gwenllian: Essays on Visual Culture* Gomer Press, Llandysul, 1994, and *The Visual Culture of Wales: Industrial Society* from his series of three volumes for The University of Wales Centre for Advanced Welsh and Celtic Studies, University of Wales Press, Cardiff 1998.
78 Gwyn Jones: *The Welsh Review*, Vol. VI, No. 2, Summer 1947.
79 David Bell: Festival Exhibition Catalogue, 1951.
80 David Bell: Festival Exhibition Catalogue, 1951.
81 Winifred Coombe-Tennant: letter to John Elwyn, 10th August 1951. [NLW]
82 John Elwyn: letter to Glyn Jones, 26th March 1950. [NLW]
83 David Bell: S.E.A. Exhibition Catalogue, 1951.
84 John Petts: Arts Council Catalogue, 1952.
85 John Petts: National Library of Wales Exhibition Catalogue, 1952.
86 John Petts: letter to John Elwyn, 11th April 1953. [NLW]
87 David Bell, John Piper and Carel Weight: Arts Council Catalogue, 1953.
88 In England, a parallel debate ensued amongst those who endeavoured to establish an English National style, in a country where 'English painters almost without exception ... work today so much in the light of French achievements ... that they are practising virtually a French art'. Lawrence Gowing: 'French Painters and English', *Penguin New Writing* No. 29, 1947 p. 148. This debate, one that is common to small insecure minorities, had persisted since the eighteenth century.
89 The Gold Medal for Fine Art today is awarded to an invited exhibitor in recognition of the achievements of and contribution made to fine art.
90 John Elwyn: letter to Glyn Jones, 26th March 1950. [NLW]
91 Rollo Charles: unmarked obituary amongst John Elwyn's papers.
92 Christopher Sandford: letters to John Elwyn, 13th and 17th October 1953. [NLW]
93 Winifred Coombe-Tennant: letter to John Elwyn, 19th August 1950. [NLW]
94 On 21st September 1955 she wrote, 'I am very old, very tired, and longing to change my world'. She died, aged 81, in 1956 and was described in an unmarked obituary amongst John Elwyn's papers as 'a pioneer woman magistrate and prison reformer, who stood for parliament and had been the first British woman delegate at the League of Nations Assembly. She was a keen Welsh nationalist, a collector and patron of painting, extremely aware of her civic duties and social position'. [NLW]
95 David Bell: 'John Elwyn', *Anglo-Welsh Review* Vol. 9 No. 23, 1958, pp.48–49.
96 John Elwyn: 'Four Works with Notes', *Anglo-Welsh Review* Vol. 9, No. 23, 1958, p. 43.
97 John Elwyn: statement for National Library of Wales exhibition catalogue, 1976.
98 Kenneth Rowntree: letter to John Elwyn, 8th October 1959. [NLW]
99 Robin Golding: letter to John Elwyn, 18th December 1959. [NLW]
100 Robin Golding: letter to John Elwyn, 25th January 1960. [NLW]
101 This involved a visit to the museum in the Department of Geology at Oxford University to draw the bones of the 'Red Lady of Paviland' (actually the bones of a young huntsman of the Old Stone Age).
102 Richard Lloyd Jones: letter to John Elwyn, 14th June 1962. [NLW]

Chapter 5

103 David Bell: 'John Elwyn', *Anglo-Welsh Review* Vol. 9, No. 23, 1958, p. 49.
104 John Elwyn: notes towards an exhibition in a letter to the author, 1994.
105 John Elwyn: notes for a television documentary, 1967.
106 Frank Whitford: *Art News*, London, 5th February 1965.
107 William Gaunt: *The Times*, London, 15th February 1965.
108 John Elwyn: interview with the author, 5th November 1995.
109 Andrew Watchorn: letter to the author, 26th August 1998. A student at Winchester from 1972–1975.
110 John Elwyn: undated lecture amongst the artist's papers.
111 There are over 100 life drawings by John Elwyn at the University of Wales, Aberystwyth. They provide the unique opportunity to observe his development and maturity throughout his professional career as an artist – as a student at Carmarthen and the Royal College of Art, and as a practising artist and instructor in the life classes at Portsmouth and Winchester Schools of Art.

Chapter 6

112 Mary lived with them until their brother-in-law David John died in October 1972. The Ceri Mill was sold in May 1973 and Mary moved back to Wales to live with her widowed sister Sally.
113 John Elwyn: letter to the author, quoting Paul Hills in *Artists of Promise and Renown*, University of Warwick (1986), 24th January 1995.
114 John Elwyn: *The Artist and Today's Public*, translated into English from Welsh notes for a lecture written circa 1980.
115 John Elwyn: notes for a television documentary, 1967. [NLW]
116 Nicolas McDowall: letter to John Elwyn, 1st March 1993. [NLW]
117 John Ormond: letter to John Elwyn, 21st November 1986
118 John Elwyn: letter to Glyn Jones, 15th December 1989. [NLW]
119 John Elwyn: 'Four Works with Notes', *Anglo-Welsh Review* Vol. 9 No. 23, 1958, p. 44.
120 John Piper: *British Romantic Artists*, William Collins, London 1942, p. 7.
121 Georges Roualt: quoted in a speach prepared by John Elwyn for the opening of the Petersfield Exhibition, 19th May 1964.
122 John Elwyn: *Imprisoned Splendour: A Study of Creative Inspiration* compiled by Jack H.Wallis, privately printed, Winchester, January 1994, p. 36.

Appendixes

I: Exhibitions

Compiled from John Elwyn's exhibition record book and supplemented by exhibition catalogues. Number in brackets refers to the total number of works exhibited with the institution during that year. In some cases the number indicates paintings deposited with regular dealers for 'stock' or inclusion in mixed shows.

ABBREVIATIONS

*	One and two person shows
ACW	The Arts Council of Wales
CASW	Contemporary Art Society for Wales
GVAGS	Glynn Vivian Art Gallery, Swansea
NM&AG	Newport Museum and Art Gallery
NLW	National Library of Wales, Aberystwyth
NMW	National Museum and Gallery of Wales, Cardiff
RI	Royal Institute of Painters in Watercolour Annual Exhibition
SEA	Society for Education through Art: 'Pictures for Welsh Schools'

1937–1938
West of England Academy, Bristol 'Portrait Drawings'

1942
National Eisteddfod of Wales, Cardigan

1944
National Eisteddfod of Wales, Llandybie [2]

1945
Cardiff NMW 'Paintings by Contemporary Artists' [2]
Welsh Federation of Music and Arts Societies, touring [1]

1946
Foyles Art Gallery, London 'South Wales Art Society' [1]

1947
Mansard Gallery, Heals, London 'Contemporary Welsh Painting'
Royal College of Art, London 'Diploma Exhibition'
Royal Academy of Art, London 'RCA Students' (also shown in Paris)

1948
New English Art Club, London [2]
Portsmouth Public Library 'Portsmouth Art School Staff' [4]
Royal Academy of Art, London 'Former RCA Students' [1]

1949
Royal Academy of Art, London 'Summer Exhibition' [2]
Paul Alexander Gallery, Notting Hill, London (with Jack Wright) [24] *
Southampton Art Gallery 'Hampshire Art Society' [2]
New English Art Club, London [1]

1950
National Eisteddfod of Wales, Caerphilly [3]
Leicester Galleries, London 'Artists of Fame and Promise' [2]
Bradford City Art Gallery 'Annual Spring Exhibition' [2]
Bladon Gallery, Hurstbourne Tarrant [2]
ACW/Cardiff NMW 'CASW: Recent Purchases' [1]

1951
National Eisteddfod of Wales, Llanrwst [3]
Royal Academy of Art, London 'Summer Exhibition' [1]
Mansard Gallery, Heals, London 'The Portsmouth Group' [4]
Paul Alexander Gallery, Notting Hill Gate, London [2]
Southampton Art Gallery 'Wessex Artists' [3]
Leicester Galleries, London 'Artists of Fame and Promise' [3]
ACW/NMW Cardiff 'Contemporary Welsh Painting' (Swansea GVAG) [1]
Bladon Gallery, Hurstbourne Tarrant [2]
Cumberland House Museum and Art Gallery, Southsea [2]
Cosham Art Group, Portsmouth [1]
Cardiff NMW 'SEA' [2]
'South Wales Group' (Newport M&AG, Swansea GVAG) [3]
Hereford Art Gallery
North Wales Group

1952
Royal Academy of Art, London 'Summer Exhibition' [1]
National Eisteddfod of Wales, Aberystwyth [2]
Leicester Galleries, London 'Artists of Fame and Promise' [2]
Bradford City Art Gallery 'Annual Spring Exhibition' [2]
Cardiff NMW 'SEA' (Newport M&AG, Swansea GVAG) [3]
ACW/Cardiff NMW 'Thirty Welsh Paintings of Today' (touring) [2]
St Anne's College, Oxford [2]
ACW/Aberystwyth NLW 'The Artist in Wales: contemporary painting' [3]
Bladon Gallery, Hurstbourne Tarrant [2]
South Wales Group (Newport M&AG)

1953
Leicester Galleries, London 'Artists of Fame and Promise' [2]
Bradford City Art Gallery 'Annual Spring Exhibition' [1]
Bladon Gallery, Hurstbourne Tarrant [2]
Swansea GVAG 'British Romantic Painting in the 20th Century' (Cardiff NMW, Aberystwyth NLW) [1]
Cardiff NMW 'SEA' (Newport M&AG, Bangor UCNW, Wrexham PL) [1]
Cardiff NMW 'Coronation Exhibition' (Swansea GVAG) [2]
Portsmouth Art Gallery 'Hampshire Art Society' [1]
Winchester College [7]
Football Association 'Football and the Fine Arts' London, Glasgow, &c. [1]
North Wales Group '1st Annual Exhibition' (Bangor UCNW, Rhyl, Chester and Wrexham PL) [2]
Winchester Art Club [1]
South Wales Group (Cardiff NMW, Swansea GVAG, Newport M&AG) [3]

1954
National Eisteddfod of Wales, Ystradgynlais [2]
Leicester Galleries, London 'Artists of Fame and Promise' [2]
Cardiff NMW 'SEA' [2]

Bladon Gallery, Hurstbourne Tarrant [3]
Winchester College
North Wales Group (Bangor, Wrexham and Colwyn Bay) [3]
South Wales Group (Cardiff, Swansea and Newport) [1]
Arts Council Gallery, London 'Thirty Welsh Paintings of Today' [2]

1955
Cardiff NMW 'SEA' (Swansea GVAG, Wrexham PL) [3]
Leicester Galleries, London 'Artists of Fame and Promise' [2]
North Wales Group
South Wales Group (Cardiff, Swansea and Newport) [1]
Bladon Gallery, Hurstbourne Tarrant [2]

1956
National Eisteddfod of Wales, Aberdare [1]
Cardiff NMW 'SEA' (Swansea GVAG, Wrexham PL, Flintshire College, Connah's Quay) [2]
South Wales Group (Cardiff NMW and Swansea GVAG) [2]
Bladon Gallery, Hurstbourne Tarrant [2]
ACW/Cardiff NMW 'CASW: Recent Purchases' [1]
ACW/Cardiff NMW 'Contemporary Welsh Painting and Sculpture' [3]
AIA Galleries, London and Portmeirion, Gwynedd [2]
Howard Roberts Gallery, Cardiff [3]
Cardiff NMW 'Members Choice: lent by CASW members' (Bangor UCNW, Swansea GVAG) [2]

1957
Royal Academy of Art, London 'Summer Exhibition' [2]
Art Exhibitions Bureau, Glasgow and the provinces [2]
Southampton Art Gallery
North Wales Group [1]
South Wales Group [1]
Howard Roberts Gallery, Cardiff 'Wales through the Painter's Eye' [4]
Bladon Gallery, Hurstbourne Tarrant [2]
Leicester Galleries, London 'Artists of Fame and Promise' [2]

1958
Southampton Art Gallery
Leicester Galleries, London 'Artists of Fame and Promise' [2]
National Museum of Wales, Cardiff, SEA [1]
Royal Academy of Art, Summer Show [2]
Glasgow Institute of Fine Art [1]
Howard Roberts Gallery, Cardiff 'Contemporary Welsh Painting' [2]
Swansea GVAG 'Welsh Painting and Drawing' [3]
Tyrrell and Green, Southampton 'Painting Now' [1]

1959
Leicester Galleries, London 'Artists of Fame and Promise' [2]
Bradford City Art Gallery 'Annual Spring Exhibition' [2]
Aberystwyth NLW (with Vera Bassett, Mildred Eldridge, Leslie Moore, Powys Evans and John Petts) [12]
Howard Roberts Gallery, Cardiff [6]
New Art Centre, London [1]
Bladon Gallery, Hurstbourne Tarrant [1]

1960
Southampton Art Gallery [1]
Leicester Galleries, London 'Artists of Fame and Promise' [5]
Bradford City Art Gallery 'Annual Spring Exhibition' [1]
Bladon Gallery, Hurstbourne Tarrant [1]
National Museum of Wales, Cardiff, SEA [1]
Howard Roberts Gallery, Cardiff 'Autumn Exhibition' [8]

1961
Hereford Art Gallery 'Modern Welsh Painters' [3]
Hampshire Pictures for Schools [3]
Leicester Galleries, London 'South Wales Group' [2]
National Museum of Wales, Cardiff, SEA [2]
Howard Roberts Gallery Cardiff 'Aspects of Wales' [10]
Cumberland House Museum and Art Gallery, Southsea 'Four Hampshire Painters' (Civic Centre, Southampton and School of Art, Salisbury) [10]

1962
Leicester Galleries, London 'Artists of Fame and Promise' [2]
Bradford City Art Gallery 'Annual Spring Exhibition' [1]
ACW/Cardiff NMW 'Welsh Painting and Sculpture' (Swansea GVAG, Aberystwyth NLW, Wrexham PL, Bangor UCNW) [3]
Howard Roberts Gallery, Cardiff 'Autumn Exhibition' [2]
Dillwyn Gallery, Swansea [3]

1963
Leicester Galleries, London 'Gallery Group Exhibition' [2]
Bradford City Art Gallery 'Annual Spring Exhibition' [1]
Bladon Gallery, Hurstbourne Tarrant [1]
Cardiff NMW, SEA [2]
Cardiff NMW 'Contemporary Art Society for Wales' [1]
Howard Roberts Gallery, Cardiff [4]
Dillwyn Gallery, Swansea
Clare College, Cambridge 'Painting and Sculpture from Wales' (Staffordshire University and Burslem Art School, Stoke-on-Trent) [2]
Keele University

1964
National Museum of Wales, Cardiff, SEA [2]
Winchester College 'Winchester Art Club' [6]
Bradford City Art Gallery 'Annual Spring Exhibition' [1]
Leicester Galleries, London 'Annual Spring Exhibition' [1]
Howard Roberts Gallery, Cardiff [1]

1965
Bradford City Art Gallery 'Annual Spring Exhibition' [1]
Leicester Galleries, London 'Gallery Group Exhibition' [1]
Royal Cambrian Academy 'Centenary Exhibition 1865ñ1965' [1]
Leicester Galleries, Cork Street, London [33] *
Howard Roberts Gallery, Cardiff 'The Young and The Established' [1]
Howard Roberts Gallery, Cardiff [45] *
Caiman Museum, Patagonia '100 Years of the Province of Chebut' [1]
Jefferson Place Gallery, Washington DC [3]

1966
National Eisteddfod of Wales, Aberafan [2]
Queen's Square Gallery, Leeds 'Five Artists from Wales' [6]
Bradford City Art Gallery 'Annual Spring Exhibition' [1]
Bladon Gallery, Hurstbourne Tarrant [2]
Manchester City Art Gallery 'Football: exhibition for the World Cup' [1]
Leicester Galleries, London 'Gallery Group Exhibition' [2]
Ash Barn Gallery, Petersfield [2]

1967
Leicester Galleries, London 'Gallery Group Exhibition' [2]
Salisbury Arts Festival [1]
Breton Gallery, Sloane Street, London [3]
Romsey Art Club [1]
National Eisteddfod of Wales, Bala 'Gold Medal Winners' (Beaumaris and Barry) [3]
Atlantic College, St Donat's, Glamorgan [2]

1968
National Museum of Wales, Cardiff, SEA [1]
Leicester Galleries, Cork Street, London [20] *
Ash Barn Gallery, Petersfield [2]
Bladon Gallery, Hurstbourne Tarrant [3]

1969
ACW 'Art in Wales: the 20th Century, the early years 1900ñ1956' (touring) [1]
ACW, 'Recording Wales, Chapels' (touring) [1]
Howard Roberts Gallery, Cardiff 'The Possessors: paintings in Welsh collections from the HR Gallery 1956–1969' [3]

1970
National Eisteddfod of Wales, Ammanford
Winchester School of Art [31] *
Ash Barn Gallery, Petersfield [1]

1971
Bladon Gallery, Hurstbourne Tarrant [6]
Ash Barn Gallery, Petersfield (with Susan French and Michael Fairclough) [20]
Winchester School of Art 'International Art Week Exhibition' [2]

1972
Royal Academy of Art, Summer Show [3]
Portsmouth City Art Gallery [2]
Albany Gallery, Cardiff [4]
Walker Gallery, Pwllheli [12]
St Peter Street Gallery, Canterbury [2]
Rotunda Gallery, London 'Bertrand Russell Centenary Art Exhibition' [1]

1973
National Eisteddfod of Wales, Ruthin [1]
Royal Academy of Art, Summer Show [1]
ACW/RNE 'Welsh Portraits' (Bangor UCNW and Aberystwyth NLW) [1]
Guildford Galleries, Guildford 'Works by Contemporary Artists' [6]
Ash Barn Gallery, Petersfield [4]
Augustine Gallery, Holt, Norfolk 'Summer Salon' [2]
Winchester School of Art
Teeside Art Gallery '1st British International Drawing Biennale' [1]
Albany Gallery, Cardiff 'Summer Exhibition' [5]
Tegfryn Gallery, Anglesey [10]

1974
Guildford Galleries, Guildford 'Summer Exhibition' [5]
Tegfryn Gallery, Anglesey [13]
Ash Barn Gallery, Petersfield [5]
Southampton University 'Amnesty International' [1]
Hiscock Gallery, Southsea [5]
Arts Council of Wales, Touring [2]
Charter Gallery, Godalming, Surrey [2]

1975
Albany Gallery, Cardiff [4]
Ash Barn Gallery, Petersfield [5]
Tegfryn Gallery, Anglesey [6]
Design and Craft Gallery, The Square, Winchester (with Garrick Palmer) [8]

1976
Aberystwyth NLW [42] *
Ash Barn Gallery, Petersfield [1]
Hiscock Gallery, Portsmouth [4]
Petersfield Art Club [1]
Tegfryn Gallery, Anglesey [14]

1977
Albany Gallery, Cardiff [5]
Ash Barn Gallery, Petersfield
University of Wales, Cardiff 'Cardiff Festival of 20th Century Music' [30] *
Tegfryn Gallery, Anglesey [50] *
RI, Mall Galleries, London [2]

1978
Tegfryn Gallery, Anglesey [4]
RI, Mall Galleries, London [3]
Hiscock Gallery, Portsmouth [3]
Ash Barn Gallery, Petersfield [9]

1979
Tegfryn Gallery, Anglesey
RI, Mall Galleries, London
Arun Art Centre [3]
Ash Barn Gallery, Petersfield 'Paintings and Sculpture' [3]
St Edmunds Arts Centre, Salisbury 'Summer Exhibition' [3]
Mostyn Gallery, Llandudno 'The Native Land' [1]

1980
Aberystwyth NLW [2]
Ash Barn Gallery, Petersfield [4]
Tegfryn Gallery, Anglesey [52] *
RI, Mall Galleries, London [5]
Oriel 700, Aberystwyth [3]
Guildhall Gallery, Winchester 'RI Members' [3]
Bill Toop Gallery, Salisbury [6]

1981
Aberystwyth NLW [3]
Ash Barn Gallery, Petersfield [4]
Tegfryn Gallery, Anglesey
RI, Mall Galleries, London [11]
Albany Gallery, Cardiff [2]

1982
National Eisteddfod of Wales, Swansea 'Brogarwch' [8]
Albany Gallery, Cardiff 'Welsh Landscape in Oils' [9]
Ash Barn Gallery, Petersfield [6]
Ruthin Arts Centre [2]
RI, Mall Galleries, London [6]
Mussellwhite Gallery, Southampton [3]
Royal Cambrian Academy of Art [2]
ACW Oriel, Cardiff 'Christmas Show' [3]
Mall Galleries, London 'Hunting Group Finalists' [1]

1983
RI, Mall Galleries, London [6]
Bill Toop Gallery, Salisbury [3]
Ash Barn Gallery, Petersfield [7]
Mid Cornwall Gallery, Biscoy Par [3]
Hayward Gallery, London 'Landscape in Britain 1850–1950' [1]
Workshop Gallery, Fishguard [6]

1984
National Eisteddfod of Wales, Lampeter [1]
Albany Gallery, Cardiff [4]
RI, Mall Galleries, London [6]
Workshop Gallery, Fishguard [6]
Mid Cornwall Gallery, Biscoy Par [4]
Ash Barn Gallery, Petersfield [6]

1985
Aberystwyth NLW [40] *
Cunningham-Knowler Gallery, Winchester [10]

Ash Barn Gallery, Petersfield [2]
Mid Cornwall Gallery, Biscoy Par [2]
Workshop Gallery, Fishguard [6]
RI, Mall Galleries, London [6]

1986
Workshop Gallery, Fishguard
Stour Gallery, Blandford, Dorset [3]
Baldwin Gallery, Clevedon, Bristol [3]
Winchester Red Cross [6]
RI, Mall Galleries, London [6]
Fry Art Museum, Seattle, USA [2]
FCA Gallery, Vancouver [2]
Ceri Richards Gallery, Swansea University [4]

1987
RI, Mall Galleries, London [4]
Workshop Gallery, Fishguard [2]
Penns Gallery, Eastbourne [3]
Winchester Red Cross [6]
Ceri Richards Gallery, Swansea University [2]

1988
RI, Mall Galleries, London [1]
Romsey Art Club [1]
Workshop Gallery, Fishguard [14]
Ceri Richards Gallery, Swansea University (with Tom Rathmell) [38] *

1989
National Eisteddfod of Wales, Llanrwst
Wintershall Gallery, Guildford [3]
Tegfryn Gallery, Anglesey
RI, Mall Galleries, London [4]
Workshop Gallery, Fishguard [10]
Attic Gallery, Swansea [5]

1990
Tegfryn Gallery, Anglesey
RI, Mall Galleries, London [6]
Workshop Gallery, Fishguard [18]
Ceri Richards Gallery, Swansea University
Attic Gallery, Swansea [15]

1991
RI, Mall Galleries, London [6]
Workshop Gallery, Fishguard [2]
Ceri Richards Gallery, Swansea
Attic Gallery, Swansea
Arlesford Gallery, Hampshire [4]

1992
National Eisteddfod of Wales, Aberystwyth
RI, Mall Galleries, London [6]
RI, Mall Galleries, London 'The Discerning Eye' [1]
Austin Desmond Fine Art, London 'British Romantic Painting 1920–1960' [1]
Workshop Gallery, Fishguard [10]
Attic Gallery, Swansea 'Diverse Landscape' (with Tessa Waite) [40] *
Arlesford Gallery, Hampshire [2]

1993
RI, Mall Galleries, London [6]
Workshop Gallery, Fishguard [5]
Attic Gallery, Swansea [4]
Arlesford Gallery, Hampshire [2]
Riverside Gallery, Crickhowell [6]

1994
RI, Mall Galleries, London [6]
Workshop Gallery, Fishguard [10]
Riverside Gallery. Crickhowell [2]
Blackstone Gallery, Newbury [2]
Attic Gallery, Swansea [2]

1995
RI, Mall Galleries, London [6]
Workshop Gallery, Fishguard
Rowley Gallery, Kensington Church Street, London [2]
Oriel Contemporary Art, Regent's Park, London [2]
Martin Tinney Gallery, Cardiff [8]
Attic Gallery, Swansea [2]
Arlesford Gallery, Hampshire [3]

1996
RI, Mall Galleries, London [2]
Aberystwyth NLW (Retrospective) [126] *
University of Wales, Aberystwyth, School of Art 'Life Class' [95] *
Martin Tinney Gallery, Cardiff [7]
David Kitchen Gallery [1]
Attic Gallery, Swansea [5]
Arlesford Gallery, Hampshire [2]

1997
RI, Mall Galleries, London
Martin Tinney Gallery, Cardiff 'Winter Exhibition' [1]
Martin Tinney Gallery, Cardiff 'John Elwyn: Paintings 1945ñ1997' [52] *
University of Wales, Gregynog 'Music Festival Exhibition' [48] *
Attic Gallery, Swansea [4]

1998
RI, Mall Galleries, London (posthumous)

2: Public Collections

National Library of Wales, Aberystwyth
University of Wales, Aberystwyth
Barclay's Bank
Pembroke College, Cambridge
Arts Council of Wales
University of Wales, Cardiff
University of Wales, Institute of Science and Technology, Cardiff
Cardiff College of Music and Drama
BBC Wales
National Museum of Wales, Cardiff
Exeter University
General Post Office
Coleg Harlech
Leeds University
Llandovery College
Ministry of Public Buildings, Whitehall
Newport Museum and Art Gallery
Nuffield Foundation
Milton Training College, Portsmouth
Southampton University
Steel Company of Wales
Glynn Vivian Art Gallery, Swansea
Tate Gallery (Curwen Archive)
Contemporary Art Society of Wales
North Wales Arts Association
Warwick University (Rugby Education Authority)
King Alfred College, Winchester

and the former Education Authorities of
Cardiff
Denbighshire
Flintshire
Glamorganshire
Hampshire
Merthyr Tydfil
Monmouthshire
Montgomeryshire
Swansea
East and West Riding

3: Holidays

1947 Prague (with Leslie Harris)
1968 France (Paris, Avignon, St Remy, Aix, Arles, Vence, etc.)
1969 Greece and Turkey (Rhodes, Crete, Marmaris, Ephesus, etc.) Crete (Heraklion and Agios Nikolas)
1970 Corfu
1971 Jersey (Gorey)
1972 Portugal (Lisbon, Sintra, Obidos, Nazaré, etc.)

1973 Brittany (Cherbourg, Quimper, Douarnanez, Concarnaux, Pont Aven and Vannes)
1973 Cornwall (St Buryan)
1974 Cardiganshire (Newquay) France (Paris, Nimes, etc.)
1975 Brittany and the Loire (Honfleur, St Nic-Pentrez, Anger, Blois, Ambroise, and Chartres)
1976 France (Gascony)
1977 Italy (Umbria, Urbino, Assisi, Arezzo, Urbino and Rimini)
1978 Sicily (Palermo, Monscale, Syracuse and Taormina)
1979 America (New York State, Saranac Lake, Montreal, Maine, Cranberry Isle and Boston)
1980 Greece (Symi and Rhodes)
1981 Italy (Gardone, Lake Garda and Siena)
1982 Italy (Verona, Padua, Mantua, Venice and Vicenza)
1983 Italy (Lucca, Pisa, Pistoia, Viareggio and Florence)
1984 Spain (Madrid, Segovia, Salamanca and Toledo) Dorset (Beer and Thorncombe)
1985 Turkey (Study Tour: Istanbul, Kusadasi, Ephesus, Izmir, Troy, etc.) Greece (Kos and Patmos)
1986 Italy (Naples, Ravello, Amalfi, Positano and Sorrento) France (Rouen, Avignon, Arles and Orange)
1987 Egypt (Cairo and cruise along the Nile, Abu Simbel, Luxor and Karnac) Italy (Milan, Padua, Verona, Parma and Venice)
1988 Italy (Vico, Equense, Naples, Pompeii and Herculaneum) Italy (Venice, Bologna, Ravenna and Ferrara)
1989 Spain (Cordoba, Seville, Granada and Toremolinos) Spain (Santander, Santiago de Compostelo, Leon and Burgos) Wales (Tenby and Montgomeryshire) East Sussex (Alfriston and Charleston)
1991 Spain (Barcelona)
1992 Ireland (touring)
1993 Manchester and Halifax
1994 Wales (Abergavenny, Aberystwyth, Berriew and Pembroke) Woodstock and Banbury
1995 Northumbria (Halifax, and tour from Durham to Berwick on Tweed) Edinburgh and Glasgow
1996 Aberystwyth
1997 Cardiff

4: Books, Catalogues and Principal Reviews

'Young Welsh artist captures the atmosphere of Wales' *Western Mail* 8th July 1949
'John Elwyn at the Paul Alexander Gallery' *South Wales Evening Post* 11th July 1949
Times Educational Supplement 12th February 1954
Studio February/March 1954
'Welsh Artists' Shop Window' *Western Mail* 7th August 1956
'Painting wins Gold Medal' *Daily Telegraph* 7th August 1956
'Art Medal Winner' *Swansea Evening Post* August 1956
The Times re. Gold Medal Award, 7th August 1956
David Bell *The Artist in Wales* Harrap, London 1957 (book)
Wil Ifan 'John mab Dafy'r Top' *Western Mail* April 1958
David Bell 'John Elwyn' *Anglo-Welsh Review* Vol. 9 No. 23 July 1958
'Variety Keynote of Welsh Art Show' *Western Mail* 15th September 1959
Cambrian News re. Welsh Art Show at NLW, September 1959
Art News and Review 30th July 1960
John Elwyn: Recent Paintings The Leicester Galleries, London 1965 (exhibition catalogue)
Frank Whitford 'John Elwyn and Orovida Pissarro at the Leicester Galleries' *Art News* 5th February 1965
Graham Samuel 'Welsh artist opens his first one-man show' *Western Mail* 5th February 1965
Terence Mullaly *The Daily Telegraph* 9th February 1965
William Gaunt 'Mr John Elwyn' *The Times* 15th February 1965
Art Review May 1965
Paintings by John Elwyn Howard Roberts Gallery, Cardiff 1965 (exhibition catalogue)
Malcolm Quantrill 'John Elwyn at the Howard Roberts Gallery' *Art Review* September 1965
Griffith Williams 'Tragedy in a dead tree-trunk' *Western Mail* 16th October 1965
'John Elwyn at the Howard Roberts Gallery' *The Times* 22nd October 1965
Conroy Maddox 'John Elwyn at the Leicester Galleries' *Arts Review* 23rd November 1968
Paintings by John Elwyn Winchester School of Art March 1970 (exhibition catalogue)
Ifor Davies 'CASW Exhibition Review' *Barn* June 1975
Glyn Jones 'John Elwyn' *Y Genhinen* Vol. 26, No. 2, February 1976
Landscapes by John Elwyn National Library of Wales, Aberystwyth September 1976 (exhibition catalogue)
John Elwyn and Betty Blandino University of Wales, Cardiff, March 1977 (exhibition catalogue)
Eric Rowan 'Craft with a touch of Mystery: John Elwyn and Betty Blandino' *Western Mail* 8th March 1977
Hywel Harries *Cymru'r Canfas* Y Lolfa, Aberystwyth 1985 (English Edition 1988)
Paintings by John Elwyn National Library of Wales, Aberystwyth, October 1985 (exhibition catalogue)
'Yr Artist Alltud' (The Exiled Artist) *Barn* December 1986
David Cole *New Wales* University of Wales Press, Cardiff 1990
Gweled Gwlad HMSO, London 1991
Rhys Gwyn 'Arlunio Cyfres III, Teg Edrych Tuag Adref Cymru', *Urdd Gobaith Cymru Magazine*
Myfi Williams *Arlunwyr Mawr y Byd* (Chapter on Wales includes John Elwyn and Winifred Coombe-Tennant)
Ann Gruffydd Rhys 'John Elwyn' *Barn* July/August 1992
Peter Lord *Y Chwaer Dduwies* Gwasg Gomer, Llandysul 1992 (book)
Edward Phelps 'John Elwyn at the Attic Gallery' *Art News* May 1992
Meuna Baines 'Y Hufen ar dop y llaeth (The cream on the top of the milk) *Barn*, August 1993
'Pethau Cain' *Golwg* 15th July 1993 (about the making of *House of Leaves*)
Peter Wakelin 'Article of Faith: John Elwyn' *Art Review* Vol. XLVIII pp. 36–37, July/August 1996
Robert Meyrick *John Elwyn: a retrospective* National Library of Wales catalogue 1996
Rhian Evans 'Artist still inspired by hiraeth 50 years on' *Western Mail* July 1996
'Stori Mewn Llun (A Story in Pictures)', *Y Cymro* 11th October 1996

5: Obituaries

Robert Meyrick 'John Elwyn' *The Times* 6th December 1997 p. 25
Robert Meyrick 'John Elwyn: Chapel days remembered' *The Guardian* 1st January 1998
Meic Stephens 'John Elwyn' *The Independent* 25th November 1997 p. 19
Roy Hancock 'Artist gained inspiration from isolated farming communities' *Western Mail* 24th November 1997
Ainsleigh Davies 'John Elwyn' *Y Faner Newydd* February 1998 pp. 4–5
'John Elwyn, artist who loved the countryside' *Hampshire Chronicle* December 1997
'Tribute to a Rural Artist' *Cambrian News* 4th December 1997
The Arts Council of Wales 'John Elwyn' *Artists Notes* No.16 Winter 1997–1998
'John Elwyn' *Cardigan and Teifi Side Advertiser* January 1998

6: Television and Radio Programmes

BBC Wales, 24th January 1955, 6.55–7.15 p.m., *Tynnu Llun* a film by David J. Thomas of John Elwyn drawing a portrait.
BBC Wales, August 1958, *Tonight*, from the Howard Roberts Gallery.
TWW, 26th December 1958, 4.25 p.m., *Orig yr Ifanc (Accent on Youth)*, John Elwyn was one of three featured artists.
TWW, 1st January 1959, live interview.
TWW, March 1960, *Pawb ei Farn,* a weekly review chaired by John Eilian Jones with guests John Elwyn, Robert Lambert Gapper and Rhys Gwyn.
BBC Wales, 8 November 1960, 11.27 p.m., *Cwmpas*, a film by Nan Davies.
TWW, 7th July 1967, 7.00–7.30 p.m., *Gorau Dawn,* Raymond Edwards interviews John Elwyn in a film directed by Geraint Rees.
BBC Wales, 9th January 1975, 8.30 p.m., *Cynfas*, a look at the arts in Wales, 18 minute film on John Elwyn.
BBC Radio Wales, *Ffresgo* by Lenna Pritchard Jones. John Elwyn talks about the Gwen John exhibition at the Barbican.
HTV Wales, 9th, 16th, 23rd, 31st January, 7th, 14th February 1997, 7.30–8.00 p.m., *A Word in Your Eye*, artists and writers on the Welsh way of life in six programmes produced by Paul Islwyn Thomas.

7: Illustrations

Illustrated Books

Leslie Harries *Tannau Teifi* Gwasg Gomer, Llandysul 1943 (cover and title page)
Leslie Harries *Chwe Drama Fer* Gwasg Gomer, Llandysul 1944 (12 black and white line drawings)
Leslie Harries 'Y Disgyblion' (The Disciples), 12 wood engravings (cut in 1944) illustrating stanzas by Harries in *Tywysydd y Plant* Vol. 60 Nos. 1–12, 1946, for the monthly religious magazine for children and young people, published by Undeb yr Annibynwyr Cymraeg (Society of Welsh Independent Churches), Swansea, January to December 1946. *Nathanael* p. 5 (January); *Mathew* p. 21 (February); *Simon Pedr* p. 36 (March); *Simon y Cananead* p. 53 (April); *Iago* p. 73 (May); *Jwdas Iscariot* p. 93 (June); *Thomas* p. 113 (July); *Andreas* p. 133 (August); *Iago ab Alffeus* p. 153 (September); *Philip* p. 173 (October); *Thadeus* p. 193 (November); *Ioan* p. 214 (December)
Leslie Norris *Norris's Ark: poems by Leslie Norris* Tidal Press, Maine, USA 1988 (1 colour, 4 black and white illustrations)
Dafydd ap Gwilym *House of Leaves* Old Stile Press, Llandogo, Monmouthshire 1993 (29 line drawings, limited edition of 250 copies)

Dust Wrappers

Dust wrappers listed here were designed especially for the book. The list does not include the many paintings that have been reproduced later as book covers.

Jack H Davies and D Jacob Davies *Cerddi'r Ddau Frawd* Gwasg Gomer, Llandysul 1940
Jack Oliver *Cerddi'r Barbwr* Gwasg Gomer, Llandysul 1943
Dafydd Owen *Beirdd y Bore* Llyfrfa'r Annibynwyr, Swansea 1945
W Llewelyn Williams *Gwr y Dolau* Gwasg, Aberystwyth 1945
Y Deryn Glas Gwasg Gomer, Llandysul
Cerddi Kate Davies Gwasg Gomer, Llandysul
Yr Arloeswr [magazine] No.1 (1946), No.7, 1960
David Rhydderch *Cerddi Cenhadol* Livingstone Press, London 1947
Glyn Jones *The Dream of Jake Hopkins* Fortune Press, London 1954
Glyn Jones *The Valley, The City, The Village* J. M. Dent, London 1956
Glyn Jones *The Learning Lark* J. M. Dent, London 1960

Radio Times

Y Corff (by the late Dewi Emrys), February 1954
The Country of the Blind (adapted from H G Wells, featuring Laurence Olivier), February 1954
O Gorlannau y Defaid, February 1954
The Sailor's Song (by James Hanley), May 1954
Beth am y Sul? May 1956
Spring Gale with Sian Phillips, date not known

8: Further reading (British Landscape)

Ian Jeffrey *The British Landscape 1920–1950* Thames and Hudson, London 1984
Ian Jeffrey/Frances Spalding/Donald Davie *Landscape in Britain 1850–1950* Arts Council, London 1983
Michael Rosenthal *British Landscape Painting Phaidon*, Oxford 1982
Malcolm Yorke *The Spirit of Place* Constable, London 1988

9: Further Reading (Art in Wales in the 20th Century)

David Bell *The Artist in Wales* Harrop and Co., London 1957
Peter Lord *Gwenllian: essays on visual culture* Gwasg Gomer, Llandysul 1994
Peter Lord *The Visual Culture of Wales: Industrial Society* University of Wales Press, Cardiff 1998
Eric Rowan *Art in Wales: an illustrated history 1850–1980* University of Wales Press, Cardiff 1985

Photographic credits:

John Elwyn:
Plates IX, XIV, XVI, XX, XXI.
Pages 21 (left), 43, 47, 67, 68, 106 (left).

John Elwyn, his family and friends, courtesy of the Artist's Estate:
Pages 12,13, 15 (left), 22, 23, 26, 38, 41, 44, 103 (left), 103 (right), 105.

Robert Greetham:
Plates I, IV, VI, VII, X, XII, XIII, XV, XVIII, XXIII, XXV, XXVI, XXVII, XXX, XXXI, XXXII, XXXIII, XXXIV, XXXIX, XL, XLI, XLII, XLIV.
Pages 14, 17, 18, 21 (right), 24 (left), 24 (right), 27, 28, 29 (top), 33, 34, 36, 37, 48, 70, 79 (top), 100, 101, 104, 108, 109 (top), 109 (bottom).

Rachel Howells:
Plate XXXVIII.

Rudy Lewis:
Plates XVII, XXVIII.

Robert Meyrick:
Plates II, III, VIII, XI, XXII, XXXV, XLIII, XLV.
Pages 2, 15 (right), 25, 30 (top), 39, 40, 75, 97, 106 (right), 107, 110, 111.

National Library of Wales, Aberystwyth:
Plates V, XIV, XIX, XXIV, XXXVI.

National Museum of Wales, Cardiff:
Page 45 (left).

Shell Art Collection:
Plate XXIX.

Michael Threlfall:
Plate XXXVII.

Untraced:
Pages 42, 46 (top), 46 (bottom), 73, 77, 79 (bottom), 80, 99.

Index

Page references in *italics* refer to Figures or Plates

Above the Mill at Adpar (1936) *14*
Adie, Vera 33
Adpar Village School 19
Adventurer, The (1954) 72, *83*(Plate XXII)
After the Rain (Gosport) (1952) 47
56(Plate X)
Afterglow at Portsmouth (1948) 38
Aftermath (1945) *30*
April Communion 16, 39
Arboreal (1968) 98
Arnold, Matthew 25
Artist's Father, The (1940) *15*
Arts Council 65, 67
Austin, Robert 69
Ayrton, Michael 29, 31, 32

Baner ac Amserau Cymru 15, 47, *47*
Bannister family 69, 74
Barn Walls (1956) *88*(Plate XXVII)
Bastien-Lepage, Jules 71
Bawden, Edward 24
Bell, David 44, *44*, 65, 66, 67, 69, 72, 78, 112
Artist in Wales, The 44
Language of Pictures, The 44
Bell, Graham 25, 32
Bell, Sir Idris 44
Between the Barns (1974) 105, *115*
Beynon, A.G. 77
Beynon, Willie 45
Blake, William 30-1
Bonnard, Pierre 31, 39
Bore Sul (Sunday Morning) (1950) 44, *45*, 66, 67
Brangwyn, Sir Frank 20
Bratby, John 73
Breughel 37
Britten, Benjamin 43
Brondeg Mills, Felindre 13
Broody Hens, The (1955) 71, 72
Brown, Loftus 72
Brown, Oliver 72
Browning, Robert 25
Bullard, Paul 35
Burns, Rodney 24
Burra, Edward 29
Burton, Charles 67
Back from the Club, Rhondda (1954) 68
Bush, Miss E.M. ('E.M.' or 'Yem') 27
Butler, George 36
Butterworth, Gillian (wife) 103-4, *103*, 107, 108

Canal, The (1953) 69, *70*
Cardiff College of Art 29
Cardiganshire Bay Blue (1957) 78
Cardiganshire Meadows (1959) *92*(Plate XXXI)
Carmarthen School of Art 20-1, 24
Carmarthenshire Farm, A 77
Carmarthenshire Green (1957) 78, *87*(Plate XXVI)
Cat and the Cock, The (1954) 71
Cattle Between the Barns (1977) *106*
Ceri Mill (1985) 97
Cézanne, Paul 20, 24, 31
Chamberlain, Brenda 67
Chapman, George 47
View in Merthyr Tydfil 68
Chardin, Jean Baptiste 121
Charles, Rollo 69
Charlton, Evan 21, 67, 73
Chwe Drama Fer (1944) 29
Clark, Kenneth 32
Clausen, George 71
Clough, Prunella 73
Cockerels and Roses (1961) 80, *94*(Plate XXXIII)
Coldstream, William 25, 32
Coldstream report 80
Collapsed Barn, The (1994) *106*
Colquhoun, Robert 31, 32
Constable, John 112
Construction (1936) 20, *21*
Contemporary Art Society for Wales 44-5, 65, 67, 72
Coombe-Tennant, Mrs Winifred ('Mam o Nedd') 36, 37, 43, 44, 45, 47, 65, 72, 112
Country of the Blind, The 70
Courbet, Gustave 41
Craxton, John 29, 30, 31, 32
Dreamer in a Landscape (1942) 30
Poet in a Landscape (1941) 30

Daly, Jehan 33
Daumier, Honoré 39
David Lloyd George (1932) 19
Davies family *15*
Davies, Sir Alun Talfan 108
Davies, Anne (mother) 13, 14, 18, 29, 39, *41*
Davies, David (father) 13-16, 18-19, 36, 39, 45
Afon Ceri 16
Calan Mai 16
Cartre 15
Cwrdd Llenyddol 16
Cwymp y Dail 16
Dyfodiad yr Hydref 16
Englyn i'r Fam 15

Etholiad Sirol Ceredigion 16
Nos Sadwrn Pae 16
Social (1936) 16
Y Bryn ar Doriad Gwawr 16
Y Gwanwyn 16
Yr Elor Gerbyd 16
Yr Hydref 16
Davies, David, & Co. Woollen Manufacturers 13
Davies, Gillian (wife) *see* Butterworth, Gillian
Davies, Katie (sister) 14, 69, 80
Davies, Margaret 72
Davies, Mary (sister) 14, 31, 69, 80
Davies, Rhys 28
Davies, Sally (sister) 14, 69, 97 97
Davies, William 'John Elwyn' *see* Elwyn, John
Deacon's Dilemma, The 16
Debatable Point, A 40
Delacroix, Eugène 121
Denis Reed in our Earl's Court Digs (1940) *25*
Derelict Barn, The (1955) 12, *84*(Plate XXIII)
Disgyblion yr Iesu, engravings for 30-1
Dr Ben Davies of Newcastle Emyln (1931) 19
Dyfed Landscape 106
Dyfed Moors 105

Eardley, Joan 73
Ebenezer Welsh Congregational Chapel, Newcastle Emlyn 16, 39, 42
Edwards, Ralph 44
Edwards, Dr Raymond 108
Egg, The (1952) 47, *59*(Plate XII)
Eifion Wyn 19
eisteddfodau
local 14, 15, 19-20
National 20, 38, 65, 66, 74
Emlyn Factory 13, 14, 17, 47
Emlyn Factory Account Book 15
Emrys, Dewi 70
Enclosed Balcony, The (1980) *116*(Plate XL)
Enigmatic Blossom (1967) 98, *114*(Plate XXXVII)
Entrance to a Farm 106
Equinoctial (1967) 98, 99
Euston Road School 25, 32
Everyman (1944) 29, *51*(Plate III)
Eyton, Anthony 37, 38

Faithful Few, The (1949) *52*(Plate V)
Family Life (1947) *33*
Family Outing, Southsea (1951) 47, *55*(Plate IX)
Farm Shapes (1961) 80, *93*(Plate XXXII)
Farmer's Wife, The (1953) 62(Plate XVII), 72, *104*
Feeding Time (1955) 71
Fernhill III: And the sun grew round that very day (1977) 107, *115*
Festival of Britain 65
Figure Studies, Winchester (1960s) *101*
Flowering Cactus (1975) *109*
Football Association 68
Forest Enigma (1963) 97, *113*(Plate XXXVI)
Forest Ritual (1963) 97, 98
Freedman, Barnett 24
Frightened Goldfish, The (1952) 47
Front, Southsea, The (1948) 38
Fry, Roger 24
Funeral Gathering in the Snow, A (1949) 41
Funeral Gathering on a Welsh Hill Farm, A (1949) 41, 42, 67
Funeral in the Snow (1953) *61*(Plate XVI), 68

Garden Episode 98
Gaunt, William 98
Gaydon, Leslie 35, 37
Germinal (1968) 98
Glamorgan (1960) *90*(Plate XXIX)
Glyn Jones (1956) *86*(Plate XXV)
Glynn Vivian Art Gallery 72
Golding, Robin 76
Greaves, Derrick 73
Green Approaches (1959) 78, *91*(Plate XXX)
Griffiths, John 70
Grigson, Geoffrey 74, 75, 76
Gross, Anthony 69
Gwilym, Dafydd ap 44, 108
Gwilym, Llywelyn ap 108

Hambledon Village – the Cradle of Cricket (1963) 77
Hanley, James: *Sailor's Song, The* 70
Harris, Leslie 29, 30, 35
Harvest Yellow 67
Haystooks in the Meadow above the Mill (1938) *17*
Helps, Francis 24
Herman, Joseph 67
Horton, Percy 24, 35, 102
Housman, A.E.: *Shropshire Lad, A* 112
Hub of the Village, The 44
Hunt, William Holman
Hireling Shepherd, The (1851-52) 72
Strayed Sheep, Our English Coast (1852) 72
Huxley, Aldous 26
Hymn Critics, The (1949) 40, 41, *53*(Plate VI)

Ieuan Gwynedd (1931) 19
In the Hill's Elbow (1959) 74, 104
In the Valley (Refugees) (1947) 36-7, *36*
Innes, J.D. 21
Inquisitive Geese, The (1956) 71

Jefferson, Alan 35
Jenkins, David 77
John Ormond (1980) *108*
John, Augustus 21
John, Gwen 21
Jones, David 21
Jones, David John 69
Jones, Doreen 29, 69
Jones, Glyn 28, 29, 40-1, 42, 69, 71, 106, 107, 108, 110
  John Elwyn's portrait of (1956) *86*(Plate XXV)
  Afternoon at Uncle Shad's, An 41
  Cwmcelyn 107
  Dream of Jake Hopkins, The 71
  Easter 107
  'Explosion' 42-3
  Learning Lark, The 71
  Merthyr 40
  Valley, The City, The Village, The 71
  Water Music, The 42
Jones, Gwyn 65
Jones, Dr Iorwerth Hughes 44
Jones, Jack 28, 108
Jones, Richard Lloyd 77
Jones, Sally *see* Davies, Sally
Jowett, Percy Hague 35
June Morning Light (1957) 78

Kandinsky, Wassily 121
  Concerning the Spiritual in Art: the Language of Form and Colour (1912) 98
Keats, John 25
King's Cross Congregational Chapel 25
Kline, Franz 80
Kooning, Willem de 80

la Dell, Edwin 69
Lamb Inn, Adpar 18-19
Lamb Inn, Adpar (1938) 18
Landscar (1964) 96(Plate XXXV)
Late August Evening Light (1959) 78
Lawrence, T.E. 26
Learning Lark, The (1960) 71, *71*
Lefevre Gallery 31
Leicester Galleries 31, 71, 77, 98, 112
Lewis, Alun 28
Lewis, Edward Morland 21, 36
Lewis, Saunders: *Buchedd Garmon* 70
Life Class at Winchester, The (1958) *100*
Life Class, Royal College of Art, The (1947) *34*
Llandysul County Grammar School 19
Lloyd George, David 76
Lonely Servant, The (1980-97) 112, *120*(Plate XLV)
Lowry, L.S. 73
Lucas, Rowland 70

MacBryde, Robert 31, 32
MacDonald, Richard 22, 26, *26*, 43
Macmurray, John 26
Mahoney, Charles 24, 35
Manchester City Art Gallery 68
Mansard Gallery, Heal's 65
Market, Santiago da Compostela, The (1989) *111*
Massacre Field (1963) 97
Matisse, Henri 29
McDowall, Nicolas 108
Meadow, The (1956) 68
Micklewright, Robert 70
Middleditch, Edward 73
Midnight Roses (1961) 80
Milky Way, The (1953) *63*(Plate XVIII), 72
Millais, John Everett: *Blind Girl, The* (1856) 72
Milner, Donald 21
Miners Returning from the Pit on a Wet Day (1951) 65
Miners Returning Home on a Wet Evening II (1951) 46
Miners Returning Home on a Wet Evening III (1953) 46, 67
Miners Returning Home over Waste Ground (1951) 47, *58*(Plate XIII)
Minton, John 29, 31, 32, 73, 74
Miss E.M. Bush (1942) *27*
Model, the Portrait Class, Carmarthen School of Art (1936) *21*
Morgan, J.T. 44, 72
Morris, Cedric 21
Morse-Brown, Sidney 20, 21, 22
Mothers, The (1954) 47, 67, 72, *81*(Plate XX)
Motherwell, Robert 80
Mr Cherry, who sailed in the Bellerophone (1951) 48, *48*
Murray, William Grant 36-7

National Advisory Council on Art Education 80
National Library of Wales, Aberystwyth 67
National Museum of Wales 65, 66, 67
New English Art Club 38
Norris, Leslie 28, 108
Norris's Ark 108
November Thanksgiving 39

Off the Main Road II (1959) 78, 79, 106
Olivier, Laurence 70
On the Dyfed Coast (1987) 110, *117*(Plate XLII)
Ormond, John 28, 45, 106

Paddock Bird (1985) 109, *116*(Plate XLI)
Palm Sunday (1949) 39, *39*
Palmer, Garrick 69
Palmer, Samuel 112
Pare, David 38, 69, 104
Pare, Vivian 38
Paul Alexander Gallery, Notting Hill 43
Peace News 29

Pet Cockerel, The (Y Ceiliog Swci) (1953) 64(Plate XIX), 66, 72
Petts, John 67, 106
Philip, Ambrose: *Imitation of Virgil's First Eclogue (The Pastorals of Virgil)* 30
Picasso, Pablo 20
Picnic in Cilgwyn Woods (1940) 25, 49(Plate I)
Pink and Grey Shapes (1959) 72, *73*
Piper, John 67, 112
Pitchforth, Vivian 24
Plan for Artists 32
Plastic People (1965) 108, *109*
Plastic People by the Sea (1964) 108
Pollock, Jackson 80
Pompeii Light, The (1951) 48

Radio Times 70
Rainbird, George 76
Rainbird & McLean Ltd 74
Red Evening, The (1960) 78
Reed, Denis 22, 24, 24, 26, 26, 27, 28, 29, 31
Religious Society of Friends, The 27
Renoir, Auguste 121
Renton, Leonard 26
Richard, Ceri 29, 36, 67
Cycle of Nature, The (1952-56)
Road to Gower, The (1963) *95*(Plate XXXIV)
Roberts, D.C.: *Wrth y Ddaear* 68
Rosenberg and Helft Ltd 24
Rosoman, Leonard 70
Rothenstein, William 44
Rothko, Mark 80
Rouault, Georges 121
Rowntree, Kenneth 74, 75
Royal Academy 38
Royal College of Art 23-6, 31-5
Rumours of a Pit Disaster in the Next Valley (1949) 42, *43*

Sadler's Almanac 18
Sailor's Return, The (1952) *60*(Plate XV), 66
Sailor's Song, The (1954) *71*
Salmond, Penelope 43
Sandford, Christopher 71
Savernake (1962) 97
Seated Figures, Cardiff Life Class (1941) *28*, 29
Seedflight (1968) 98
Self Portrait Studies, Portsmouth (1950) 37
September (1996) *112*, *119*(Plate XLIV)
September Evening Light (1956) 78
Settling a Small Point over a Hymn Tune 40
Shell & BP Guide to Britain 74
Shell County Guides 74, *75*, 76
Shell Guides to the Countryside 74
Shell Wayfarer Guides 77
Shoni Winwns (Johnny Onions) (1958) 74 *89*(Plate XXVIII)
Sickert, Walter 36, 72
Simon y Canaanead 30
Smith, Matthew 72
Social Tea Party, A (1949) 16 *52*(Plate IV)
Society for Education through Art (S.E.A.) 65, 66
Sorrell, Alan 24
Southern College of Art, Portsmouth 35, 37, 43
Southsea Front (1951) 47, *55*(Plate VIII)
Spencer, Gilbert 24, 35, 44
Spencer, Stanley 112
Stapledon, Olaf 26
Steegman, John 44
Stillness of the Roots, The (1944) 30, *50*(Plate II)
Suliau Mebyd (Sundays of my Youth) *a.k.a. Before the Meeting* (1950) 44, *54*(Plate VII), 66
Sun and Snow (1953) 67-8, *68*
Sutherland, Graham 29, 32, 104, 108
Sweeper, The (1952) *58*(Plate XIII), 73

Thomas, Caitlin 29
Thomas, Dylan 28, 29, 107
Fernhill (1946) 107
Thomas, Gwilym 27
Thomas, Joyce 25
Thompson, J. Walter, advertising agency 36
Thornton, Robert John 30
Three Generations (1953) 67
Topiarist, The (1985) 109
Tredegar's Workmen's Institute 44
Tree Architecture (1954) 72
Tywysydd y Plant 30

Undeb y Annibynwyr Cymraeg 30
Up to Date News before the Meeting (1949) 39, *40*
Upland Farm (1993) 106, *118*(Plate XLIII)
Usherwood, Ralph 70

Vaughan, Keith 31, 32
Veterans, The (1985) 107, *107*
Vuillard, Edouard 31, 39

Walters, Evan 21
Ward, John 33
Watchorn, Andrew 100
Weight, Carel 43, 67
Wells, H.G. 70
Welsh Committee of the Arts Council 38, 66, 67
Welsh Hill Farm 106
Welsh Joint Education Committee 66
Welsh Review, The 65
West of England College of Art, Bristol 21
Wet August Light (1956) 78
Wet Day Miners (1950) 47
Wet Summer II (1985) 67
White Goats, Cos, The (1985) *110*
White Leghorns 72
White Washed Walls (1958) *80*, 106
Whitford, Frank 98
Whitsun Festival Interval 16

Wilkins, Dr F.J. 77
Williams, Waldo 28, 107
Winchester School of Arts and Crafts 69, 71, 99-102
Windfalls (1956) 67, 73, *85*(Plate XXIV)
Wool Dyers, The (1950) 45, *57*(Plate XI)
Wordsworth, William 25
World War II 26-31
Wright, Jack 26, 43
Y Corff (The Body) (1954) 70, *71*
Ydlan yn Sir Aberteifi (The Rickyard) (1954) 72, *82*(Plate XXI)
Yellow Silence (1957) 78, 79
Yesterday's Gossip (1949) 41
Young, Edward 74, 76-7

Zobole, Ernest 67
Zwemmer Gallery 31